Juncture In Time

Robert T. Jefferson

Library of Congress Control Number: 2009925875
Publisher's Catalog—in—Publication Data
Juncture In Time / Robert T. Jefferson
ISBN-13: 978-1-934956-15-1
ISBN-10: 1-934956-15-5
1. Religion.
2. Christianity.
I. Title

This book was written, printed and bound
in the United States of America.

For my children and grandchildren,
that they may see the return of
God's reality to the Western world

Influential Ideas for the Third Millennium

Epicureanism - A materialistic system of belief which teaches that personal happiness is the highest good.

Materialism - The doctrine which holds that nothing exists other than physical bodies and physical processes.

Naturalism - The doctrine that scientific laws are adequate to account for all phenomena.

Historicism - The relativity of goodness and badness in time.

Rationalism - Human reason is the sole medium by which man can arrive at any truth. Faith in God-like authorities is unalterably opposed to reason.

Secularism - Indifference to or rejection of the reality of goodness in religion.

Individualism - The doctrine opposed to the Common Good which holds that the interests of the individual are or ought to be superior to all others.

Existentialism - Mankind lives alone in a universe of such complexity and vastness as to be incomprehensible. Consequently absolute Knowledge of good, bad or fair play is impossible.

Optimistic Humanism - The denial of the existence of human badness (sin).

Marketism - The doctrine which holds that the consumer is the center of significance. The well-being of society is best served when each person pursues his or her own interests.

Catholicism - Roman Catholic doctrine holds perfectly to Christ's teachings. Catholicity is unity in His Word through the power of the Holy Spirit. It is the One True body of Christ as shown by the fact that His body is present in the fullness of unity throughout the world.

ACKNOWLEDGMENTS

To my sister, Ruth Ann, I owe a debt of gratitude for her suggestions to improve grammar and spelling. And to my son Alan and his wife Anne I owe recognition of their time and computer skills devoted to formatting the style of presentation I chose.

Also I am grateful for my "voices in the wilderness" who continue to warn us of the corruption of liberty and of other dangers threatening Western civilization.

This book owes its existence to these many authors, syndicated columnists, to the Institute for Theological Encounter with Science and Technology (ITEST), the New Oxford Review, the National Geographic Society's Story of Man Library, the Catechism of the Catholic Church and newspapers published by Catholic Dioceses; and, the Bible.

Over the past thirty years I collected books and newspaper articles, attended ITEST Workshops, read the Journalist's Code and read my monthly issues of New Oxford Review. These are my resources used to write this book; all confirming my suspicions.

My thanks go to the following men and women in the order that they appear: Michael Novak, C. S. Lewis, St. Augustine, Joseph Cardinal Ratzinger, Pope Leo XIII, Hilaire Belloc, Harry Adams, Cal Thomas, George Will, Pope John Paul II, Morris Berman, William Bennett, Jeffrey Burton Russell, G. K. Chesterton, Linda Bowles, Andrew Wollman, St. Paul, Pope Pius XII, Kenneth Whitehead, Dorothy Sayers, Thomas Woods, H. W. Crocker III, Regine Pernoud, Charles Darwin, John Whitehead, Fulton J. Sheen, Andrew Mallor, Edward Jefferson, Sherry Kerns, Judge George Greer, Ron Galloy, the Lichter-Rothman Report, Pope Paul VI, William Jennings Bryan, John Thavis, Stanley Marrow, Kurt Godel, Stanley Jaki, E. F. Schumacher, John Henry Newman, Harry Disston, Martin Luther, Paul Vitz, Harry, Pope John XXIII, George Weigel, Russell Shaw, Pope Pius XI, Mortimer Adler, Nancy Pearcey, Charles Colson, , Daniel Haifley, Michael Denton, Michael Behe, Robert Brungs, Lazarus Macior, Francis Collins, Paul Langsfeld, Steven Kuhl, Sirach, Thomas Sheahen, Joan

6

Kelly, Will Rogers, Thomas Martin, Robert Clark, Martin Esslin, Virgil Blum, Robert Brown, Reed Irvine, Irving Kristol, Olivia Gans, Vincent Rue, William Clinton, the father of Rachel Scott who was killed in the Columbine High School shooting, Max Rafferty, Andrew Coulson, Stephen Carter, Gorden, Robert Gallo, Bob Wood, , Daniel Haifley, Mike Huckabee, Adam Smith, Eric Gill, Rodney Stark, Seymour Lipset, Russell Kirk, Joseph Tussman, , Daniel Haifley, Albert Hobbs, John Kennedy, Donald Wildmon, Peter Gott, Hans Asperger, Christopher Hitchens, Peter Kreeft; and, Ezekiel.

———————————

Above all I thank God for giving my life a higher purpose.

This project started in 1983 with about 50 letters to the editor written over the span of 10 years, and no purpose other than binding them for my children to read.

Juncture In Time has had more help on it's way to publication than I could not have imagined.

TABLE OF CONTENTS

INTRODUCTION

This collection of letters and commentary has something in common with the Pensees (Thoughts) of Blaise Pascal.

Pascal lived from 1623 to 1662 in France. He was a gifted mathematician, but he is best remembered for the notations he kept to record thoughts about his worldview. He didn't live to publish Pensees. His notes were preserved and published by others. Pascal used reason alone to fit together a part of the puzzle showing the whole Christian Worldview. It has been said of Pascal's thoughts, agreeing with them or disagreeing misses the point. The point is, in the end we understand better our task on earth regardless of our background.

I believe Blaise Pascal would have agreed that societies are persuaded to "act more wisely if we spell out for each other our visions of human nature and destiny, in all their variety, in civil discourse and in respect for one another." (Quote from Michael Novak's column published in The Indianapolis Star, March 27, 1987.)

———————

I believe our primary task on earth is to accomplish, each in his or her own way, that for which every devout Christian prays in the Our Father, "Thy Kingdom come on earth." Peace everywhere on earth will be realized when this task is accomplished. God has promised to help if we repent and believe.

I believe that Christians and others are failing in their task. Today, a disunited Western Man is creating a grossly sensual (pagan) culture - a Movement away from God. If this in fact is correct, it would follow that a way is needed to prevent all mankind from moving backward.

Movement away from the reality of God reverses the gains of the past four thousand years by destroying their foundation. Moreover, it eats away by degrees the broad intellectual tradition developed during that span of time. The Movement is called heresy or Mortal Sin.

This defines the magnitude of our problem as we enter the twenty-first century. We knowingly replace God's reality with our own. We remove God in order to have ethics as our plaything.

The scientist in me offers a treatise that methodically examines

Western Man as though he is a fallen bridge. The cause or nature of the problem is corruption (corrosion) due to Mortal Sin. It is counter-productive to cite the many valuable properties inherent in ironwork, or in men and women, since these are not at fault. Denying sin is also counter-productive, as denying proof that the bridge failed.

One fact stands out. Corrosion of "Goodness" evident in man's inhumanity to man during the century just past, far exceeded inhumanity in the history of any prior century. The period of twentieth century AD was the bloodiest in history. Man-made reality proved to be a nightmare.

C. S. Lewis saw Western Man approaching a critical juncture in time when he wrote: "The twenty-first century will be one of two things. Either it will be the best since the thirteenth, or the worst since the twenty-first BC before the call of Abraham and the founding of Judaism."

Goodness and Fulfillment uncovered by Lewis in the thirteenth century was the culmination of more than a thousand years of Catholic tradition.

Scientists, when faced with particularly difficult problems, adopt a position that says no idea is too far out for consideration. The problem is turned upside-down and backward. My position accepts mankind as a free agent whom God designed to be with Him forever in heaven.

PREFACE

God created man, and gifted him with everything he needs to succeed in his task. Our task, or purpose on earth, is to live out our moral potential in a shared process that will be completed in heaven. There is a bonus if enough people live-out their moral potential God's way. There is a penalty if they do not. The bonus is the answer to The Lord's Prayer, "Thy kingdom come on earth as it is in heaven," i.e. justice and peace in families, then everywhere, and if steadfast, for all time.

In other words mankind was designed and created by God to cooperate in the achievement of perfection on earth; not God-like perfection, but human perfection working in partnership with God. Peace on earth is a collective goal worthy of our God-given talents and our faith. Augustine said, "When God crowns our merits, He crowns His own works" (Confessions, Part 9, 13.34)

This is a simple concept to understand but a formidable and multifaceted, ongoing task to accomplish - a doable task if each generation reverses their emphasis from humans need God to God needs humans working together toward fulfillment. It is formidable in that it really is about human dignity and respectful relationships - sinful people trusting sinful people and selfish people trusting God. It is all about faith and prayer. The essence of Faith is conversion - turning from heresy to Divine Truth about how each is to fulfill his or her own moral potential God's way.

Genesis records that on the first "day" God said, "Let there be light," and there was light. God saw how good the light was. Does God need to tell humans that the crowning (potential) good of His design came when He said, "Let there be man"?

We are accustomed to hearing that humans need to obey God's Commandments. The penalty for disobedience (without remorse) is disorder and eternal damnation. We are not accustomed to hearing that God's Commandments are the foundation of His Plan for humans. They serve the same purpose as His Commandments for the physical universe.

God's command to every particle of matter is: Thou shall attract every other particle with a force that is directly proportional to the product of their masses and inversely proportional to the squares of the distances between their centers of mass. If gravity refused to obey its Creator the universe would end in a state of utter confusion.

The outcome is no different if humans refuse to obey their Creator. Man would end in disorder and mankind in failure. The same attention God gave His galaxy, and in fact the whole universe, is also at work providing for the welfare of the creatures He created in His image and likeness. May we not then conclude that God's Commandments are for our good, not His? And, being for our good, we can agree that obeying the Commandments, starting with the First Commandment, is a matter of common sense.

Conversely, we can agree that the outcome of any civil law disparaging God's Commandments is disordered and a disservice to mankind? Satan needs humans working together to dismiss God and common sense.

This view is developed in a later chapter to assist the main argument: "Thy kingdom come on earth as it is in heaven" is man's work, not God's work. He gave us everything we need to succeed, including the Church He instituted to prevent the foundation (of His Plan for humans) from falling into heresy.

God gifted mankind alone with free will. We are free to deny all of this, including eternal suffering, but we are not able to change it.

The twentieth century was witness to changes of massive proportion compared to other centuries in history. The United States became the envy of most other nations for its virtually unlimited personal freedom, its high (if not the highest) standard of living, its status as The Superpower .... Yet, the United States is a failure. We, God's people, failed to halt the runaway regression of our own moral attitudes and of civility. We allowed the evil in Secular Humanism to undermine our faith in Divine Truth and untie the laces that hold the nation together. The knots undone are spiritual authority, responsibility, marriage, and dignity. We bequeath a corrupt national culture to our children and grandchildren.

Restoring life to this "culture of death" is a difficult human-relations problem all about loving God and obeying His Commandments. I approach the problem in the detached manner of my profession, as though it is a scientific analysis of any fallen thing.

The resemblance of fallen man and mortal sin to a fallen bridge and its corroded ironwork is useful. The scientific solution for both problems requires knowledge developed over hundreds, even thousands of years. Corroded ironworks have been discovered dating from one thousand BC. Mortal sin dates back to Adam and Eve.

Truth about both is discoverable by trial and error. And, scientific tests are always designed to fit a particular theory developed by closely observing nature's way. Nature's way is knowable.

Note that denying nature's way increases the problem.

Every scientific analysis starts with what is known: (1) We know God exists. Proof is established by natural reason as we witness His Signature in the infinite diversity around us; and, as Science ponders matter in orderly, harmonious motion throughout the universe. (2) Truth about harmony and order in nature is discoverable by deliberate extrinsic action, rarely by accident. However, man exists as a child of God with free will. Harmony or truth arises in humans intrinsically, by deliberate choice. (3) The premise advanced here is that the rational choice for sinful man is obedience to infallible authority carried for two thousand years in apostolic succession only in the one worldwide Church instituted by the Son of God. (4) Morality is what the head of God's One, Holy, Catholic and Apostolic Church says it is. Logic concludes that men and women can neither define natural law nor invent morality for themselves, because they did not make themselves. Their Maker alone has that privilege and the final word on the ethical manner in which they must live to enjoy peace on earth. (5) Spiritual solidarity (unity) and responsibility (along with faith and prayer) are keys for restoring a sinful. dying culture.

"Speak Lord, for thy servant heareth" (1 Sam 3:9) is the only logical attitude if we can prove by reason that God has spoken.

Reason encourages faith (as with sunrise).

A humble mind is awed by all that it comprehends about the physical universe. It recognizes matter in orderly and purposeful motion and variety that is awesome. Infinitely intelligent design has spoken.

Know that this humble mind (in the words of Joseph Cardinal Ratzinger) is "the microcosm designed by God to embrace the whole world."

Supernatural power speaks every time God gives us His miracle of life.

Isaiah, the greatest of God's prophets, said - "Woe to those who call evil good, and good evil, who change darkness into light, and light into darkness, who change bitter into sweet, and sweet into bitter" (5,20).

Divine justice spoke with Isaiah's voice.

God speaks to us through His infinite love evident in the beauty of a rose, brilliance of a diamond, the innocence of a child (and recent wonder at the DNA/RNA code). His love is most evident in His gift of unique talents essential to dignify each child of God before his equals and before God.

Dignity is essential as a collective goal, otherwise peace on earth is unattainable. Distributive justice (as a collective goal) must come before human dignity is possible. Distributive justice comes about when the state and society work together for common good, i.e. to help everyone achieve true fulfillment of their God-given talents. True fulfillment is man's crowning merit and eternal reward.

"St. Augustine taught that God's love is impressed on our hearts, and His law transferred to our consciences, just as the image from an Emperor's ring passes over to the wax, yet does not leave the ring." (See p. 68 in The Splendor of Truth, an Encyclical letter of John Paul II).

Twenty-first century battles will not only be about defeating the lies of heretics, as it would first appear. They will be about freedom to speak and act upon the truth that is God's Word. They will be about salvation. The enemy's battle plan is man-made morality promoted as a vision of hope attained when men and women declare their independence from God.

"Me first-ism," the culture of twentieth century AD, evolved over many centuries, influenced by the Renaissance in fifteenth century Italy, the Protestant Reformation in sixteenth century Germany, two events in eighteenth century France, a revolution and "Enlightenment," and the Industrial Revolution in nineteenth century England.

Over the span of half a dozen centuries Western Man slowly moved away from God. God's relevance, as in "Thy will be done on earth," became "My" will is done on earth.

Without God there is no hope for sinful man, because there is no truth without God. Without truth salvation is practically impossible.

A powerful Immoral Minority is busy forcing their secular vision of a Godless reality on everyone and everything by means of institutions they dominate. The most blatant example is the secular media. Other examples are Science, the entertainment industry, the Supreme Court and the political party of abortion. We have God's Word that suffering for generations to come and salvation lost are consequences wherever "Me first-ism" corrupts God's truth.

By denying God's existence the Immoral Minority denies Salvation history. They corrupt liberty guaranteed in the U.S. Constitution by making it a license to annul the Commandments (and all that religions teach). They declare false the Christian worldview committed to serving a just and a loving God, and serving Common Good. Miracles God performed are myths.

A secular reality must create a universe that self-exists, then use subterfuge to evade the truth. When is a lie not a lie? Answer: When fraudulent words, pictures and ideas are used to convey scientific knowledge, i.e. science teaches that the universe self-exists. Or, the Supreme Court perverts moral law by making abortion legal. Or, when President Clinton perverts civil law by committing perjury for political gain and democrats in Congress proclaim, "political gain by any means."

Such demoniac means are chosen to anesthetize consciences and in the process quiet fears of God's wrath.

C. S. Lewis wrote in 1947 - "The twenty-first century will be one of two things. Either it will be the best since the thirteenth, or the worst since the twenty-first BC before the call of Abraham and the founding of Judaism." (This quotation is found on page 189 in C. S. Lewis for the Third Millennium by Peter Kreeft, published by Ignatius Press, San Francisco.)

My treatise deals with the new paganism, the down side of his predictions; although, it does recognize that Lewis presents an either-or situation and he expressed hope for the best. I hope for the best too.

However, of immediate concern is abundant evidence showing that self-worship (the new paganism) has already charmed Western cultures. Dignity, honesty (the hallmark of character), duty to others and common good are being sacrificed to the gods of pleasure. Seduction of traditional excellence of character and traditional holiness is widespread, extending even to the Whitehouse and to the Church.

The new paganism will result in near total damnation of Western man.

Modern paganism differs from ancient paganism in that *we know* the Creator and *we know* that relentless disobedience challenges God's infinite Justice. Ancient disobedience arose in part from invincible ignorance of God and His perfect Justice. Today, short of lunacy, there is no way that relentless ignorance of one's duty (before God) can be anything but blameworthy.

Satan's influence (sin) was everywhere in the twentieth century. It is said that he chose that century to do his greatest harm. Believing this, Pope Leo XIII (who reigned at the end of the nineteenth century) gave Catholics a prayer for the twentieth century (the prayer I said at Mass forty years ago with other Catholics) -

"Saint Michael, archangel, defend us in battle. Be our protection against the wickedness and snares of the Devil. May God rebuke him, we humbly pray; and do thou, O prince of the heavenly host, by the power of God, thrust into hell Satan and all the evil spirits who roam through the world seeking the ruin of souls." Amen.

Western man has arrived at a critical period in time holding a false view of right and wrong and of body and soul. We possess the power of the atom and the will to destroy hundreds of thousands of innocent lives by pushing buttons; and, we have the ability to manipulate DNA to make new life in our suicidal image. We routinely manipulate the Constitution, the economy and the Word of God.

All of this flies in the face of wisdom and early history from 33 to 1517 AD - the period that saw peasants and philosophers of the

Western world gradually converted to One Church the Son of God gifted to mankind for all time. Conversion aids were faith, reason, martyrs, miracles, fearfulness (of God's wrath), forgiveness and (the keystone) one earthly authority to preserve Divine truth about moral behavior. These attributes combined to raise spiritual Solidarity (Oneness) throughout the Western Empire to overcome Satan's folly. Individual rights and dignity still prized today as our sacred heritage gained ascendancy in law, customs and cultures during this period.

"Within that household the human spirit has roof and hearth. Outside it, is the night." (Quote from Hilaire Belloc.)

Less than one hundred years after Christ's death the truth of His teaching had influenced the lives of whole communities. Distributive justice was a distinguishing component of His teaching. Public worship was inspired. The words and form of many first century liturgical rites are repeated today. The rites of baptism and the Eucharist were already well established as Sacraments. In short, by 150 AD the Church Jesus gifted with the Paraclete had achieved a reputation for spiritual and intellectual soundness. By 350 AD the hierarchy of Bishops was resolved.

Here there is greater appeal for the mind and the heart of man than in any form of pagan worship (ancient and modern).

Spiritual and intellectual energy reached its zenith in the thirteenth century. Thomistic scholasticism provided mankind a systematic theology, i.e. a comprehensive synthesis of wisdom found in the works of ancient Greek philosophers, recounted by Justin in the second century, and in theology revealed in the Bible's Old and New Testaments, and in theology from patristic letters of St. Augustine, St. Jerome and others who listened to God. The means for university schooling to instill spiritual and temporal perfection in following generations slowly developed beginning with St. Benedict. It continues today in Benedictine and other monasteries.

Lewis called the thirteenth, the century of excellence. The Western Empire was united spiritually and intellectually as recorded in medieval accounts of Cathedral builders and culture builders. Faith was reinforced by many miracles enacted through the intercession of the Queen of Heaven.

That the Queen of Heaven was courted for her favors is a common topic of medieval authors -

"She knows each one, beggar and prince, by name. Christ is very sublime and just; but, 'Mary knows' about everyday ignorance and absurdity." "Humanity is corrupt for all time; each person differing from others only in the degree of their sins." "All know they are criminals; if not, there would be no need for religion and very little need for the State." "Mary was human, but she is different from any other being on earth or in heaven. She made life bearable."

(Quotation from a book titled Mont-Saint-Michel and Chartres by Harry Adams, published in the United States by IndyPublish.com.)

God knows that Humanity is corrupt for all time. But, we need not despair. God provided a means for obtaining absolution (see Jn 20, 21-23).

As another medieval author from Harry Adams' book said, "the Cathedral builders (our great, great .... grandparents) took to heart this gift Jesus gave to the Apostles." I borrowed his words for a letter addressed to the editor of the local newspaper -

December 28, 2005

Dear Editor:

I have four articles on my desk to help write this letter. One is titled Judge prohibits teaching Intelligent Design in schools. It is an AP article in the Dec. 20 Goshen News. Another is Secular state will not reflect religious beliefs, a syndicated column by Cal Thomas in the Dec. 27 Goshen News. The third is the lead editorial on the same page, Intelligent decision on intelligent design. The fourth is a letter written more than 700-years ago, The Gothic Cathedral of Mary at Chartres.

Cal Thomas wrote: "The culture in which we now live no longer reflects the beliefs of our grandparents generation." I thought the reader would appreciate the opportunity to reflect on the culture of much earlier generations. The fourth article, written by Archbishop Hugo of Rouen, France to Bishop Thierry, describes the "organization" of the Cathedral at Chartres:

"The inhabitants of Chartres have combined in the aid of the construction of their church by transporting the materials from the quarry to the building site. The blocks of cut stone were of considerable size requiring one thousand persons or more to move the waggons.

Who has ever seen! - Who has ever heard tell, in times past, that powerful princes of the world, that men brought up in honour and in wealth, that nobles, men and women, have bent their proud and haughty necks to the harness of carts, and that, like beasts of burden, they have dragged to the abode of Christ these waggons, loaded with wines, grains, stone, wood and all that is necessary for the wants of life, or for the construction of the church? But while they draw these burdens, there is one thing admirable to observe; it is that often when a thousand persons are attached to the chariots - so great is the difficulty - yet they march in such silence that not a murmur is heard, and truly if one did not see the thing with one's eyes, one might believe that among such a multitude there was hardly a person present. When they halt on the road, nothing is heard but the confession of sins, and pure and suppliant prayer to God to obtain pardon. At the voice of the priests who exhort their hearts to peace, they forget all hatred, discord is thrown far aside, debts are remitted, and <u>unity of hearts</u> is established.

But if anyone is so far advanced in evil as to be unwilling to pardon an offender, or if he rejects the counsel of the priest who has piously advised him, his offering is instantly thrown from the waggon as impure, and he himself ignominiously and shamefully excluded from the society of the holy." >

The Archbishop's letter is longer as is mine, but you get my point - the culture of our (great, great, great, ---) grandparents generation is, as Cal Thomas wrote, irrelevant.

I underlined "unity of hearts" to emphasize the point Cal Thomas made. He said, "It is futile to try to make a secular state reflect religious beliefs of the past."

The Confessional State (above) would require an act of God.

Assume for the moment God restores Christian unity. How would it go? Many Christians will ask, By whose authority do you assemble? The answer is of course, "Jesus Christ." They will ask, "Which Jesus

Christ?" Which denomination's Bible do you proclaim? Stalemate. We agree God really has the power to restore spiritual Solidarity as in the century of excellence, yet we insist on being pro-choice.

Treatise argument: The consequences of a bastardized reality without mortal sin and Satan in its vocabulary, and without a mechanism for solidarity in partnership with God and His Church, are vastly different from the consequences of an ideology based on belief in God's love and in His terrible wrath - as different as our penalty is from our bonus, untruth from truth, license is from liberty, and a war-torn modern world from a world at peace; as different as moral vacuum is from ethical conduct.

Think about this: Progress (toward dignity, justice and true happiness), and the way progress and true liberty are sought after, is radically different in these conflicting ideologies. One moves Modern Man toward a forged temporal happiness (Success) selfishly gained through injustice for his neighbors and, eternal punishment. The other moves "Everyman" toward temporal selflessness, the forerunner of distributive justice, peace; and, eternal happiness (real Success) in the minds of our medieval ancestors. Trust in natural law and faith in One infallible authority are poisoned in one ideology and are nourished in the other.

Treatise proposition: Success and Failure are about choices; whether to live the truth, or live a lie, (salvation or damnation) within a framework imposed by God and the reality of His love imprinted in every heart. Wherein His Natural Law is joined with every conscience, His Commandments struck on tablets of stone and His judgment is eternal.

Garbage is the word that best fits the consequences of choosing a truth-less, God-less reality. I explained my observations and conclusion in a letter published January 29, 2003 in the local newspaper -
Dear Editor:

I was asked (about 30-years ago), "What's it like to be born and grow up in the United States?" I was born in 1928 and was educated and worked here since that time. The co-worker who asked the question was born, educated and worked in Japan. We collaborated on a research project.

My answer was, "It was fun." I explained "fun" as, "life made sense to me." There are no bad memories and no frustrations that I remember. My family lived through the great depression as most poor families lived - one day to the next (no one told us we were poor). We lived through the "cold war," but we had confidence that comes from trust both in leadership and in our sources of information.

If my co-worker had asked that question today my answer would be different. Now I feel that I'm living in a pile of garbage. Let me explain -

I don't remember a time when I wasn't curious about how things work. Understanding properties and uses of materials was key to fixing problems I was paid to fix. Understanding how things work and how things fail logically begins with the truth about the thing itself. It's fun to discover that truth always makes sense.

For the past 40-years life in the United States has not made sense. Truth is made to appear dependent on circumstances. This so-called culture of death, and political correctness we live by, makes it very difficult to communicate the truth about serious social problems that will burden my children and grandchildren. (This difficulty is one reason God-fearing people are not succeeding in their task.)

There are obvious differences in fixing material failures and fixing social failures. However, both are similar in the fact that progress logically starts with the truth about the problem. Truth is knowable through testing. If tests are designed authoritatively, the procedure is followed exactly and the equipment properly calibrated the result is true and verifiable. The result is garbage where the test of (and authority for) truth is manipulated. Manipulating truth is a bad idea. Without truth there is no hope.

I read in newspapers and hear on television repeatedly that we are a united country. I say this information is garbage. Repetition is a mark of denial of truth. The truth about our social problems is we are not a spiritually united country. >

Bad ideas, like heresies, are contrary to God's Truth. They cause mankind to live without hope in a pile of garbage. Bad ideas lead to bad choices, poor governments, failed economies and to hell. Willful tampering with God's test for truth (His Commandments and His gift of conscience) is a bad choice like willfully choosing self-importance over humility.

I take Webster's definition; that is, garbage is inaccurate or useless information, and track the rate of increase in "garbage" over the last seven hundred years (dating from the century of spiritual unity C. S. Lewis saw as the standard for excellence).

A thought: Perhaps Divine Justice set a limit of these four thousand years from the second millennium BC through the second millennium AD in which to recycle garbage, i.e. for man to get his act together.

An analogy: Mankind is a traveler through time on a road that leads to paganism or away from paganism. Modern Man enters the road at the junction/juncture or period called twenty-first century AD free to choose his or her direction.

Freedom to choose is a gift from God with strings attached. The issue for Modern Man of choosing paganism is temporal as well as everlasting failure.

I believe the Western world has chosen to deny salvation history to live in mortal sin. We have permitted evil to undermine our ability to speak and act upon the moral truth that is God's Word.

I see activist judges killing 40 million babies. I see Capitalism as a ship without a moral rudder. I see sin causing more sin. And, I see the product John Calvin saw in the sixteenth century when followers of Martin Luther subjected God's Word to manifold interpretation. Calvin saw "Reformed Christians," burdened with utterly depraved minds and selfish desires, caught up in anarchy. He set himself the task of restoring order by formulating the theology of Protestantism.

I see broadmindedness that is absurd.

Modern Man must reclaim all that was so much in evidence seven hundred years ago. The key is persuasion, not coercion. All of Creation speaks to us of God's existence and his love for mankind. Truly, the only logical attitude is to listen.

I have collected newspaper articles and articles from Christian publishers that pierce the smokescreen laid down by heretics. Letters and articles are presented in the chapters that follow, organized into a systematic account of observations about America's culture of death.

We are "voices crying in the wilderness."

Perhaps an observation reported by George Will in the June 23, 1980 issue of Newsweek best captures best that which I found -

"A diluted faith cannot compete with the distractions (I call them strange gods) of the modern world. As the West sleepwalks into a decade in which moral confidence and steadfastness will be increasingly needed and decreasingly found, and as a cry for 'leadership' issues from millions who probably would not recognize it if they saw it, and probably reject it if they did, the Roman Catholic Church of John Paul II becomes more fascinating."

The encyclical letter of John Paul II (The Splendor of Truth) also warns us that true freedom has strict limits set by God.

By definition, Subjectivism rejects (in fact excludes) God and the Word of God from its concept of reality. It is the worst of today's bad ideas because it leads directly to Mortal Sin and to hell.

C. S. Lewis saw spiritual solidarity in the thirteenth century. People everywhere in the Western Empire were as one in their outward and inward devotion to God and His Church. He saw gradual weakening of that unity in following centuries as devotion turned inward to man's worldly accomplishments then to self-worship.

George Will saw in the modern world an increasing need for faith in God and in reality ordained by God; moral confidence he called it.

My letters further propose to incorporate the ancient teaching of the Catholic Church, i.e. men and women cannot discharge their duty to seek religious truth unless they enjoy protection from external coercion and freedom from judgment. But, my letters (and accompanying articles) also incorporate God's reality, namely the totality of real things and events. The Western world really has become a killing ground where the lives of millions are terminated because they are inconvenient.

My treatise is delivered in two-parts. Part one covers arguments to defend and support (as I would defend and support a scientific study) the theory that the rational choice for restoring life and the Common Good to this depraved culture is solidarity and prayer, each person working together under one infallible authority, with mutual respect for all. I explain why the problem is all about the by-product in liberation of conscience, namely, failing to obey God's Commandments, particularly the first two Commandments.

I claim as the solution: Restore true freedom by restoring faith in God's reality. Furthermore (as with a scientific study), I claim objectivity and good judgment in the use of resources dealing with Western history from the crucifixion of God's Son to the twenty-first century - A Junction and a Juncture in Time.

Part two is about persuading my readers that Western civilization really has come apart at its cultural seams due largely to runaway regression of morality, civility and goodness. The "bad news" is, as Morris Berman wrote in his book titled Dark Ages America: "We are in a state of advanced cultural disintegration, or what might be termed spiritual death. Given the emptiness, alienation, violence, and ignorance that are now pervasive in this country, it is hard to imagine where a recovery would come from." (His book was published in 2006 by W. W. Norton & Company, Inc. New York.)

I say recovery will come from the only source available. It will come from voters working in partnership with God and unified in His Spirit.

> Post Script: Time marches on. My generation is nearly gone. This book looks for validation from those of my generation who are witnesses to pivotal changes in customs and cultures.
>
> The world's material wealth financed a hot, quasi-nuclear war, then financed a cold quasi-nuclear war.
>
> Our children are witnesses to suffering and death that surpass anything in human history.
>
> Our grandchildren are witnessing the consequences of 40-years of pivotal change in morality, civility and goodness.
>
> My book does not describe greed surrounding the governments $700 billion dollar mortgage bail-out, or greed surrounding oil and gas production, or greed on Wall Street. It closed prior to the November 4, 2008 election that saw a politician gain the office of President on his promises instead of on his honesty and capability.

CHAPTER 1

FAITH IN REALITY

Faith, how and why it works, is an interesting subject worthy of study. How does one come to faith in the reality of one God? Can faith change one's life? Can faith change a corrupted Western Empire?

It is good practice to begin studying how and why faith works by reviewing what others with credible knowledge have said. Faith in one God is a topic that has been around for four thousand years. There is too much information. The subject can be simplified:

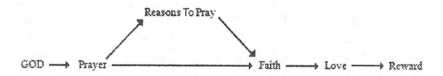

God loves each of us individually. This is what the Fathers of the Catholic Church taught from the beginning. They teach us truth ratified by the Holy Spirit. (Faith must rest on Truth for a solid foundation.)

Faith is a gift available by petition. It is available to each of us who pray out of desire to believe. Faith is an act of mutual love.

God wants us to be with Him in heaven. Why? His Love is why. We are commanded to do our part. How? Example is the best teacher. God revealed this through His Son who said, "As I have done for you, go and do likewise." Jesus lived the good life of God's obedient servant so that through His example I might come to faith. Likewise, I must live the same way in order that you might find reasons to pray for the grace to believe.

Your faith and mine are directly influenced by contributions others (of past generations) have made to our understanding of God, His love for us and His Plan. My responsibility before God is to help (not hinder) your faith formation. The reward for living the way Jesus lived is two-fold - "Thy Kingdom come on earth;" and, my happiness in heaven.

God is The Perfect Architect and Master Builder. His plan for and construction of the physical universe is an open book. Greek philosophers possessed God-given talents to "read" the universe, and appreciate some of what His plan means to mankind. Mind and heart are tools God designed to accomplish this. He made minds capable of discovering enough about Him, through His design, to want to believe - and more. He made hearts specifically to love Him and to love sinners enough to help them believe.

Faith and Love have the power to make peace in a world full of sin.

Interacting with others strengthens faith. We come to faith through reasons to trust in infallible authority. "Homework" and objective reasoning are essential. As more is learned about a mysterious God each person discovers that his or her prayers were necessary in order to receive faith to trust and act. The decision to commit one's life to God comes from trust in His plan and from our gift of love given back to God.

Is my prayer requesting God's help, prompted by many reasons I find to believe, love, and trust, plus His direct touch on my heart, plus good works (mine and others) all there is to know about faith? No.

These are mechanisms by which each of us come to God in body and soul. Faith, love and trust are the ultimate motives for obedience. Faith and trust strengthen our conviction that God alone has the right to dictate truth (Reality), because He is our maker. Faith and Theology intertwine. Theology is the science of God and all of revelation.

Twenty-first century battles are about faith in Reality only God is privileged to dictate. A real God created the universe then caused living creatures to rise from the "dust" of His creation. He breathed a soul into a male creature and created a human being. God used a rib from the man to make a woman. These are real events by a cause itself uncaused.

God is the Supreme Being who can neither deceive nor be deceived. The Good News and the real vision of hope for mankind is that this Supreme Being favored men and women ahead of everything else He created. He gave souls that never die to mankind alone. He gave men and woman free will together with conscience, intelligence and other faculties by which they know with certainty that God exists necessarily. All of mankind have a common purpose revealed in the reality of God's Plan to live as obedient subjects under His governance, and a common destiny that is salvation if our purpose on earth is fulfilled. Man knows sin is real and he knows the penalty for disobedience is eternal punishment. He knows with conviction that nations fail because sin begets sin. But, it is in our fallen nature to choose sin and rebellion regardless of conviction or consequences.

God revealed His infinite Mercy and how His Mercy works. He forgives sins and restores sinful men and women (and their nations) to favor through His grace granted on the conditions of confession, personal and collective remorse, contrition and recompense. Objective historians and theologians see Divine Mercy at work in the rise of civilizations. They see the reality of Divine Justice at work in civilizations that fail.

Choices together with consequences plot the course of human history. Learning about reality (Divine Mercy and Divine Justice) from the laboratory of Salvation history is our "homework." Learning begins with The Easter Story and Justice, published April 20, 1994 in the Goshen News, Goshen, IN -

Dear Editor:

Easter commemorates an act of love that we have been taught from an early age to appreciate. Easter is about justice too, which we also need to understand and appreciate and respond to, because the suffering and death of Jesus on the cross is very important for understanding the problems our country faces today.

Justice is an impersonal concept, just as gravity or thermodynamics are impersonal concepts. Once we understand the principle or law we can predict accurately the consequences that follow. Once we understand the meaning of justice where it concerns God, as in the Easter story, we can predict the consequences of everyday existence in America in this year of 1994.

Postscript: Or in the year of 2009.

We have much difficulty understanding and accepting suffering caused by floods, earthquakes, and other impersonal occurrences of nature. We have even more difficulty accepting suffering caused by cancer, where you and I are innocent, personal victims. Jesus was an innocent, personal victim.

Why did He have to suffer the horrible death inflicted upon Him? Because He loves us. But also, because it was necessary, and He was obedient. He accepted such a death because He understood that it was necessary. In the divine wisdom and justice of God this sacrifice was the only way to balance the scale. The evidence of Easter strongly suggests that our disobedience of God's commands is so serious an offense against our Supreme Ruler that justice required the sacrifice of His only Son in this cruel manner.

Reflect on that this Easter week, and pray for God's help. Rein in your ego and be objective. Study the facts Easter teaches us about God's justice the way you would study the meaning of a falling apple.

Robert Jefferson

The crucifixion of Jesus is an historic event, witnessed by many and recorded by some, which took place in Easter week of the thirty-third year of our Lord. It did happen, and it was unarguably a demonstration of infinite justice and mercy. The fact that it did happen (it was authentically recorded) constitutes a rational defense of Christianity.

The divine measuring scale was balanced on what we now call Good Friday. Accordingly, on the third day we now call Easter Sunday, the souls of large numbers of innocent men and women suffering in hell were released to heaven as described in The Apostles Creed: "I believe ---- He (Jesus) suffered under Pontius Pilate, was crucified, died, and was buried. He descended into hell (to raise up many innocent souls) and on the third day He and the innocent souls ascended into heaven. ----."

I suppose God could have exercised the other option His Justice allowed. God could have terminated mankind and assigned all souls to eternal "fire." But, as Jesus revealed, the Father loves each of His children.

Consider the complete passage from the Lord's prayer: "Thy kingdom come, THY WILL BE DONE, on earth as it is in heaven."

It is important that we understand the impact Divine Justice (God's wrath) has on a future that man controls. THY JUSTICE WILL BE DONE ON EARTH is unmistakable in this portion of the Lord's prayer. God "needs" mankind to perfect ("Crown") His design for peace everywhere on earth, each one choosing to obey God's commands. History and Scripture teach that "the wages of sin is death." (Romans 6, 23) Punishment "kicks in" with hell on earth (pain, suffering, war and injustice) when significant numbers of the population disobey God's Commandments and fail to pray for forgiveness and mercy.

Denial of the reality and meaning of the passion, crucifixion, resurrection and ascension of Jesus serves pride, mankind's ultimate failure. Selfish pride in man's accomplishments, particularly in his inventive genius, is a grave problem. Its ancient names are Tower of Babel and Renaissance. Modern names are Enlightenment, Relativism, Individualism, Gay Rights and Abortion Rights.

Each of these manifestations of pride say: "Let us beset the just one, because he is obnoxious to us. He sets himself against our doings. He reproaches us for transgressions of the law and charges us with violations of our training." (Wisdom 2,12)

Pride makes us disciples of the ideology of denial.

Defeating the age-old Ideology of Denial

First, the ideology of denial must be clearly understood for what it is: Proud men and women freely choosing to deny and thereby escape from the reality God made, particularly His infinite Justice and His infallible authority on earth, in order to deny the reality of the Last Judgement, temporal and eternal punishment and efficacious confession and prayer.

The habit of denial is a simple way to say it. (Webster's definition of habit: An acquired mode of behavior that has become nearly involuntary.) The habit of denying real things and events can have dire consequences, as many will discover who deny the reality of fealty owed to God and deny the Last Judgement. Qui s'excuse s'accuse: He who excuses himself accuses himself.

It is characteristic of human nature that men and women become comfortable with bad ideas and bad habits, even willful ignorance, to the point where they invent senseless ways to keep them. Of course one's habit of denying the existence of God makes it likely, even at the moment of death, that the individual simply never bothers about whether God can be deceived.

The sin of our first parents was pride. The sin of the people who built the Tower of Babel in the twenty-first century BC was pride. The sin of Renaissance Man and Enlightened Man was arrogant pride. The sin of the Enlightenment Age was and is towering pride that rejected God and the reality of His gift of conscience. Today, sinful pride is nearly inseparable from technical genius and towers that dwarf Babel's; and, from the pompous view of progress as a world government without God and a right of each person to his/her own interpretation of God's Commandments.

Warning was given six hundred years ago by Blessed Juliana of Norwich when the Renaissance directed attention away from God. Borrowing from Saint Augustine he said, "God crowns mans merits. Renaissance Man crowns himself."

Modern Man crowns his demerits.

Those who favor the secular view of progress should not be permitted to escape responsibility for its "demerits," e.g. four hundred percent increase in illegitimate births, tripling the percentage of children living in poverty in single parent homes, two hundred percent increase in teenage suicides, quadrupling divorce rates and five hundred percent increase in violent crimes. (Statistics from Index of Leading Cultural Indicators by William Bennett, published by Simon & Schuster New York, NY.)

The certainty that hearts can be judged underlies this methodical discussion of America's cultural garbage. Assignment of responsibility is based on certainty that the fruit of sinful hearts is knowable and is subject to public condemnation irrespective of bogus rights.

Today, Americans are living in a culture of death made legal by our nation's judicial system. Appellate Courts, State Supreme Courts and the U.S. Supreme Court have, in the last forty years, routinely confounded tenets of the Constitution. Activist judges have remade God's Plan in step with Canadian and European lawmakers as opposed to the God-based Constitution of our founding Fathers. Their purpose is to block legitimate cultural interests of elected lawmakers (the

Congress) and a majority of God-fearing citizens. The stakes are high; namely, the destiny of our souls. God's Word on virtues and vices really is essential for those who rule over mankind.

Rulings of activist judges shaped the key that opened the door to promiscuous sex, partial-birth abortion, sodomy and the AIDS epidemic, students killing students, euthanasia, etc. - forty years during which these Satanic Demerits unloaded a toxic and putrid pile of garbage.

These are the bitter fruits of a quarter century reported in The Journal of the American Medical Association: Fifty million Americans, ages 12-65, are infected with an incurable sexually transmitted disease (STD). Ten million new cases are reported annually in the 5-29 age group. STD's increased from three to seventy since the door opened to Satan's helpers. (STD's are passed from mother to fetus according to a Department of Health and Human Services Bulletin).

Moreover, these problems are made worse by a culture-induced wishful feeling that sex freed from lasting commitment and freed from religion is good; and, with condoms, sex is safe forward or backward. The Medical Institute for Sexual Health states: "Condoms fail to provide full protection from AIDS and many of the STD's known today."

These are the wages of sin - bitter fruits along the road to hell.

Dozens of books have been written documenting how the Ideology of Denial turned the very best ideas into evil deeds. Jesus teaching on love of neighbor (social justice) is one example. The public conscience in early Christian communities properly translated love of neighbor into selfless common ownership and distribution of all goods based on need. Communism conceptualizes a system in which goods are owned in common and are made available to all as needed. Problem: Communist leaders misused their free will to choose. They took ownership of all goods, and the distribution thereof, but denied the lesson of selflessness Jesus taught. Twentieth century Communism, Fascism and Socialism were terrible man-made tragedies, and great lessons teaching how and why nations fail.

The battles of this century truly are about Salvation.

There is no longer a word in the languages of modern Western nations to encompass their cultural garbage as they enter the twenty-first century. Traditionally, troubled times such as these were called Evil times. However, today rationalists tell us that reality is shaped by Relativism. Good and evil are not real. Truth, eternal life and other realities ordained by God, and Mortal sin, these are figments of one's imagination. Salvation is meaningless. Theology is a waste of time. Life everlasting, the resurrection of the body, forgiveness of sins, the Communion of Saints, the Holy Catholic Church, God the Holy Ghost, etc. are ideas used to control ignorant slaves.

A tenet of my treatise holds that those who promote Relativism in order to excuse their Mortal sins do great harm to their country.

Relativism rids us of humanness, i.e. knowledge of truth about right and wrong. "We believe and do whatever pleases us" is a forty-year old battle cry reminiscent of immorality before the fall of the Roman Empire.

Freedom is liberty to choose one's own truth regardless of the dictates of conscience. (President Lincoln called this tyranny.) It is liberty without duty imposed on mankind alone to return the Creator's love. Freedom without responsibility is a shameful, undignified thing.

Understanding that egoism motivates the Ideology of Denial is step 1. Accepting the premise that peer pressure of Satan's Collective moves cultures toward egoism, cynicism, sin and damnation is step 2. The third step in defeating the Ideology of Denial and its stepchild Relativism, is to infer logically that the peer pressure of oneness in partnership with God and the gift of His inerrant Church by the grace of God restores unity, hope and the wisdom to advance Western culture toward order and life, i.e. true love, true peace and salvation.

Zealous belief in God or in man, though sinful by nature, leads to social transformation is not a new idea. Duty for everyone is to reshape their sinful lives and become zealous believers that Oneness in God will crown our Merits.

Man's whole history of sin and grace is not properly understood unless we humbly admit that authentic liberty, natural law and everything else that is good begins with God and ends (for good or for evil) with man.

As C. S. Lewis wrote in Mere Christianity: "I must say what I think true. If you look for truth, you may find comfort in the end; if you look for comfort you will not get either comfort or truth - only soft soap and wishful thinking to begin with and, in the end, despair."

CHAPTER 2

THE TWO VIEWS OF REALITY

The two views of reality previously identified are God's view (right side up) and man's view (upside down). My view is centered on God. At first glance my idea of reality is an imposition, because everyone has their own idea based on personal experiences and values - no two are exactly alike for the reason that no two people are exactly alike.

However, God is logical. He designed the universe and started time by setting the universe in motion. Man is nothing if he is not the curious observer. Long ago man observed order in everything around him and his heart understood that his life and purpose must be centered on its maker. Modern Man learns to center life and purpose on himself.

If I describe in detail my idea of reality with a totally objective conscience, with human history in the background and with humility, it will be evident that I am close to your idea and the idea of every clear-thinking submissive adult. The personal values I treasure most are timeless (first salvation then common sense, truth, justice and lawful authority, lawful behavior, natural law, kindness, good health, world peace, happiness, etc.). These values that I treasure are not mere personal ideas. These are the virtues and values we have in common with early Greek philosophers, our Hebrew brethren and with others of our species. Salvation, conscientiousness of right and wrong and the rest are real gifts God has given to no other earthly creature.

Each is free to rationalize his or her purpose subjectively with talents or whims. If with our God-given talents, and prayer, he or she finds a common reality and one purpose -

"To live out one's moral potential God's way in a process that will be completed at the end, in heaven."

(Quotation from A History of Heaven, page 127, by Jeffrey Burton Russell, published in 1997 by Princeton University Press, Princeton, NJ)

Not everyone ends in heaven, but that was not intended and is beside my point. My heart cannot be judged by other men. This does not mean society cannot or ought not judge those whimsical acts issuing from my aberrant talents. Common Good is real and attainable by only one route. Society, i.e. the public conscience, must exercise its right to demand that I behave in an accountable manner - accountable to both God and neighbor.

We are near-sighted specks in a universe filled with stars and other wonders. We are half-blind subjective observers. But many are unable or unwilling to accept with humility wisdom made available by God Himself, i.e. God's breath of life produced "A unique being among the animals," (as G.K. Chesterton wrote in his book The Everlasting Man). We are the creators God made in His image. We have timeless souls that are capable of artistic expression. Our problem comes when men and women deny God and create their own right and wrong and their own accountability out of nothing.

Over the past three hundred years an Enlightened reality has found acceptance throughout the Western world. This reality finds misery in the traditional and historic explanation for Chesterton's unique being, and with the fact that mankind will live forever.

Enlightened Man puts his anguish aside by believing and promoting (with Satan's approval) the idea that man is an accident without a cause and life ends at death. This is the other side of the matter.

Enlightened Man is not accountable for his existence and behavior; therefore, love freely returned to a Creator is nonsense. Love freely given is merely an option, not a command (not to worry about a fictitious eternity in hell). Edmund Burke called this enlightened view "atheistical fanaticism." It is uncritical devotion to one's own insufferable self. Right and wrong are what I say they are. This is Relativism, one of the twenty-first century's biggest problems.

I call this Satan's madness.

Those who habitually gamble against the reality of God and His Plan for mankind and against the immortality of their own soul discover their error after death. They must learn before death that studied or morally culpable ignorance of God and invincible ignorance of God are not the same. They must learn that studied ignorance about

Truth is highly contagious and harmful if permitted to spread through civilized society.

For thousands of years people throughout the civilized world have known God's name. When Moses asked His name God answered, "I AM WHO AM" (Yahweh). God's Word, His authority, His grace, our faith and intellect, our humility, our prayers (personal and public), our conscience, History and Science all play a role in Salvation. His grace rests on our integrity and humility.

We are obligated to use our God-given intelligence and free will to recognize and follow the signposts on His road, i.e. the historic account of the life of Christ, the scientific account of assemblies of "irreducibly complex cells" waiting to receive His breath of life, predictability throughout nature, and other signposts. There really is "One Solitary Life" which showed us by example, and told us by word-of-mouth the truth about His Father's unique plan.

ONE SOLITARY LIFE   (Author unknown)

He was born in an obscure village, the child of a peasant woman. He grew up in another village, where He worked in a carpenter shop until He was thirty. Then for three years He was an itinerant preacher. He never wrote a book. He never held an office. He never had a family or owned a home. He didn't go to college. He never visited a big city. He never traveled two hundred miles from the place where He was born. He did none of the things that usually accompany greatness. He had no credentials but Himself.

He was only thirty-three when the tide of public opinion turned against Him. His friends ran away. One of them denied Him. He was turned over to His enemies and went through the mockery of a trial. He was nailed to a cross between two thieves.

While He was dying His executioners gambled for His garments, the only property He had on earth. When He was dead, He was laid in a borrowed grave through the pity of a friend. Nineteen centuries have come and gone, and today He is the central figure of the human race.

All the armies that ever marched, all the navies that ever sailed, all the parliaments that ever sat, all the kings that ever reigned, put together, have not affected the life of man on this earth as much as that One Solitary Life.

If this Solitary Life and Christian doctrines rooted in it are merely "your ideas not ours," as atheists and secularists claim, the tale is skillfully constructed, most elaborate, most familiar, most believed, most suffered and died for and the most useful myth ever devised. It is more reasonable to question the motives and integrity of those who willfully distort and upset the history of Truth, than to reject the intelligence of literally half of the people of earth starting with Abraham and Sarah; and to reject the basis for judicial and moral restraint used by civilizations for millennia. No Truth and no Justice is found in such distortions.

C. S. Lewis turned from atheism to Christianity when he realized atheism is too simple. But he believed God's Reality was also too simple. Upon careful examination he discovered that God's reality looked simple in the way a tree looks simple. Ask a botanist about a tree and you will sit for hours while he answers. The answer is intelligible but far from what the audience expects.

So it is with God's Plan. His infinite love, grace and mercy, and infinite intelligibility everywhere, are truths far from what mankind could ever have imagined. But, these truths stand to reason as does that part of God's managerial skill dealing with His appointed Overseer who has, with heavenly assistance, absolute earthly authority for all sacred knowledge for all time.

Those who deny Jesus' long-term managerial skills and Apostolic authority in earthly succession do so at great risk. Unity in one body under one head may or may not be the key to salvation, but most certainly it is the key to solidarity for banishing secularists. This is the solution advanced in my treatise for fixing the "corrosion of Goodness."

We discover that Divine Law revealed to mankind by "One Solitary Life" in no way contradicts the Ten Commandments given to the Hebrews by God the Father. Jesus perfected man's understanding of the Father's will, in that we learn the motive for obeying the Commandments is love of neighbor out of love for God. Since love of neighbor is essential for the Common Good we also learn that the

Hebrew life of obedience acts to perfect the public conscience as well. Should we be surprised?

Should we be surprised that God really does work His will on earth through the efforts of sinful men and women acting in One Body under One Head? God appointed Moses as One Head and helped him free the Israelites from slavery.

Should we be surprised that Satan works his will on earth too, through sinful men and women who act as though they had no intellect, no soul and no conscience?

My focus is on the tyranny of secularists and atheists who choose to promote a Godless reality. Their intention is to deny the reality of God and their own souls. Their strategy is to influence rather than inform, particularly about their loss of hope without God. Their wild pursuit of convenience and pleasure entices others. In two or three generations the personal effects of evil (moral decay) and loss of hope become endemic, ending in a culture of death.

My focus is also on restoring solidarity powerful as it was in Poland in 1987 and powerful as it was throughout medieval cultures.

People of medieval Europe knew that God made them masters of their own acts so that each could freely return to God His act of love. For a thousand years selfless love in devotion to God and neighbor was a visible part of civilized Western cultures.

Pagans were impressed by the unselfish acts of God's people. In times of great misery they marveled at a religious belief that encouraged heroic acts of love and mercy accorded even to their oppressor. Through this example, in time and in God, thoughtful pagans were converted.

The Catholic Church is a work in progress. By the thirteenth century the Western Empire was solidly united in one religion with one head. The vast majority knew the personal effects of sin and were united in the knowledge that sinful acts cause moral decay. So much so that, mindful of the Second Commandment and right order, any neighbor who was relentless and remorseless in his or her denial of God and His Commandments was banished from the community until they came to their senses. They knew that public conscience before personal conscience is the right order.

President Lincoln was mindful of right order when he spoke about liberty vs. tyranny in his April 18, 1864 Baltimore address -

"The problem with liberty is that one man says liberty permits him to do what pleases himself and the product of his labors. Another man denies his conscience; saying, liberty permits him to do as he pleases with other men, and with the product of their labor. This is tyranny."

The pattern of societal illness in America, and throughout Europe, is well documented. I studied this pattern of religious bias and misinformation for thirty-five years. My ideas about virtues and values need to be upside down to understand the constant endorsement of immorality and no-fault legislation by the secular media and others.

The following quotation is from a letter by Linda Bowles in the June 1996 issue of the American Family Association Journal -

"There is no mystery. For 30 years, we have allowed the systematic, step-by-step dismantling of a structure of morals and standards carefully put in place to protect us from the primeval forces of our dark side.

No-fault living has become the order of the day in America. Sin is an archaic idea.

Right and Wrong as moral concepts have been abolished. Moral discernment has been deemed judgmental and discriminatory. God is scorned - but tolerated if He stays in His place."

On one hand I saw what C. S. Lewis saw, customs, Christian tradition, and a worldview shaped around God's reality that brought Western civilization to its highest refinement in the thirteenth century. On the other hand I see today what Linda Bowles saw years ago - a secular worldview shaped around man-made reality with monumental changes in customs and Christian traditions. Western civilization is turned upside down at this critical juncture in time. Today, broadmindedness borders on reckless.

Popularity of No-fault living is a good test for moral decay in a culture. A nation's culture fails when Truth about man's faults is thought to be intolerable.

How refined are Western cultures today? There is no answer because the two camps will never agree on the meaning of refined. If "cleansed of impurities" is agreed upon, the argument becomes, "what impurities?" Sin, one camp replies; adding, God cleanses men and women of their impurities. The other camp replies, God does not exist therefore no such impurities exist; adding, we win because we made No-fault living the norm.

The Western world is entangled in the contradiction that is Atheism. Eventually it destroys every democratic government. President Washington in his Farewell Address offered wise council. National morality he spoke of cannot be expected to prevail over atheism where the national culture is bewitched by broadmindedness about right and wrong.

I read a "Pastor's Pen" article in my local newspaper (October 29, 2005) about broadmindedness tolerated in the name of love. The author, Lutheran Pastor Andrew Wollman, called today's Churches "a Hodge-podge of mixed views and confused theologies and varying opinions."

Knowing what your church confesses is important

"What would happen if you went up to your pastor and asked him this question: 'Pastor, what do we believe in?' Now, any Christian pastor could hand you a Bible and say, 'We believe in God, and this is his word.'

That sounds like a good answer, of course, but I'm afraid it's a bit incomplete. We Lutherans have a famous question we like to ask. 'What does this mean?'

In other words, probe a little further. If your church and that other church and all the rest of the churches are holding up the same Bible saying, 'We believe in this,' how is it that we're believing different things? Certainly God doesn't speak different truths to different people. His word is as He is; unchangeable and eternal. And if we all believe the same thing, there would be only one denomination for all of us. But as it stands, there are multiple versions of Christianity out there.

Many Christians go their whole life not really knowing what their church confesses. Oh, they have the gist of it; they know it has something to do with Jesus, but other than that, not many people could give you any specifics about the theology of their church. Perhaps it's because of this age of relativism. Perhaps people by and large don't really care about the specifics of what their church believes, teaches and confesses. 'As long as we just get along, enjoy each other, attend ice-cream socials, and sing a lot - have fun! That's the main thing.'

Is it? Is that really the main thing? In Romans, Paul warns us not to even congregate with people who bring a teaching different from the one inspired by the Holy Spirit, and voiced or sanctioned by Jesus Himself (Rom. 16:17). So God places the first emphasis upon His word, not on fun and social good times. Getting the teaching right. Ice-cream socials and church picnics and fun youth groups should be the result of, not in spite of, doctrinal agreement.

Today it's more common for us to ignore and tolerate differences in theology, and believe this is some form of love. It feels more loving to accept differing views of God's word than to insist upon God's one and only view. It smells of arrogance, and people can't stand that kind of stink.

I know of one church that doesn't believe in infant baptism; but when one of its members do, they allow that member (out of supposed love) to go elsewhere to have their baby baptized. The message is: 'You can still be a member here; even though you don't agree with our confession of faith.' What they should be saying is, 'Everyone here agrees that babies shouldn't be baptized, so if you insist upon having your child baptized, you should really join a church that agrees with your belief.' But that sentence is not seen as integrity at work, but intolerant and unloving.

Our churches are becoming a hodge-podge of mixed views and confused theologies and varying opinions, all the while relishing in the fact that they tolerate all of it in the name of love. Nowhere does Christ teach this kind of love. Do you know what your church teaches about infant baptism? About the Trinity? About the Lord's supper? Jesus Christ? Grace? Angels? Good Works?

Find out. It matters. God is not going to accept you into His heaven just because you are a member of some visible church. He wants you to be engrossed in His truth; not immersed in contradiction; for this immersion ultimately drowns. Ask your pastor about these topics of faith; listen very closely to what he says, or what he hands you to read. Compare it with Scripture.

Be careful though. One of our worst enemies happens to be a gift God gave us called Reason. It wasn't bad when God gave it to us but we tainted it with sin. So now we have this uncanny ability to reason away God's truth. We can look directly at a verse and claim that it means something other than what it says, simply because of our sinful reason. So make sure God's word is ruling over your reason, rather than the other way around (2Tim.3:16-17).

Don't align yourself with a church simply because they do fun things, or there are a lot of nice people there, or because you walk away feeling good. When I walk away from Dairy Queen, I always feel good. Fattening, unhealthy food always does that for me. But faith deserves more attention. It is a higher gift than feelings; and it needs to be fed pure, nourishing food, not fattening food that's full of fluff and feels good. Discover what you've been ingesting. Ask him: Pastor, what do we believe in?"

From Pastor Andrew Wollman I read deep concern about broadmindedness as regards mixed views, confused theologies and varying opinions among Christians, all in the pretext of love. He believes as I do that God's word is as He is: Unchangeable; eternal. And he speaks the unspeakable. He said: "If we all believed the same thing, there would be only one denomination."

Insisting upon God's one and only view is an important part of my message. Those who are diligent with their homework discover that this attitude was universally taught by the apostles and universally accepted as an article of faith until the Reformation in the sixteenth century.

Pastor Wollman said of this attitude; "It smells of arrogance, and people can't stand that kind of stink." He finds it deplorable, as do I, that modern Christians ignore theology.

Pastor Wollman did not take the next step from universal belief in God's whole truth to the sufficiency of God's power and His grace to make it happen in spite of free will and sin. Imagine, God putting His faith in sinful men and women?

He points to the "famous question" Lutherans ask: "What does this (verse) mean?" And: "If we (Christians) are holding up the same Bible, how is it that we are believing different things?" Certainly God knows His children fight and argue. He knows they are prideful and arrogant. May we not presume that in His infinite love the Son of God would do precisely what the Bible says? He set in motion a group of holy yet sinful men and gave them the Holy Spirit as counselor to organize all men and women, Jews and Gentiles, teaching them God's whole truth for all time.

We turn to history books to learn the rest of the story. As the Lutheran pastor said: "Probe a little further."

I say, do your homework.

CHAPTER 3

HOMEWORK

Resplendent and unfading is wisdom, and she is readily perceived by those who love her, and found by those who seek her. She hastens to make herself known in anticipation of men's desires; He who watches for her at dawn shall not be disappointed, for he shall find her sitting by his gate. For taking thought of her is the perfection of prudence, and he who for her sake keeps vigil shall quickly be free from care; Because she makes her own rounds, seeking those worthy of her, and graciously appears to them in the ways, and meets them with all solicitude. (Wisdom 6:12-16)

The best way to begin homework is with "the perfection of prudence," i.e. good judgment in the use of resources.

For example: Knowing the truth of what the "Pius War" is all about depends first on one's good judgment in the use of resources. Pius XII was Pope while Adolf Hitler was in power. Following World War II the Pope was slandered in numerous books and plays written by vengeful enemies of the Catholic Church. John Cornwell's book titled Hitler's Pope, The Deputy, a play by Rolf Hochhuth that opened in 1963, and a dozen more come to mind.

Pius XII is still portrayed as anti-Semitic and a contributor to the Holocaust, based totally on gross misinterpretations of the few resources (personal letters from Holocaust survivors) available at the time. Much later (by 1995) most of the letters and original documents surrounding "Hitler's Pope" had been released by families, by the German and Russian governments and by the Vatican and made available to historians. A book about the role Pope Pius XII played in opposition to the Holocaust and in contributing to saving the Jews, titled The Pius War, was published in 2004 by Lexington Books, Lanham, MD. It was edited by Joseph Bottum, William Doino Jr. and Rabbi David Dalin. A statement at the beginning of the book is: "The Pius War was a long and arduous struggle, vituperative and cruel, but in the end the defenders of Pius XII won every major battle. Along the way, they also lost the war."

I know the feeling. Good judgment in the use of resources does not win the battle for truth where bashing the Catholic Church ranks ahead of baseball as the national pastime. Recent events teach that truth about the past is found little by little, and about the Church, not at all.

Second, knowing the truth depends on prudence in probing a little further into God's whole truth and on one's ability to be objective. The Pastor's Pen reminded us that God doesn't speak different truths to different people.

Throughout history men and women have defined themselves and searched for true happiness in various ways influenced by their parents and by the counsel of wise men; and, by a well-formed conscience. They looked to Philosophy, Theology and to Natural Science in all that they saw around them.

Ancient Greeks saw that man is a rational animal who gains happiness through speculation about the natural world and about himself.

Socrates was the first to theorize that ethical conduct, i.e. avoiding immoral behavior and choosing proper moral actions, is ordered out of spiritual yearning for happiness. He reasoned that the betterment of society will follow when everyone sees to the betterment of his soul. Socrates possessed a well-formed conscience. He was truly a martyr in that he sacrificed his life for the sake of this principle.

Plato (a student of Socrates) reasoned that true happiness lies in knowledge of reality - all that is outside of one's self and unchangeable.

Knowledge of reality gained by these and other ancient philosophers derived from their own observation of purpose, predictability and order throughout nature and from their conscience. Aside from Revelation and Divine Tradition, order, purpose and conscience declare the existence of One outside of ourselves with authority over nature and all of creation - a Supreme Being. This was and is genuine knowledge belonging to mankind's essential nature. Denial of genuine knowledge is ludicrous.

Ancient Hebrews gained knowledge of God's power through their prophets, with whom God the Father communicated directly. They believed that man possesses free will, but he is bound to a life of obedience to Yahweh, where obedience guarantees inner peace and acceptance. The Word of Yahweh is genuine knowledge. Denial of the Word is forbidden.

The Catholic Church is two thousand years old. It derives from Hebrew tradition brought to new life in the person of Jesus, who was, and is, the personification of selfless love.

The Word of the Son of the Hebrew's God is genuine knowledge. Denying the Word endangers one's eternal happiness.

The Apostles lived with Jesus for three years; and witnessed through His teaching and ministry, the fulfillment of all that the Hebrew prophets foretold about the Messiah. The Apostles were slow to understand.

Before He ascended into heaven Jesus "opened their eyes." He empowered Peter as their leader, and the other Apostles (and Saint Paul) to go out and teach God's Word to Jews and Gentiles alike in every nation. Peter and his successors appointed and, by Divine authority, consecrated Bishops, each to teach The Word to their flock. Their minds were subject to intercession by the Holy Spirit who, as it were, mediated their arguments. God in the person of the Holy Spirit was the reason sinful people could trust sinful people and selfish people could trust God.

There was one flock and one shepherd, as foretold -

"And all who believed were together and had all things in common; and they sold their possessions and goods and distributed them to all, as any had need.

And day by day attending the temple together. And breaking bread in their homes, they partook of food with glad and generous hearts, praising God and having favor with all the people." (Acts 2:44-47).

Thus, a new tradition or pattern of thought about God's love slowly took root with grace obtained through the Holy Spirit. Jews, Gentiles and even pagan conquerors throughout the Western Empire were gradually persuaded to enter into this new tradition, because selfless love as an attainable goal appealed to all reasonable people.

These men, who followed in the footsteps of Saint Paul and the apostles, taught from memory and wrote letters to the churches they started, recalling and explaining (free from error but not from arguments) the words and acts of Jesus, as He ministered to the people. These letters and acts are the Epistles and Gospels contained in the New Testament of our Bible. They are, as St. Paul wrote to Timothy, "useful for teaching - for reproof, correction, and training in holiness." (2 Tim 3:16)

The consecrated ones institutionalized the sacred actions (Sacraments) commanded by Jesus (Eucharist, Penance and Anointing of the sick, for example). The Catholic Church proclaimed and defended God's Words aided by faith, granted through His grace, and through reason. That tradition was passed on, shielded from error by the Holy Spirit. By the hand of God it is Divine Tradition.

The Catholic Church flourished and spread across Asia Minor, Italy, Spain and much of northern Africa and northern Europe. By the second century the Church Jesus instituted truly was Catholic, meaning it was acclaimed universally. Hilaire Belloc wrote: "Within that household the human spirit has roof and hearth. Outside it is the night."

From the beginning this "Household" was not closed to religious freedom. As early as the fourth century the philosopher Lactantius, together with the Church Fathers, taught that love for God and neighbor is not open to coercion. Emperor Constantine issued the Edict of Milan in 313 AD granting everyone freedom to follow their religious convictions.

"Only with a free mind can one truly serve God" is a foundation stone of Western Scholasticism. But first, it is with God's gift of a free mind that we are able to find Him.

Grasping and compiling Truth that is God from letters the apostles wrote (some in Greek and in other languages) from inspired teaching of Church Fathers and from deliberations of Bishops was a 300-year process. Authenticity was of primary importance. Incorporation of all that Hebrew prophets and the Psalms taught about the Messiah was necessary. The Roman Synod of 382 AD was called by Pope Damasus to formalize this sacred Bible and proclaim it immutable.

Saint Jerome (347-419 AD) translated the various languages of all that was compiled into Latin. This Latin Vulgate Bible embodies core beliefs responsible for the spread of the faith throughout the Western Empire. It is our Inheritance.

We have for homework the official history of Divine Tradition God helped man to build, including the official text of the Church contained in the Vulgate Bible. He promised to protect it from Satan for all time. Persecutions and its many battles are well documented, particularly the battles over choosing from the whole Church an assembly of Bishops gifted with grace of the Holy Spirit to commission one Bishop, as Peter's successor, to rule on earth over interpretation of the moral law of God.

We have the Word of Jesus recorded authentically in the New Testament that the Holy Spirit will exalt His Body, the Church on earth, making it One, Holy and Catholic (it was Apostolic from the start). And, the power of God will keep it free from error in faith and morals and not subject to another Church for all time. To deny God's power is heresy.

Divine tradition is nothing if it is not about overcoming many obstacles (including personal sin) and resolving many heresies to save (as in Salvation) all of mankind. Gnosticism, i.e. an elite few possess special knowledge of salvation, is one heresy. Arianism, i.e. denial of the divinity of Jesus; Pelagianism, i.e. denial of Original Sin and free will; and Modalism, i.e. denial of the Holy Trinity, are other heresies.

Perhaps the best demonstration of the Holy Spirit's power to safeguard Truth and overcome obstacles manifested itself during the Council of Nicaea. This Council of Bishops dealt with questions raised by a priest named Arius: "Was Jesus truly God?" And, "Did God become man in order to save mankind from their sins (which only God can do) and bring them to eternal life?" Arius said: "How could this be since it is obvious that Jesus was simply a man?"

Over half of the Eastern Bishops in the third and fourth centuries were caught up in doubt about the true nature of Jesus. Arius and others rebelled saying, "Jesus was not (as the Apostle John taught) 'in the Father from the beginning' (John 1: 2). And, when Jesus said 'Whoever has seen me has seen the Father' (John 14: 7-10), He did not mean He was one in being with God the Father. Jesus was merely a man and no mere man can be truly God."

The ecumenical Council of Nicaea (in 325) defined for all time the infallible dogma that correctly expresses the faith of all who call themselves Christians. First called the Symbol of Epiphanius after the bishop of Salamis, it is now called the Nicene Creed -

> "We believe in One Lord, Jesus Christ, the only Son of God, eternally begotten of the Father, God from God, Light from Light, true God from true God, begotten not made, one in Being with the Father ---."

Note that the Muslim world is caught up in the heresy of Arianism. Also note that the Protestant world is caught up in denial that the Church mirroring Christ's authority on earth is One, Holy, Catholic and Apostolic - a declaration universally acknowledged as early as the fourth century after Christ, and affirmed in 381 by the power of the Holy Spirit at the Council of Constantinople.

Catholic tradition embodies the spectacle of little men standing up to and converting Roman emperors, not by the vengeful power of Moses' God, but through the love of Jesus. A volume in The Story Of Man library titled Great Religions of the World (published in 1971 by The National Geographic Society) reveals that Catholicism was made the State religion of the Roman Empire of the West by Emperor Theodosius I shortly before the end of the fourth century.

The fourth and fifth were pivotal centuries for the Catholic Church in that the primacy of Rome essential for religious unity throughout all of the Roman Empire, both East and West, was established for the first time by edict of Theodosius I and his co-emperors Gratian and Valentinian. His edict follows (copied from One, Holy, Catholic and Apostolic) -

> "It is our will that all the people subject to the government of our clemency shall follow that religion which the holy Peter delivered to the Romans, as pious tradition from him to the present times declares it, and as the pontiff Damasus manifestly observes it, as also does Peter, bishop of Alexandria, a man of apostolic

sanctity; that is, that in accordance with the apostolic teaching and gospel we should believe in the deity of the Father and the Son and the Holy Spirit, of equal majesty, in sacred Trinity. Those who follow this law we order shall be included under the name of Catholic Christians. All others we pronounce mad and insane and require that they bear the ignominy of teachers of heresy; their conventicles shall not receive the title of churches; they shall be chastised first by divine vengeance, and then by the punishment of our indignation, with divine approval."

Contrast the fourth century with the twenty-first.

Catholicism had the support of many (but not all) fourth century Emperors and their subjects. Christians of the fourth century believed in the deity of the Father and the Son and the Holy Spirit, not on faith alone, without reason, but on faith granted through the grace of God and reason. They believed the Words of Jesus, protected from error by the Holy Spirit and taught with absolute authority by the apostles, St. Paul and their duly appointed successors. They and generations to come believed the Truth of God contained in the Vulgate Bible saves souls from eternal damnation.

Sacred Trinity and Divine Tradition were accepted not only because they are worthy of devotion, but also because such devotion is in fact judicious.

Twenty-first century Catholicism is merely one of many Christian traditions, and the Vulgate Bible is merely one of many Christian bibles holding that mankind was created free, in the image and likeness of God.

Modern Man excels in re-forming God in man's politically correct image.

Kenneth D. Whitehead wrote at the beginning of his book titled One, Holy, Catholic and Apostolic, published in 2000 by Ignatius Press, San Francisco: "Who could ever imagine doing such things?" These are the words of Saul become Saint Paul to King Agrippa II.

We have the benefit of hindsight. "Such things" are awe-inspiring in Catholic tradition. "Such things" are dreadful in Enlightened tradition.

The high point in Enlightened tradition came when secularists (influenced by Satan) dismissed God's Word from creation.

The high point in Catholic tradition came when the Church Fathers, through the grace of God the Holy Spirit, finally recognized the necessity for One Infallible and Continuing Authority for God's Word on earth.

It is good judgment to use for homework letters written by Bishops and Popes, in particular the fifth century letters of the Bishop of Hippo (St. Augustine), who lived when the first Bible was unchangeably expressed in Latin. Unity and the solution for overcoming Secularism's culture of death and eternal punishment are there in the Vulgate Bible.

These letters, and the Bible, tell the true story of the faithful and record important events, obstacles and arguments that shaped the course of Catholic and Eastern Orthodox doctrine.

Many pagans were converted. As King Edwin of seventh century Northumbria proclaimed to his people -

"This new teaching reveals more certain knowledge (than from our gods) of what went before this life and what follows. It seems only right that we should follow it."

This quotation is found in National Geographic's Story of Man Library. It is on page 336 in the book titled Great Religions of the World. King Edwin possessed common sense.

Faith, reason, one accepted authority and the power of the Holy Spirit checked the spread of error over time. Western Man advanced in very small increments from disbelief to belief in the reality of God; and, from credulity to the exquisite perception of sacred truth made understandable in the Summa Theologiae of Thomas Aquinas, and in sacred images displayed in Gothic Cathedrals that adorned the land.

St. Thomas took the mystery out of mysterious events - the Eucharist for example, where Consecrated human hands change bread and wine into the body and blood of God's Son. St. Thomas knew by reason alone that God possesses the ability to produce this change for all time. How? St. Thomas called it Transubstantiation. The substance of bread and wine genuinely change. The accidents (color, taste, etc.) do not change.

Choose to doubt the supernatural abilities of God's Son, and suffer throughout eternity; or, choose to accept them, and be eternally comforted by God's love.

Thomas Aquinas was a champion of wisdom contained in works of early Greek and Roman philosophers. Many of these treasures had been saved from barbarian plunder. They were carefully reproduced in Benedictine monasteries. St. Thomas and other determined men of his time (Dante is one) blended this wisdom of antiquity with revelation and scholasticism in their quest to move mankind closer to God's reality.

Through Revelation and a facet of Catholic tradition called scholasticism (and common sense) Christ's One Body on earth did convert the Western world. Peer pressure born of customs played a role.

Cathedrals and Basilicas erected throughout the Western world were "hymns in stone" that continue to this day to glorify God's Son and His mother. The architecture became known as the Catholic Style.

By the end of the thirteenth century the customs, beliefs - the pattern of Western life, had succeeded in producing what Dorothy Sayers called Whole Man (in her book, Begins Here, published in 1941 by Harcourt, Brace & Company, New York). Whole Man believed, with great conviction, not only that God exists, but that He works His will slowly and methodically, with input from men and women everywhere and for all time.

Whole Man was an image and likeness of God in a body unified in God and subject to Church teaching. He truly was the product of supernatural solidarity. He was called to live and die by God's will as it is proclaimed free from error by the Church instituted by the Son of God.

God was heartfelt and so real that His presence in the Eucharist, in the celebration of Holy Mass was not doubted. God was active in daily life, both feared, knowing that each day by their sins they offended Him; and loved, knowing that by regretting their sinfulness and asking forgiveness for each sin He forgave them.

Acting on that conviction, Whole Man was the culmination of a

Western culture focused on God's Plan, superior in wisdom to any the world had fashioned to that time and since that time. However, this "evolution of wisdom" is history in labor. It blends man's joy with sin, sacrifice and suffering.

It is prudent to read about the many benefits of the metamorphosis of medieval cultures from darkness to light in man's quest to live as God wills. I recommend the book titled How The Catholic Church Built Western Civilization by Professor Thomas E. Woods, published in 2005 by Regnery, Washington, DC. I also recommend Triumph (over sin) by H. W. Crocker III, published in 2001 by Prima Publishing Roseville, CA (a division of Random House, Inc.).

The story that describes the formation of Catholic tradition is still being written just as the story describing the formation of Protestant tradition is still being written.

––––––––––––

Joy in the century of excellence was short lived. The fourteenth century Italian Renaissance started a long, pain-filled retrogression of Whole Man into Humanist Man - man making himself a value apart from God (not a new phenomenon in human history).

Innocent women and children were slaughtered by medieval (and post medieval) men on orders of a Pope or a Holy Roman Emperor or a Muslim Caliph. Post medieval Kings (Protestant, Catholic and pagan) ordered the same blood shed. Protestant, Muslim, pagan and Catholic mobs likewise.

Man's plan invariably competes with God's Plan (and vice versa).

This is the dark side of human nature. Free Will and a free mind are ongoing obstacles common to all of the good (and evil) that men and women do. That some men and women (Protestant, Hebrews, Muslim, pagan, Catholic, etc.) succeed spiritually, "beyond their own wildest dreams," is freedom wonderful to behold. Bashing those who obey God is understandable for anyone in touch with their dark side.

Sayers postulates seven phases of "History-in-labor" following Whole Man's spiritual success. Each phase (paraphrasing her words) shows us the ideology of denial - pride; each with a different face.

Humanist Man has a smug face that basks in the glory of ancient

Greek and Roman ancestors. Humanist man idolized the works of Classical Antiquity and all that its pagan philosophers, orators and architects accomplished. He envied their pagan conception of happiness.

Humanist Man was out of place (an anachronism) in human history. Humanist Man lived in a vibrant Catholic civilization with the thorns of its God in his flesh. Its religion and its strict discipline were burdens on his ego.

Humanist Man chose to rid himself of the thorns and the burdens by denouncing all that men and women had accomplished in the preceding 1000 years, i.e. the Middle and Dark Ages. He ignored the fact that knowledge of the marvelous works of Ancient Greece and Ancient Rome he envied would not exist if Benedictine monks during the Middle Ages had not preserved and copied them.

Humanist Man and his progeny would reject absolute authority and the supernatural and unworldly ideals of the Scholastics in order to embrace a pagan life of comfort and pleasure. It was as though his was a new age of light separated from the old by 1000 years, with nothing important between. Thus began Western Man's break away from God.

I discovered in my homework a book titled, Those Terrible Middle Ages by Regine Pernoud, a distinguished French historian and scholar. The book was published in 1977 in France. Its English translation was published in 2000 by Ignatius Press, San Francisco. The author adds to my conviction that the seven faces of Sayers "History of man in labor" Begins Here with Humanist Man's battle plan. This effort to slander and weaken the authority of Whole Man's God grew ever more outrageous. It gained favor with both nonbelievers and believers as the means to make their rebellious lives more pleasurable. Each face was more distorted than the one before.

Early in the sixteenth century Martin Luther's "faith alone" (sola fides) contested the wisdom, power and instituted authority of the Son of God by granting to each person his or her own subjective approach, not only to God's Word, but to the binding authority on earth for God's Word - a distortion of their Catholic heritage, i.e. fifteen hundred years of Divine Tradition. Solidarity was corrupted. Churches and nations were split apart.

Rational Man was born late in the 16th century out of the slow, calculated process Humanist Man used to make "self" a value totally independent from God.

Rational Man grew slowly over the next three hundred years fathering, through a Frenchman, Rene Descartes (1596-1650) and his slogan "I think therefore I am," a creative but irrational "intellectual" movement that later came to be known as Enlightenment. "Oneself is the only reality" (Solipsism) was Enlightened Man's joyful message. Enlightened Man's joy: "Without sin no mechanism is needed to explain that readily observed component of the fallen nature he proudly worshiped."

In hindsight Enlightened Man produced moral disorder, not the joy of a "new moral order" his Movement had promised. He seized Natural Law from God thereby elevating (in small increments) Individualism, Secularism and Relativism to the highest practicality.

Whole Man was no longer whole.

Individualism provided fertile ground for "I'm Number One," a child of Solipsism and for Situation Ethics, Relativism's child.

"I think therefore I am" changed the philosophy of life dedicated to our all-loving God to Godless rationalism (with much encouragement from Satan); and, changed the object of life from salvation to liberation. Liberated Man said: "If there is no God then all is permitted. There is no Satan. There is no sin." Liberated Man justified a Right to create reality because, after all, God is nothing more than an idea within one's mind - an idea one wills to be. Reality is, "everything goes."

Jean-Jacques Rousseau (1712-1778) romanticized liberty and emotional participation in life saying: "Turn to (Godless) nature for inspiration." Seek from worldly things not the works of the Gods that inspired Plato; instead, release one's emotions to soak-up nature's limitless wonders freed of the burden of indebtedness.

Near the close of the eighteenth century Immanuel Kant (1724-1804) taught that there is no prevailing moral law outside of man. Judgment and eternal happiness are false products of the spiritual cravings of the mind.

One hundred years later, in 1882, the German philosopher Friedrich Nietzsche gave Secular Man the long-awaited news - "GOD IS DEAD!"

Dead is God, the Creator of the universe, who raised man above all other forms of life. God, the patient Lover, gifted ancient philosophers with humility and the resolve to discover Him in nature. God, the protector, who made Abraham the father of a people chosen to carry His Word throughout the whole world. And God, the Provider, who (when asked) assisted men and women everywhere with faith and reason to perfect His Plan on earth.

Biological Man, or Homo sapiens, was also born in the latter half of the nineteenth century aided by a proud midwife called "Science." His strategy was to confiscate Darwin's Theory of Evolution (1859) for Enlightened Man to use in his war against Christian teaching, particularly the "wrath of God," and against eternal punishment for those who do not believe in a Last Judgment.

Charles Darwin's scientific theory of Evolution turned wishful thinking atheists into pseudo intellectuals.

Economic Man, a social disorder also unleashed in the latter half of the nineteenth century by the Industrial Revolution and Karl Marx (1818-1883), was the response to a secular world.

The Oedipus complex created by Sigmumd Freud followed in quick succession. Rebellious children (Communist, Socialist and Secularist) wreaked havoc throughout the twentieth century. They liberated words from their rightful meaning - valueless values, intolerant tolerance, duty-free freedom; and political correctness freed from common sense are a few of many examples. All standards of sober thought are suspended (they said) where Christian teaching butts-in.

Enlightened Homo sapiens evolved into members of the herd. Jean Paul Sartre (1905-1980) declared that all events are fixed in advance for all time in a manner (genetically) so that human beings are as powerless as cattle to change them. The Beat Generation shouted "Life is absurd."

The loving, all powerful, uncompromising (often terrifying) God of our ancestors was dismissed from reality and replaced with smoke. The result was that ancient and medieval traditions that had, by the 13th century, made Western culture rich with God's grace and man's humility, were by the twenty-first century snared in an arrogant Ideology of Denial.

A two-video set titled Grasping for the Wind, by John H. Whitehead (available from Gadfly Productions, P.O. Box 7482 Charlottesville, VA 22906) dramatizes the decline of Western cultures and to a large extent the decline of Western civilization due in large part to the Enlightenment Movement of the late 1700's and early 1800's, and Secularism from that point on. It is a harsh and somewhat painful review of two hundred years of cultural changes in Europe and America that proceeded from "I think therefore I am." (Descartes got it exactly backwards.) Biological Man accelerated the movement and every day, on the hour, we hear it's drumbeat telecast by the Secular News Media.

Whitehead presents an accurate picture of human nature in the twenty-first century, absorbed in its own arrogance, relieved of all obligations and limitations.

Modern technology multiplied the destructive force of war a hundred-fold and made the world into a battlefield. This hell on earth ought to be a wake-up call. Products of silicon chip technology easily become a thousand distractions blocking acknowledgment of sin and its harmful social effects. Consider the maze of modern gadgets, developed not to serve God, but used (most of the time) to worship strange gods.

God-fearing people would do well to examine their consciences, particularly with regard to the Commandment forbidding the worship of "strange Gods." Denying these facts of modern life delays and in many instances prevents the self-rebuke we must feel in order to make a good confession and receive (from God's agent) forgiveness and absolution.

The twentieth century was far more developed materially than spiritually. In man's enthusiasm over progress in knowledge and power he embraced a defective concept of Natural Law; consequently, of Natural Justice and of civilization itself. The defect is: "I'm Number One."

G.K. Chesterton said -

"The coming peril is something that is coming of itself. America is now by far the wealthiest of States and, in the degraded condition of our day, therefore the most influential. The peril is standardization by a low standard."

He spoke in the Great Hall of London's University College. The date was June 28, 1927.

Modern men and women, secular and sin-filled, carry into the twenty-first century an upside down, head-in-the-sand, defective view of reality - a view that Whole Man would easily defeat; except, according to Protestant tradition, Whole Man lost his head. Ignored was the fact that the head (crowned with thorns) belongs to the all-powerful Son of God.

This all-powerful Son of God gifted Whole Man with unity in the Holy Spirit so he could stand firmly against the enemy. Unity is absent at this historic moment beginning the 3rd millennium of Christ's time. Modern Christians are but a remnant of that physical organism through which Christ acts, because too many have become too broadminded.

A comment of Bishop Fulton J. Sheen (Life is worth living) bears repeating -

"America, it is said, is suffering from intolerance. It is not. It is suffering from tolerance of right and wrong, truth and error, virtue and evil, Christ and chaos. Our country is not so much overrun with the bigoted as it is overrun with the broadminded. In the face of this broadmindedness, what the world needs is intolerance."

Bishop Sheen died in 1979.

Protestantism, Catholicism and Judaism, each battling separately, will not reverse the heresy known as Scientific Materialism spreading through the Western world. This new paganism is far more destructive than the old paganism, because it teaches that men and women, aided by Science, do not need God.

Both Sayers and Lewis died before the rebellious children of the twentieth century turned Western civilization totally backward.

The twenty-first century is about to unveil Postmodern Man - a Homo sapiens clone without a soul or conscience. A monumental failure. Thus the dream of Immanuel Kant may live in infamy …. and God may say, "Enough."

CHAPTER 4

EDDIE

Here, one example is given of Western civilization turned totally backward. It is about Baby Doe who society and the Supreme Court of Indiana deemed to be worthless, and it is about Eddie, an enigma born in the same boat. It is about infanticide. The enigma, or riddle is suffering.

The tragedy of "Baby Doe" provides convincing evidence of improper civil justice and reckless arrogance in a divided nation indifferent to God. Infanticide is a terrible idea.

Perspective 1: *Bloomington Tragedy Brings Right To Life Debate Close To Home*
From the Editorial Page of the Columbus, IN Republic.
By George Will, Washington Post News Service.
April 21, 1982.

WASHINGTON - The baby was born in Bloomington, Indiana, the sort of academic community where medical facilities are more apt to be excellent than moral judgments are. Like one of every seven hundred or so babies, this one had Down's syndrome, a genetic defect involving various degrees of retardation and, sometimes, serious physical defects.

The baby needed serious but feasible surgery to enable food to reach its stomach. The parents refused the surgery, and presumably refused to yield custody to any of the couples eager to become the baby's guardians. The parents chose to starve their baby to death.

Their lawyer concocted an Orwellian euphemism for this refusal of potentially life- saving treatment - "Treatment to do nothing." It is an old story: Language must be mutilated when a perfumed rationalization of an act is incompatible with a straightforward description of the act.

Indiana courts, accommodating the law to the Zeitgeist, refused to order surgery, and thus sanctioned the homicide. Common sense and common usage require use of the word "homicide." The law usually encompasses homicides by negligence. The Indiana killing was worse. It was the result of a premeditated, aggressive, tenacious action, in the hospital and in courts. Such homicides can no longer be considered aberrations, or culturally incongruous. *They are part of a social program to serve the convenience of adults by authorizing adults to destroy inconvenient young life.* (Italics added to emphasize a point I make). The parents' legal arguments, conducted in private, reportedly emphasized "freedom of choice."

The freedom to choose to kill inconvenient life is being extended, precisely as predicted, beyond fetal life to categories of inconvenient infants, such as Down's syndrome babies. There is no reason - none - to doubt that if the baby had not had Down's syndrome the operation would have been ordered without hesitation, almost certainly, by the parents or, if not by them, by the courts. Therefore the baby was killed because it was retarded.

I defy the parents and their medical and legal accomplices to explain why, by the principles affirmed in this case, parents do not have a right to kill by calculated neglect any Down's syndrome child - regardless of any medical need - or any other baby that parents decide would be inconvenient.

Indeed, the parents' lawyer implied as much when, justifying the starvation, he emphasized that even if successful the surgery would not have corrected the retardation. That is, the Down's syndrome was sufficient reason for starving the baby. But the broader message of this case is that being an unwanted baby is a capital offense.

In 1973 the Supreme Court created a virtually unrestrictable right to kill fetuses. Critics of the ruling were alarmed because the Court failed to dispatch the burden of saying why the fetus, which unquestionably is alive, is not protectable life.

Critics were alarmed also because the Court, having incoherently emphasized "viability," offered no intelligible, let alone serious, reason why birth should be the point at which discretionary killing stops. Critics feared that the Indiana homicide demonstrates: The killing will not stop.

The values and passions, as well as the logic of some portions of the "abortion rights" movement, have always pointed beyond abortion, toward something like the Indiana outcome, which affirms a broader right to kill.

Some people have used the silly argument that it is impossible to know when life begins. (The serious argument is about when a "person" protectable by law should be said to exist.) So what could be done about the awkward fact that a newborn, even a retarded newborn, is so incontestably alive?

The trick is to argue that the lives of certain kinds of newborns, like the lives of fetuses, are not sufficiently "meaningful" - a word that figured in the 1973 ruling - to merit any protection that inconveniences an adult's freedom of choice.

The Indiana parents consulted with doctors about the "treatment" they chose. But this was not at any point, in any sense, a medical decision. Such homicides in hospitals are common and will become more so now that a state's courts have given them an imprimatur. There should be interesting litigation now that Indiana courts - whether they understand this or not - are going to decide which categories of newborns (besides Down's syndrome children) can be killed by mandatory neglect.

Hours after the baby died, the parents' lawyer was on the CBS Morning News praising his clients' "courage." He said, "The easiest thing would have been to defer, let someone else make that decision." Oh? Someone had to deliberate about whether or not to starve the baby? When did it become natural, even necessary, in Indiana for parents to sit around debating whether to love or starve their newborns?

The lawyer said it was a "no-win situation" because, "there would have been horrific trauma - trauma to the child who would never have enjoyed a quality of life of any sort, trauma to the family, trauma to society."

In a "no-win" situation, the parents won: The county was prevented from ordering surgery; prospective adopters were frustrated; the baby is dead. Furthermore, how is society traumatized whenever a Down's syndrome baby is not killed? It was, I believe, George Orwell who warned that insincerity is the enemy of sensible language.

Someone should counsel the counselor to stop babbling about Down's syndrome children not having "any sort" of quality of life. The task of convincing communities to provide services and human sympathy for the retarded is difficult enough without having incoherent lawyers laying down the law about whose life does and whose life does not have "meaning."

The Washington Post headlined its report: "The Demise of 'Infant Doe'" (the name used in court). "Demise," indeed. That suggests an event unplanned, even perhaps unexplained. ("The Demise of Abraham Lincoln?") The Post's story began: "An Indiana couple, backed by the state's highest court and the family doctor, allowed their severely retarded newborn baby to die last Thursday night...."

But "severely retarded" is a misjudgment (also appearing in the New York Times) that is both a cause and an effect of cases like the one in Indiana. There is no way of knowing, and no reason to believe, that the baby would have been "severely retarded." A small fraction of Down's syndrome children are severely retarded. The degree of retardation cannot be known at birth. Furthermore, such children are dramatically responsive to infant stimulation and other early interventions. But, like other children, they need to eat.

When a commentator has a direct personal interest in an issue, it behooves him to say so. Some of my best friends are Down's syndrome citizens. (Citizens is what Down's syndrome children are if they avoid being homicide victims in hospitals.)

Jonathan Will, 10, fourth grader and Orioles fan (and the best Wiffle-ball hitter in southern Maryland), has Down's syndrome. He does not "suffer from" (as newspapers are wont to say) Down's syndrome. He suffers from nothing, except anxiety about the Orioles' lousy start.

He is doing nicely, thank you. But he is bound to have quite enough problems dealing with society - receiving rights, let alone empathy. He can do without people like Infant Doe's parents, and courts like Indiana's asserting by their actions the principle that people like him are less than fully human. On the evidence, Down's syndrome citizens have little to learn about being human from the people responsible for the death of Infant Doe.

The United States of America is a nation with eighty percent of its citizens faith-filled in their belief in God the Father almighty, and in His Son our lord Jesus Christ. Our faith in God, the creator of all that we see around us, is scientifically sound and consistent with the belief of preceding generations traced back four thousand years. Our faith in God's Son, our lord Jesus Christ, is historically sound and consistent with the belief of preceding generations traced back two thousand years. God the Father and God the Son are real and necessary for peace on earth. The twenty percent who would have you believe otherwise need to be educated.

Post-Modern America faces a very serious problem. These indispensable Truths are being undermined by a mere twenty percent of the adult population. George Will writes about the problem from the perspective of his son Jonathon, a Down's Syndrome child. His article warns us of the danger when those who know God tolerate the evil in killing inconvenient babies. No judge, no politician and certainly no news manager has a right to question the "meaningfulness" of an imperfect child, particularly in a cultural climate that thrives on feeling good about oneself.

Perspective 2: *"Baby Doe" Challenges Us*.
Printed in the Criterion, (a Catholic newspaper).
By VRD, editor, dated April 23, 1982

The case of "Baby Doe" of Bloomington is a tragic one. Tragic for the infant who died because he was not born perfect. Tragic for the parents, who immediately after his birth, faced an agonizing and no-win decision they will live with forever. And tragic for the human community, as it clumsily tries to cope with growing technological power over life and death.

The case also brings clearly into focus an enormous challenge which faces us and which goes well beyond factual education in the life issues.

Heaven knows, just enabling people to understand what medicine can do and what moral principles should guide them as they make life/death decisions is complicated enough. But the need goes deeper than simple knowledge. Once, we innocently believed if we could prove that abortion killed a living child that would end its widespread practice. We know today how wrong we were. (Why today? Because, today we understand that the culture of death serves personal convenience.)

So facts about unborn life, theological principles and (in the case of "Baby Doe") proof of the potential of a Down's syndrome child won't, by themselves, change very much. Instead, the change must be of minds and hearts, a reshaping of the deeper values by which people live.

There is this attitude that parents own their children. We see it manifested in the abortion laws which give a pregnant woman total decision-making power over her child's life. We see it in the weak, unenforced laws on child abuse, in reluctance of neighbors and teachers to report obvious cases of abuse and in the court's willingness to return a beaten, sexually abused, even tortured child to its "natural" parent. And we see it in such cases as "Baby Doe."

As long as parents believe they "own" their children, the little ones may not have much of a chance.

There also flourishes a "quality of life" mentality that exalts physical perfection and intellectual excellence and shuns weakness. We are, at times, victimized by our own affluence and fascinated by our material goods. We inordinately respect success and cannot tolerate waiting, suffering or failing.

Can such pervasive attitudes be changed? Can the good values we hold somehow be meshed with traditional Christian belief in honor for the aged, compassion for the vulnerable, of willingness to nurture potential in the less endowed? Can we build a community which welcomes everyone and devalues no one?

It surely is no job for the faint-hearted or the technician. It's an undertaking for the hope-filled, and they won't finish in their lifetime. And the challenge is not only to preach it, in season and out but to live it joyfully so that others may also believe. >

The job is to reverse six hundred years of "History in labor."

Dorothy Sayers and C. S. Lewis both found that the object of freedom in medieval times was honor owed to ones real nature as a child of God. A thousand-year spiritual revolution stemming from the teaching of Christ, passed down from His Apostles, produced a medieval culture based on honesty and disciplined integrity toward oneself and others.

The object of freedom today is liberation of conscience. Personal convenience has all but displaced personal honor.

Perspective 3: *Life or Death of Baby Can't Be Legislated, Attorney Says.*

A UPI wire story, dated April 15, 1983

Efforts to legislate whether parents can make decisions that mean life or death for physically handicapped babies are misdirected, a lawyer in such a case said.

Andrew Mallor represented the parents of "Infant Doe," a Downs Syndrome baby with a detached esophagus whose death a year ago today spurred a national controversy over the medical care of handicapped babies.

Mallor called national response to the case "frightening."

A rule, enacted last month and struck down in a federal court ruling Thursday, would have required the posting of signs in some seven thousand hospitals that get federal funds, saying it is illegal to stop feeding or treating infants because of handicaps.

Margaret Heckler, secretary of Health and Human Services, immediately announced that the Reagan administration would appeal.

The American Pediatric Association has challenged the rule in a lawsuit in the Washington, D.C. federal court that issued the opinion.

"I would concur wholeheartedly with the association," Mallor said. "It's frightening to think a rule of this type could be passed without thinking of the effects it would have on future cases."

"We, as a society, haven't evolved to the point where we have all the answers," Mallor said. "Legislation of this type prevents family, clergy and friends from trying to make a decision. It greatly intrudes on the province of a doctor to make a recommendation to a patient."

Infant Doe was the name a court used to hide the identity of the week-old boy who died at a Bloomington hospital April 15, 1982, after his parents asked doctors to suspend food and medical treatment.

The child died hours before court-appointed lawyers were to ask a U.S. Supreme Court justice for an emergency order that might have kept him alive. The Indiana Supreme Court upheld a trial court's right to back the parents' decision.

Besides the Reagan Administration federal rule, a number of states are considering legislation designed to protect handicapped infants, said Sen. James Butcher, R-Kokomo, whose own bill was enacted by the Indiana Legislature.

The so-called Infant Doe bill states that all handicapped people under age 18 qualify under the state's "children in need of services" law.

"There appears to be a growing interest in other states," Butcher said. "If nothing else, the case has made most of our citizens aware there is a problem and we need to look hard at what is happening in some of our hospitals across the country."

A Marquette University law professor has drafted a model Infant Doe law so courts can review parents' decisions about medical care of their newborns.

Mallor criticized groups supporting the passage of such legislation.

"The Baby Doe case came at a time when you had many pro-life groups around," Mallor said. "It was a political response from those people who are anti-abortion. It's not a response to this case so much as using this case, maybe abusing this case, for political purposes."

Mallor said doctors asked to comment on a medical situation such as Infant Doe's all agreed that it was in the child's best interest not to treat him. (A lie printed as fact.)

The significance of Infant Doe's death has been exaggerated, largely because a court seal on the case has kept people unaware of all the facts, Mallor said.

"When the public thinks of a baby, their perceptions are of a healthy child not getting any nourishment," Mallor said. "This child did not breathe at birth. He was going to have brain damage. (Opinion passed on as fact by the secular media.) He required multiple, prolonged, painful operations that could have been painful, horrible with no quality of life."

Senator Butcher insists Infant Doe would be alive today had his defect been other than Down's Syndrome. "If Baby Doe was born with a club foot, there's no doubt in my mind the operation on his esophagus would have been performed." >

My comment: If Terri Schiavo's death by slow starvation on March 31, 2005 is a benchmark of progress, America's judges and attorneys are giving us a hard, sorrowful look at the twenty-first century.

George Will's article and my two articles below, titled "My life or death response" (published April 20, 1983 in The Republic) and "Two views of life and death in the United States" (published March 31, 2005) were not treated the same as Mallor's "Life or Death news." Our articles were merely opinions assigned to the Editorial page. Mallor's article had the imprimatur of the UPI and commanded a page reserved for reliable information.

My life or death response

Dear Editor:

On April 15, the anniversary of the death of Infant Doe, The Republic printed an article describing an interview with Andrew Mallor, attorney for the parents of Infant Doe. "It is frightening to think a rule of this type could be passed without thinking of the effects it would have on future cases," he said. (The rule is about posting signs in hospitals saying it is illegal to stop feeding or treating infants because of handicaps.)

Mallor and others believe "legislation of this type prevents family, clergy and friends from trying to make a decision." In plain language this means kill the child, and forget about disagreeable details such as morality. Mallor arrogantly criticizes groups that support the passage of such legislation. He also said doctors, asked to comment on a medical situation such as Infant Doe, all agreed it was in the child's best interests not to treat him. The UPI article goes on to quote other Mallor statements, ending with: "This child was going to have brain damage.... with no quality of life."

What is "quality of life?"

Life is full of difficult decisions. It has been this way for thousands of years, and it isn't likely to change. What does change is our response to duty and pain. I remember when Americans accepted their responsibilities, and the pain and hardship that followed. They grew stronger, and the nation was strong.

Today, many Americans take extreme measures to avoid pain and hardship in their personal lives, without considering the effect on others. This makes them weak (in my opinion) and lowers the quality of life for everyone.

While reading the Mallor article I wondered why it was selected for publication, particularly on the anniversary date. Arguments in favor of parents killing a handicapped child, or aborting their unborn children, are no longer news. They have become common. Nor is it news that some doctors support efforts to kill handicapped infants. Not all doctors, but enough so that the moral standard of the American Medical Society, and the American Pediatric Association is lowered.

Allow me to suggest something that would be news. Print the other side of the issue, not on the Opinion Page, but on the same "information pages" where the UPI's Mallor article was printed. You can begin by interviewing me.

Two views of life and death in the United States

Dear Editor:

Why do I believe that I am wrong to apply logic to understand life and death court rulings? Perhaps the reason is that I might discover by applying logic that there really are two very different worldviews about life and death dividing this nation (and Western nations in general); and, that most of the people who manage our thoughts are strongly biased toward the view that the universe and mankind are simply the result of a series of accidents.

This worldview dismisses all knowledge of duty owed to a loving Creator and instead insists on elevating (in civil society) one's personal interests ahead of all other interests. Decadence and death of the soul logically follow from such corruption of moral freedom in civil society. As a nation we dare not permit man's will to win over God's will. Having it both ways is illogical.

The court ruling in the Terri Schiavo case is a recent example of corruption of logic. Modern Medical Science describes life and death as natural stepwise processes, where each step is understood and readily observed to follow a logical order. The issue with Terri Schiavo comes down to one question. Is she actively dying? Are her bodily functions shutting down? (The need for nourishment in terminal patients depends on how far along their bodies are in shutting-down, and thus, the "need" for nourishment in a patient who is dying is readily observable.) Those who have first hand knowledge of Terri Schiavo say she enjoys having a full stomach   .

State and federal courts have ruled that self-interest of her husband is more important than (observable) evidence that the body of Terri Schiavo is fully functional. (There was no sign that her body was shutting-down.)

Thirty years ago the Supreme Court dared to rule that self-interest of a pregnant woman is more important than (observable) evidence that her fetus is functioning, i.e. it is alive. (Otherwise, the pregnancy would terminate itself by miscarriage.)

Self-interest of mother first, husband second, woman's parents third, and the woman's innocent infant last, confuses freedom of conscience with the pursuit of happiness (as in pursuit of sex).

Those who pervert truth and logic at one end of the spectrum, and get away with doing so, will eventually succeed in perverting truth and logic at the other end. This is the predicament in the Netherlands where Infant Euthanasia (the latest tyranny) takes an alarming number of "unworthy" babies from their cribs.

Now perverting truth and logic is part of the Bioethics curriculum at Princeton University.

We, as a nation, are suffering from death of the soul. The first step toward reversing this process is prayer. Next, identify by their conduct those who pervert truth and logic. They are perverts and liars. >

As George Will said, "When a commentator has a direct personal interest in an issue, it behooves him to say so."

I have a personal interest in the "Baby Doe" issue, details of which were expressed in a letter my wife and I wrote to Edward T. O'Meara, upon reading about the starvation of "Baby Doe."

April 20, 1982

Most Reverend Edward T. O'Meara:

My wife and I request a mass be said to honor the six day old baby who died in Bloomington. We have a 25 year-old son, Ed, who was born with the severe handicap of cerebral palsy. At his birth we did not think of ourselves as victims, but as parents with a heavy responsibility. Twenty- five years is too long a time to have clear memories; I do remember that it wasn't easy. Mental retardation was one concern. Today Ed is preparing to receive a degree in theology from Marion College. He is an outstanding member of the community, and has received a number of awards. The latest was the Governor's award given to select volunteers, which he received from the mayor of Columbus, Indiana.

I said we did not feel victimized that day 25 years ago. But we are victims today, and we protest. We protest against a judicial system that confuses death by starvation with death by natural causes. We protest that newspapers say "permitted to die," when an innocent victim is "intentionally put to death." And we protest that our children and grandchildren will reap the ruin that comes in retribution for a million abortions every year. It would be wonderful to see Christians unite in One Body over "Baby Doe," an infant not even permitted a name, and to vote as One Body.

Respectfully,
Robert T. and Thelma A. Jefferson

Eddie is a story all by himself. He earned a Masters degree in Adult Education from Ball State University in 1985. He writes letters too, typing slowly with a jerky finger. His letter was published in 1976 in our Columbus, IN newspaper, The Republic -

EDDIE

Handicapped Student Wants Chance To Do For Himself

I am a student at Columbus North high school, and I am handicapped. I am very interested in working with the handicapped and the retarded of Columbus, but there is a problem. When I am out helping people, the public thinks I need help.

I recently attended a basketball game as part of the Special Olympics, which is a contest for the retarded. I went as a volunteer to help. I wanted to get some lunch across the street, but I was stopped and taken back.

I can understand why they stopped me, but they did not listen to me try to explain. They took me in to the game and called someone to come and get me. This is not the first time this has happened.

The handicapped person is just like everybody else, he wants to do things for himself. I think the public needs to be aware of the handicapped person and what he can do. I think people would be surprised.

Edward Jefferson

Ed has a speech impediment.

Eddie was news, even at the early age of eight. The following letter by Sherry Kerns was published in our local newspaper -

A Lesson to be Learned

I saw him across the street and wondered what sort of game he was playing. But when the sun caught the metal on his feet I realized the lurching walk was no game. He had braces on his legs.

He crossed the street, walked up our driveway, rang the bell and asked if I'd like to purchase some chances on a drawing which would be held by the Gorman School for the Handicapped PTA. He explained the donations would go toward wheelchairs and crutches.

I invited him in. He sat down and began a conversation. His speech was halting and labored. Each word was spoken slowly and carefully. He told me proudly that I was his thirty-first customer. When I asked his name I couldn't quite understand so he spelled it for me - EDDIE.

It was a struggle for him to get up from the couch because of the weight on his legs. He thanked me and said he hoped I would win.

I watched him walk down the driveway and the longer I watched the cloudier my eyes became. This emotion I felt was not sympathy or pity. I was proud of Eddie. His outlook and pleasantness would put all of us cynics to shame.

He was just a boy. His name was Eddie. He was physically handicapped and his smile was unending.

My hat is off to you Eddie, and to your parents for instilling in you the joy and love of living. We could all learn from you. >

Eleven years later the article below, by Staff Writer Sheryl Shelton, appeared in the same newspaper (the Republic). The time was spring 1977 -

Jefferson Selected for Award

A Bartholomew county youth afflicted with cerebral palsy, who "gives himself to life..." will be honored tonight as the state's "Outstanding Gold Teen of the year."

Selected to receive the $1000 W. Rowland Allen Memorial Scholarship is Edward (Eddie) Jefferson, 19, son of Mr. and Mrs. Robert T. Jefferson of Road 500N.

The award is given annually in honor of Allen, who died in 1973, and who worked and was a leader in the Mental Health Association for over 30 years.

Traveling to Stouffer's Inn for the special event will be Jefferson's parents and brother Alan, a fourth grader at St. Columba Roman Catholic School.

The award will be given in Indianapolis during the annual meeting of the Mental Health Association in Indiana, at which Authoress Mary MacCracken will guest speak.

Among those sending letters to the state Mental Health offices, highly recommending Jefferson for the scholarship award, were William Mihay, chairman of Bartholomew Gold Teens to the Muscatatuck State Hospital and Training Center for the Mentally Retarded at Buterville, Horace E. Broome, director of community services at Muscatatuck, and Elizabeth Kerns, administrator at Columbus Convalescent Center.

Jefferson will graduate May 22 from Columbus North High School, and plans to earn a degree in special education at Ball State

University at Muncie.

For the past five years, Jefferson has made bi-monthly trips to Muscatatuck and has given five hundred hours of volunteer service to patients.

Regarding Jefferson as "an inspiration, and a good friend of mine," Mihay said of the youth, "being physically handicapped with cerebral palsy, he is better able to understand the problems of handicapped people and to help them without appearing to be patronizing or pitying."

At Muscatatuck, Jefferson's responsibilities ranged from delighting patients as Santa Claus, to assisting with such volunteer activities as Special Olympics, Petty Zoo and the annual Phi Delta Pi Carnival.

Lauding Jefferson as "bright, honest and uncomplaining," Broome said Jefferson "would make you proud to have been a part of his life."

At the Columbus Convalescent Center, Jefferson has worked as a "very successful" Gold Teen volunteer, donating close to 175 hours assisting the elderly with physical therapy, pushing them in wheelchairs and playing games with them, especially euchre, which is his specialty.

At Columbus North, Jefferson has been involved with the youth section of the Association for Retarded Citizens, and while a student at Northside Junior High School was manager of the swim team.

For the past three years he has worked as a volunteer at youth and adult camps for the handicapped sponsored by Developmental Services.

Jefferson is a member of St. Columba and is vice president of the Catholic Youth Organization. >

Dad's note: I am truly grateful that Andrew Mallor, attorney for the parents of "Baby Doe," or Indiana's highest Court, or Pinellas, Florida Circuit Court Judge George Greer, or the American College of Obstetricians and Gynecologists, or George Felos attorney for the estranged husband of Terri Schiavo had no say in 1957 regarding Ed's "Quality of Life."

I have Ed's permission to copy an article he wrote in which he retraced a painful, yet rewarding four-month period of his life.

My Suffering: A Gift From God

One of the major doctrines of the Catholic faith is that of the

death and resurrection of Christ. This is recalled at each liturgy in the proclamation of the mystery of faith. Through penance and sacrifice, especially during lent, we are invited to share in the suffering of Christ.

I have lived with cerebral palsy all thirty-two years of my life. People would tell me that through my disability I was fortunate to share in the suffering of Christ. But I didn't fully understand what that meant. I did not see myself as disabled, and had never related my pain with the suffering of Christ. Because of a four-month hospitalization, now I can personally identify with Christ's suffering. During this time there were several occurrences that have strengthened my faith in the divine Will of God, and in the Eucharist; and the support that comes from the Church as community. My faith in Our Lady has also been strengthened.

On the evening of March 7, 1989 I went out to dinner with my family, and to a movie. I came home and went to bed. About 1:00 am I woke up with severe chest and lower-back pain. To wake up with chest pain was not uncommon, but this was different. I knew something was wrong. The pain was so strong that I could not straighten my legs.

My dad took me to the emergency room where I was admitted for observation. The next day I was in constant pain, and late in the afternoon I went into respiratory arrest. I was put on a respirator and my vital signs improved. This was the first of many times where I was not physically able to help myself. I was unaware that I had gone into respiratory arrest.

The pain continued for 2 days, well beyond the usual level for my cerebral palsy. Then, for no apparent reason (no medical explanation), the pain was gone. The improvement made me realize that I had no control of my own life - over the will to survive - this is actually part of the soul. I found faith enough to accept God's hand. The strength of the Real Presence in the Eucharist is another essential quality of the soul. It is a vital part of the will to survive. But I'm getting ahead of events as they happened.

Eight days later I was transferred to the university's Hospital in Muncie, Indiana. I was going to Ball State at the time, and I had a doctor who knew my medical history. Later my lung collapsed and I had to have surgery. My dad asked the doctor if they could wait until I was stronger. The doctor told him if they didn't operate I could die.

On Good Friday I was in the intensive care unit and in severe pain. Because of the pain medication, I was not aware of what was happening around me. A good friend told me that she was in my room at 3:00 PM. She felt that Calvary was present in the room.

My surgery was scheduled for Easter Monday. Several layers of a rind-like substance had to be removed from my lung in the same way one might peel an orange. Once all of the layers were removed my lung expanded. When I was told of the procedure, and I realized that it took place on Easter Monday, I knew that just as I had suffered with Christ on the cross of Good Friday, so too, on Easter Monday I received new life in His resurrection.

During the same surgery a tracheal tube was placed in my throat so they could hook me to a respirator; on which I was completely dependent. During this time I thought a lot about how small but how vital is a breath of air. The image that came to mind is from the book of Genesis where the author says, ".... the Lord God formed man of the dust of the ground and breathed into his nostrils the breath of life, and the man became a living soul." The doctors and nurses knew how to take care of me while I was on the respirator, but it was God who had given me back the breath of His life.

This is God's breath of life. There are other people who depend on respirators and receive the same care as I had, but when they are taken off they do not live. Or, there are people who live only a short time. My mom, for example, was in a coma and was placed on a respirator at the same time as my hospitalization. She was taken off the respirator in July and she lived until August 15th, which is the feast day of the Blessed Virgin Mary. Mom had a great devotion to Our Lady. I believe she is with Mary and at peace in Heaven.

Because of the tracheal tube I was unable to eat. They had to insert a tube into my stomach through which I was fed. Later I had to relearn how to swallow. At first they gave me clear liquids and then I moved on to soft foods. It was difficult for me to eat without choking. The nurses had to use a suction tube to remove the food when I choked. I did not know from one bite to the next whether I would choke.

The day they started giving me soft foods a good friend, who was a nurse on a different floor, brought me Holy Communion. The possibility occurred to me that I might choke. But this fear was dispelled with the realization that I was about to receive Christ. I had no trouble receiving the Eucharist on that day or any other time in the hospital. Despite my friend's medical training, the possibility of choking did not occur to her.

This was an emotional experience. I cried because it meant so much to be able to receive Our Lord. During the first 6-weeks I was not able to receive Communion. The ability to receive Our Lord again felt like I had come out of a spiritual desert. Before this time I was in so much pain and confusion that I found it impossible to pray. Later in my hospital stay I looked forward to visits from people of my parish who brought me Communion.

The Eucharist, as mentioned earlier, is part of the soul. Sometimes this is referred to as "spiritual nourishment." Jesus said, "I am the bread of life. He who comes to me shall never hunger and he who believes in me shall never thirst."

My parish community was very supportive with their prayers, both for my recovery as well as for mom. Different people from the pastoral care team came two or three times each week. Each time someone would come they told me I was mentioned in the offertory petitions at every mass.

The first time I went to mass upon my release it was a real homecoming experience. As I sat in church before mass, two feelings overwhelmed me. After not being able to attend for four months it was refreshing for me to be physically present in my own faith community. As I looked around I realized that all these people had been praying for me. This first mass was also the feast of Corpus Christi, the feast day of the Body and Blood of Christ. I gained a greater appreciation of the strength that comes from the Eucharist and now my homecoming was even more significant.

When my mom passed away I was not able to attend her funeral. I did attend Mass at my parish. Two priests concelebrated the Mass. They said the prayers of burial for mom at the end of Mass. I heard the prayers and I heard them say her name, but I felt numb, as if the reality of her death had not hit me. I could not believe what I was hearing. I was glad to have the support of my parish that day.

My hospitalization drew me closer to Our Lady. A friend came and we prayed the rosary. This brought me great peace. This was one experience that proves to me the protection of the Blessed Virgin.

During my hospital stay I had five different surgeries. One was for a hiatus hernia. The day before the surgery my sister and a good friend were in my room as the doctor explained the procedure. He said the operation may not help and, that I could die. He also said the operation would take at least 3 hours, and they were concerned about my lung. Being under anesthesia for a long period could cause more damage to my lung.

This was the first surgery where I could understand what was going to happen. I was afraid. I had my scapular tied to the rail of my bed. Instinctively I reached up and held it. At this time I still had my trache and I could not talk. I spelled out on my communication board, "I am afraid. I want this with me." Before I went to surgery my dad tied the scapular to my arm.

The surgery went much better than expected. It lasted an hour and a half, and there was no further damage to my lung. I attribute the success to Our Lady and to the scapular.

During much of the time in the hospital the physical pain was most evident to those around me. I received various medications to control pain. I remember the greatest suffering was emotional and spiritual.

There were people who came to visit and to pray with me. I remember that it was very difficult to pray verbally. My visitors were very sincere, yet I felt that they didn't understand what I was experiencing. As I said, I wandered for a time in a spiritual desert. I remember thinking about the last words of Jesus before He died on the cross, "My God my God, why have you forsaken me?" While in my desert, I knew many people were praying for me. Support that comes from the prayers of a faith community is another quality of the soul.

The whole experience was, in a very real sense, a long series of emotional ups and downs. While I had the tracheal tube I couldn't talk, and with cerebral palsy communicating by pointing to words on a board was awkward, and very slow, and very tiring. There were times when I wanted to talk to friends, but the effort was too great. It was frustrating to lay there and look at my friends.

The hardest thing for me to face was losing my mom. Muncie is a two and a half hour drive from home. At first my parents came once or twice a week. When I was strong enough to be moved out of the intensive care unit I noticed that there was something wrong with mom. Each time I saw her she seemed more withdrawn. Dad brought her to see me in May for what was to be her last visit. That day she was not withdrawn. Dad was out taking care of some business for me and, with my trache gone mom and I talked normally.

Mom was admitted to the Goshen hospital in June. Her kidneys and liver were failing rapidly. During the next two months I was torn between wanting to be with mom and making my own recovery.

Saturday, July 1st dad called to see if I could come home. Arrangements were made and a friend drove me to Goshen the next day. By this time mom was in a coma and on a respirator. I noticed that mom had the same bed in intensive care that I had in March. I could not separate my feelings for mom from the memories I had in that room, hooked to perhaps the same respirator. I kept telling her that I loved her. At the same time I wanted to get out of my wheelchair and pull out her tubes so she wouldn't have to suffer. I said good-bye, and felt that I would not see her again.

I had to return to Muncie the next day. The following day she came out of the coma and was taken off the respirator. Her vital signs were stable. She was transferred to a round-the-clock professional care center in Goshen, where she improved to the point that she recognized some of her visitors, and talked to them. During this time I was on an emotional roller coaster.

I spoke with either my dad or my sister by phone two or three times a week. I was able to follow and relate with her improvements and her set backs. My prayer was that God would take her, because what the doctor saw as "good signs," I saw only as prolonging the inevitable. And yet, when I heard that mom could talk, I prayed so that she would live. It was a hopeless feeling.

One night, in the midst of my confusion, a verse from scripture came to mind; Christ said, ".... unless a grain of wheat falls to the earth and dies it shall not produce fruit, but if it dies it will bring forth much fruit." In this passage Jesus invites us to share not only in His death but also in His resurrection.

Through my suffering and "death" experiences I have come to understand two separate "gifts" we receive in suffering. The first gift; suffering is a powerful prayer. I knew that in my suffering I had been helping mom. Through our love relationship, even though we were over a hundred miles apart, we were very close in spirit. This closeness transcended distance. I also began to offer my suffering as a prayer for a retreat community for disabled people I belong to.

The second "gift" my suffering and pain revealed is: I am alive by the will of God. To better understand what happened to me I talked with several friends and asked them what they observed from their visits in the hospital and later.

When I first entered the hospital in Muncie my dad called a good friend of mine who lived nearby to let her know about my surgery. She learned that I might not live. My friend said that her prayer for me was a source of confusion. It was exactly the same confusion I felt praying for mom. It was a humbling experience, because she is a very dear friend; and, because I saw clearly that the prayer Jesus prayed the night before He died. "Father, Your will be done," is the perfect prayer.

I had been in so much pain that I was not aware of my condition day-to-day. My counselor told me that there were times while I was in intensive care she felt she would not see me again. And yet I did not die.

Other people have had similar life-and-death experiences. I am overwhelmed when I read about them. I was so close to death from the surgeries and I was not accepting the fact at the time, or I sometimes drifted through those months without knowledge of happenings around me. This makes me appreciate the value of my life, and it showed me the role suffering can play. On Thanksgiving day of 1989 I was most grateful for God's gift to me of my life.

Through this series of surgeries I feel closer to Christ, and to His suffering. I was joyful because I was able to share in His death and resurrection. I am closer to my faith community - my Church. The feast days have greater significance because of the insights I received from my suffering. ⊱

Ed died at age 47 from respiratory failure. He never married. He could not afford an automobile, or a house. The business world saw only his disability. He never found a job although he applied many times to many employers.

Without name or voice, Baby Doe has the eloquence of one who knows only the dark side of mankind; and, with halting voice Eddie invites us to share in the suffering of Christ. Minds and hearts of heretics caught-up in the culture of death are unmoved. Other minds and hearts are distressed over Baby Doe and puzzled over Circuit Court Judge George Greer's order to starve Terri Schiavo. They know good things (aseptic operating rooms devoted to saving lives) are used to offend God. Moreover, they know that Justices of this nation's courts deserve millstones for making infanticide lawful.

There is no mystery here. The dark side of mankind is slowly winning the age-old struggle over Truth. Satan's strategy was (and will always be) to discredit absolute authority the Son of God instituted on earth, thereby creating confusion. Today, without Solidarity, Whole

Man is a shadow of his former self, no longer effective against the ticking bombs of Satan.

Nations must acknowledge the truth in words Cardinal Joseph Ratzinger wrote twenty years ago (The Ratzinger Report) -

"We know that the 'spirit of the world' is evil, and the father of lies is at the helm."

George Will believes killing inconvenient babies by starvation or abortion will not stop. I agree. He pointed to mutilation of language in order to "sell" the public acts that are incompatible with common sense.

I am reminded of A Prolife Semantics Guide by Ron Galloy, published in New Oxford Review (February 2006) wherein he quoted Pope John Paul II's encyclical The Gospel of Life:

"The moral conscience, both individual and social, is today subjected, also as a result of the penetrating influence of the media, to an extremely serious and mortal danger; that of confusion between good and evil, precisely in relation to the fundamental right to life."

Galloy's guide gives twenty-six examples of his maxim taken verbatim from the secular Media: "If you want to change the way people think about abortion, just change the words.

Their purpose is unmistakable - Abortion is said to be 1) a reproductive right; 2) a right to choose; 3) a privacy right; 4) a woman's right to do as she pleases with her body."

The reader learns that killing an unborn child is a right granted by the U.S. Constitution.

His Guide calls attention to the word "unwanted," in "unwanted children," frequently used in mainstream news about abortion. He said what everyone should say -

"The term 'unwanted' puts children in a negative light."

"Abortion advocates would have people believe that unborn children are without intrinsic value and only the woman's situation or feelings determine her child's worth .... In reality, wantedness measures *the character of the wanter* (his italics), not the value of the child. For those participating in procreative acts the only question is whether they will be accountable or unaccountable parents where life is conceived."

Galloy knows most religions teach with clarity and persistence that infanticide, abortion and euthanasia are unspeakable crimes. By what authority then do managers of mainstream news promote abortion as "health care" and turn comfort, as in "aid" to soothe a bedridden wife, into poison, as in "aid" to kill a bed-ridden wife? Compassion in dying? Who is the recipient?

My letters and the work of others confirm that the mass media (or mainstream as they prefer) is hell-bent on changing the culture by denying the basis for moral standards and by insisting that control of one's conscience matters most. Their worldview is Relativism - ethical truth (morality) is not what God says, but whatever men and women say. Social conscience becomes what the mainstream media manages.

Secular news-makers trash my conscience (a gift from God). My conscience informs me about Truth that abortion, infanticide, genetic cleansing and genocide, adultery, sodomy, euthanasia, pornography, etc. are wrong and harmful, because they offend God and diminish Common Good. Moreover, Natural Law and reason inform me that unbridled materialism, Secularism and same-sex marriage harms civil society.

If my informant is correct, this nation's secular media is an unreliable resource for news about social issues (as unreliable as Joseph Gobbles' managed media was for social issues of Germans during World War II). The secular media is the enemy of all who are fighting to reverse this culture of death.

Time and again I questioned this malicious assumption while searching for more confirmation. Confirmation was found. George Will's article (April 21, 1982 Washington Post News Service) makes reference to a changing culture or "Zeitgeist" that sanctions infant homicide; two modern popes, John Paul II and Benedict XVI warn of the big lie; Linda Bowles believes that right and wrong are nullified as moral concepts when the secular media makes celebrities of serial murderers (from her June 1996 letter); and, G.K Chesterton said in June 1927, "standardization by a low standard is our peril."

It is reasonable to assume that Satan needs humans working together to oppose God. How? By exploiting our sinful nature. Twisting evil into good and making truth Jesus revealed mere opinion comes natural to those who deny God, or those who view religion and God with indifference and their conscience as a pleasure-seeking "friend."

The magazine Public Opinion (1983) published profiles of editors, reporters, bureau chiefs, news executives, TV anchormen, producers and film editors taken from the work of S. Robert Lichter and Stanley Rothman. Lichter and Rothman talked for one hour with each of 240 of these men and women who edit morality, asking for their views on social issues, political issues and cultural change. Noteworthy results were as follows -

54% saw nothing wrong with adultery.

86% never (or seldomly) attend church or synagogue.

When asked, "Who directs American Society?" the consensus was, business first, themselves second and unions third.

When the question was rephrased: "Who do you think should run the country?" they placed themselves first.

Nothing has changed. In an article titled The Future of Newspapers published in the March 17, 2006 Goshen newspaper Cal Thomas wrote -

"Research based on recent interviews with 547 print and broadcast journalists showed that 94% believe God is meaningless in their intellectual view of 'hard news.' Their agenda, as they reveal it, has no room for God."

I believe their Ideology of Denial and their ability to corrupt truth by changing words explains why the conscience of American society is in mortal danger.

Lies and innuendo reported as hard news about men and women elected to high office harm civil society. The arrogant treatment president Bush received from the mainstream media when he said he believes in God is an example. Remember, president Bush was elected by a majority who also believe in God.

This nation has, as all Western nations have, acquired (over the latter half of the twentieth century) an evil spirit so conspicuous that Pope John Paul II expressed concern over the destiny of his flock.

I wrote earlier, "twenty-first century battles will be about salvation --- and defeating the lies of heretics;" and added, "God needs humans working together (God's way) toward fulfillment of their moral potential."

Today, God's standard of morality is being trashed with one lie after another. To expect that I will believe these lies is as much an insult (and malicious) as expecting me to believe that Godless people should run the country.

Speaking/writing about Godless people running the country raises a perplexing issue. We turn to Godless people to learn the facts at a time when Europe faces extensive Islamic immigration and (in a few generations) world-wide terror on a scale much more destructive than the war in Iraq.

Godless people, by their own admission, have no room for God or for religion or for eternal life. They do not choose to understand the religious zeal that drives Muslims who, although misguided by false prophets, fervently sacrifice their lives for a make-believe end. The Godless media is not competent to report on a religious war. They choose to ignore the power religion has in man's struggle over good and evil. The danger is, as Will Rogers said, "All I know is just what I read in the newspapers."

Dependable information I need, with respect to the war on terrorism, I do not receive due to incompetent reporting. This is the other side of this worthless "media coin."

America must start paying attention to Europe. Islamization of the Western world is an explosive threat as old as Islam. Eight Crusades, from the 11th into the 13th centuries, were wars directed against the heresy of Islam by Whole Man. They are best described as a union of people and sovereigns of the Western world under the direction of the popes to save Christian civilization.

The Crusades drove the Religion of Islam out of medieval Europe but did not put down the heresy. Failure was due to deviation of avaricious leaders from the original purpose, i.e. conversion through persuasion. Spoils of War sidetracked both sides. (See "Crusades"

in the New Catholic Dictionary, page 272, published in 1929 by the
Universal Knowledge Foundation.)

———————

I end this chapter with a medical opinion/announcement on
genetic cleansing given by the American College of Obstetricians and
Gynecologists twenty-five years after the 1982 Indiana Supreme Court
ruling. The information below was contained in an article published
in the Opinion column of Today's Catholic dated January 21, 2007
titled -

Beware of some so-called medical breakthroughs

Recent news from the medical field reported in the article reminds
us that we need to be very cautious about the motives behind some
so-called medical advances.

"The American College of Obstetricians and Gynecologists
announced that it recommends that every pregnant woman be
tested to determine whether her unborn child may have Down's
syndrome.   Previously, that recommendation applied only to
women older than 35 or those with genetic anomalies in their
families.

ACOG recommended a new blood test combined with an
ultrasound that allegedly identifies babies with Down's syndrome
with 80 percent accuracy. The new procedure is being promoted
because it does not carry the risk of miscarriage that older testing
through amniocentesis did.

This news was reported in the secular media as a tremendous
breakthrough. A doctor discussing the new recommended testing
on television was excited, giving the impression that the early
detection of Down's syndrome would somehow help the unborn
child or the child's parents. When the newscaster asked an obvious
question, the doctor seemed miffed by his naivety and replied that
this of course would allow "termination" in the first trimester,
when the "procedure" is easier, safer and cheaper.

It was sobering to learn that one baby escapes "termination"
for every 199 babies who test positive. Moreover, studies have
shown that a small number of aborted babies who test positive
did not have Downs Syndrome. To date false positives from

tests for genetic defects range from 3-percent in the AFP/free Beta screening test to less than 1-percent in the amniocentesis test (although unborn babies fare no better from amniocentesis, because it causes spontaneous abortion in a fraction of 1-percent of women tested."

So, this great medical "breakthrough" in genetic cleansing of Down's Syndrome babies really is no different than the "breakthrough" of gas chambers used to rid Europe of Jews and devout Christians by Nazi Germany during the second World War. America wins based on percent of population "cleansed."

What a terrible commentary it is on Western civilization in the twenty-first century that we place so little value on human life, especially on the most vulnerable humans who require extra care.

What a loss it is to society to be deprived of the valuable lessons to be learned from disabled people and to be deprived of their love. What a loss to miss the opportunity to care for someone else and to exercise the virtues that assist our own salvation.

Perhaps no one better expresses this terrible loss than the families of a baby with Down's syndrome. Internet blogs are a resource for testimony from parents, siblings and extended families of children with Down's syndrome. They speak of their loved ones as "blessings," as cherished people who give a special meaning to life, free spirits who show others how to love and how to enjoy the simple things of the world.

Many families speak of the considerable accomplishments of children who once were given little chance of a "meaningful life." And, many adults with Down's syndrome have said that they are shocked and offended that someone else might proclaim that their own very valuable life was not worth saving.

I believe future DNA/RNA studies will identify the specific section of the genetic code responsible for the development of Down's Syndrome, and stop there, without searching for pieces that flow from God's goodness. For example, pieces of the code responsible for attributes parents and siblings recognize as "blessings," namely innocence, free spirit, a loving nature, etceteras.

Maria of Sound of Music fame said: " Whenever God closes a

door, somewhere He opens a window."

Post Modern Man is embroiled in an age-old clash between moral conduct sinful man ordains by an act of his will and the moral conduct God ordained. As Jiminy Cricket said, "Let your conscience be your guide."

CHAPTER 5

FREE WILL AND CONSCIENCE

Free will is God's gift that allows us to seek or ignore and accept or reject Him. We have the ability to know His supreme Goodness and the freedom to choose to return His love, or we can deny Him; and, we can obey or ignore the new Commandment His Son revealed: "Love your neighbor as you love yourself." God's gifts of free will and dignity require us to respect our neighbor's dignity as well as our own.

Logic (another gift) guides us to an understanding that choices shape our earthly lives as well as our eternal destiny. Life-long disregard of both our duty to properly form our conscience and our duty to obey our conscience constitutes injustices against God, our children and neighbors; and, causes eternal punishment. Insecurity, mental anguish, loss of trust and, in extreme cases, suicide are temporal effects.

Freedom of choice is owed to human dignity. "Being empowered by God with reason and free will humans are privileged to bear personal responsibility." (A quote taken from Declaration on Religious Freedom, the encyclical of Pope Paul VI, dated December 7, 1965.) The pope cautions -

"In accordance with their dignity as persons all men should be at once impelled by nature and also bound by a moral duty to seek the truth, especially religious truth."

It is the judgment of a well-formed conscience that directs him or her to the truth about good and evil. It is the judgment of reason that directs us in our duty, and the will to do what is good and pleasing to God and to accept responsibility for evil deeds.

Thomas Aquinas explained why this is so: "We have authority over our own actions in that out of infinite love God made us in His image and likeness." (See his Summa Theologica I-II, 91,2c.)

Such is the splendor of human beings alone in this vast universe. We are rational and willful. We are aided by a properly formed conscience to know and to choose the truth. Therefore honoring, appreciating, and returning God's love is our duty.

God gave us His loving gift of salvation merited through the sacrifice of His own Son on a cross. Conscience is our guide. He gave us grace to persevere and a Mortal Man with infallible authority to teach.

God gave men and women everywhere the right to appeal to a standard of behavior we call the "Rule of fair play." He gave fallible men and women the ability to understand natural law, His Commandments, and other supernatural truths. He gave us the ability to communicate His Words to non-believers and the freedom to choose duty over self.

Every human act carries a conscious impulse to do good and avoid evil and, corresponding perceptible impressions on the mind - satisfaction or guilt accompanying each moral choice we make.

This is the essence of "humanness."

It is humanness that distinguishes mankind from "man-like animals" and from every other living thing God made. God breathed a soul into (perhaps preexisting) bodies of the first man and woman to create our first parents. Men and women who lived 5000-years ago in Babylon, the cradle of civilization, were their offspring.

Socrates was their offspring. He lived 2500-years ago, centuries before the Son of God lived on earth. He knew about good and evil (see Homework). Socrates possessed the morality of spiritual aspiration, i.e. knowing the truth about good and evil he aspired to a morally good life. Without knowledge of the Triune God, he recognized in his own humanness a transformation in progress toward that which is most rational. In other words, toward an end holding the most good (which is the work of a personal conscience). Furthermore, he recognized that his own Greek government must strive to attain the most good for its citizens.

We too are offspring of the first "human" parents. It is rarely acknowledged that Cro-Magnon Man cannot be classified as the first "human" merely from the fact that skeletal remains resemble those of other tall erect "man-like" hominids. The reason is obvious. Anthropologists cannot know that an erect fossilized skeleton (35,000 to 250,000-years old) possessed spiritual gifts from God, i.e. free will, a soul and a personal conscience; or, the Rule of fair play.

Evidence of civilization in remnants from the Cro-Magnon period is necessary to prove that Cro-Magnon "Man" was human. Archaeologists and anthropologists have not found evidence of civilizations or, respect for personal dignity, earlier than Babylonia.

Civilizations arise along many routes. All owe their existence to God's gift of a personal and public conscience.

The Dilemma of human dignity in an irrational world

Canon Law #747 states: "To the Church belongs the right always and everywhere to announce moral principles, including those pertaining to the social order, and to make judgments on any human affairs to the extent that they are required by the fundamental rights of the human person or the salvation of souls."

This is Freedom of Religion from the side of the coin owned by the Catholic Church by virtue of its morally infallible teaching authority, and owned by most religions by virtue of their traditions.

On the other side of the same coin: "Every human person, created in the image of God, has the natural right to be respected as a free and responsible being. All owe to each other this duty of respect. The right to the exercise of freedom, especially in moral and religious matters, is an inalienable requirement of the dignity of the human person. This right must be recognized and protected by civil authority within the limits of the Common Good and public order" (#1738 Catechism of the Catholic Church).

The dilemma comes in permitting those who make little distinction between good and evil and show little respect for human dignity, to influence modern cultures. This is outside the limits of the Common Good and public order. This is irrational justice masquerading as broadmindedness - a scandal against long established morality.

Conscience informs the mind about good and evil. Therefore, choosing to block one's conscience about an evil deed causes the mind to invent illogical ways to justify the deed.

Jesus admonished His disciples saying, "Scandals will inevitably arise, but woe to him through whom they come. He would be better off thrown into the sea with a millstone around his neck than giving scandal to one of these little ones." (Lk 17, 1-2)

Injustice, failure and defeat in this Postmodern age is in denying our proper and collective right to defend Truth dealing with the salvation of souls. "Abortion is normal, even good," is one of many recent examples of illogical inventions that must convince the public conscience to cry out for common sense. We live in an age marked by arrogance, irreverence and insensitivity. Few see or feel duty to respond to God's command in Mt 10: "The gift you have received, give as a gift." The gift we have received (God's love) is to be given as our gift to help those who are demoralized.

October 7, 1980 (thirty years ago)

The Republic
Columbus, IN
Dear Editor:

In a book by William Jennings Bryan (1860-1925) titled The Value of an Ideal, I found these words: "The country is suffering today from a demoralization of its ideals. Instead of measuring people by the manhood or womanhood they manifest, we are too prone to measure them by the amount of money they possess, and the demoralization has naturally and necessarily extended to politics. As a result the public conscience is becoming seared and the public service debauched." Bryan went on to suggest that "we place against money something stronger than money. And what is stronger than money? A conscience is stronger than money. We must appeal to the conscience - not to a democratic conscience, or a republican conscience, but to an American conscience, and a Christian conscience, and place this awakened conscience against the on-flowing tide of corruption in the United States."

The problems Bryan saw have magnified many times, so that today the evidence of demoralization is everywhere. But there is hope. Awakening of the Christian conscience Bryan hoped for is taking place in the conservative camp, by the younger generation, and elsewhere.

Our normal pastime with the elections so close is to argue about the outcome, and hope that certain problems will go away if this party or that party is elected. Unfortunately, awakening of the Christian conscience is outside the realm of politics.

The hope referred to above is in the people. It was Abraham Lincoln who said: "Let the people know the facts and the country will be saved." I believe that significant numbers of people (in the Minority) recognize the personal and societal dangers in a nation without family discipline, without moral discipline, without monetary discipline, etc. We have experienced first hand, or have friends close to us who have experienced, the heartaches attached to single parent households, the stigma of spouses and teen-age children whose lives are controlled by drugs and alcohol, the debilitating stress from unrelenting debt, and so forth.

Significant numbers of God-fearing people recognize that humanism and secularism stem from pride and greed, and represent failure; that taking the life of an unborn child is inexcusable; and, that a corrupt society justly deserves the wrath of God (millstones).

Mankind has lived with pride, lust, greed, etc. for thousands of years, sometimes repenting and sometimes not. History gives unmistakable proof that the choice is personal and is bound to the morality of the individual, which morality, to paraphrase Bryan, stems from the ideals each person values. Demoralization of ideals, if widespread, will destroy this nation.

Robert Jefferson

Perhaps that is what Thomas Jefferson was thinking when he said: "If a nation expects to be ignorant and free, in a state of civilization, it expects what never was and never will be" (letter to Colonel Charles Yancey, January 6, 1816). In Notes on the State of Virginia Jefferson wrote: "I tremble for my country when I reflect that God is just."

Churches that teach God's Word, and all who listen, should know (and do know) that both the Old and New Testaments describe abortion, sodomy, etc. as acts of "grave depravity" (cf Gen 19: 1-29), as "the exchange of the truth of God for a lie" (cf Rom 1: 24-27); and as, "an abomination." (cf. Lev 18: 22).

Christians, Jews and Muslims should know (and do know) that Old Testament prophets warned the chosen people about God's terrible wrath inflicted on the depravity He found in Sodom and Gomorrah. His wrath is timeless. It awaits all who choose to reject Him.

We shrink from the law of God and willfully choose to live by immoral laws of the State made (it seems) to twist love into hatred.

Repentance was a common sight near the end of the Middle Age. Why? Because most of the people, from nobleman to peasant, were faithful Catholics who believed above all else that they were sinners subject to failure. They gave thanks to Christ for His great sacrifice. Confession of one's sins to a priest, resolution to live a better life; and penance, were signs of that faith and their bitter regret for having offended God.

A monk who witnessed the year 1000 wrote -

"It was as if the whole earth, having cast off the old were clothing itself everywhere in the white robe of the Church,"

(Quotation found on page 160 in The Age of Chivalry, published by National Geographic Book Service.)

Who has ever seen such humility, devotion and acts of love; who has ever heard tell in times past. Or ever again, I add in hindsight.

Late in the Medieval Age the state and everyone subject to the state affirmed and defended the proper role of the Church in moral affairs. Simply stated, that role was to bring inerrant Truth about salvation to sinful men and women already gifted with salvation.

Pilate said, "Truth. What does that mean?"

Coptic legend has it that Pilate later converted to Catholicism and was a martyr for his faith. If this legend is based on fact his conversion was due to his own convictions and faith through the grace of the Holy Spirit.

Treatise Proposition from page 20: Success and failure, i.e. the common good of society, is about choices; whether to believe and live the truth about good and evil, or not believe, and live a lie; whether salvation, or eternal punishment, within a framework imposed by God's gift of conscience and the reality of His love imprinted in every heart. God's Plan for mankind unfolds in Natural Law (God's book of nature), in His gift of personal conscience and in His Commandments.

The problem is this: Today, liberation of conscience from God's moral guidance is a bad idea promoted as freedom of choice. Conscience, personal and public, is liberated and bad ideas are sanctioned by judicial process and by advancements in technology said to be self-justified. I call this garbage. It is much more dangerous for our children than failure of Social Security.

In God's Plan liberation of conscience is tantamount to foolishness and everlasting defeat.

After thirty, forty or five hundred years, living dangerously becomes accepted custom, even fashionable. Customs shape a nation's culture and the course its citizens take. Self-indulgence and indifference about good and evil are signs of insanity.

Are we really "as powerless as cattle to change?"

St. Paul warned: "They had knowledge of God; yet they did not glorify Him as God or give Him thanks." They claimed to be wise, but turned into fools instead." (Rom I,21-22)]

The riddle of life: We're not so dumb, but we're dumb.

Pope John Paul II gave Modern Man a moral wake-up call. The Vatican released his Encyclical on October 5, 1993 titled The Splendor of Truth (available from Saint Paul Books and Media, Boston, MA). A week later an article by John Thavis in Today's Catholic gave an analysis of the 137-page encyclical. The article is reprinted below -

Encyclical, Veritatis Splendor offers lesson on morality
and limits of freedom

At the heart of Pope John Paul II's new encyclical, Veritatis Splendor (The Splendor of Truth), lies a lesson on human freedom and its limits, addressed to audiences inside and outside the church.

To the pastoral corps of bishops, priests and theologians, the document reverberates with the warning that the foundations of moral theology are being undermined by error, ambiguity and neglect.

To the 959 million Catholics around the world, the encyclical lays down basic principles of the church's moral teaching and draws the clearest line yet against dissent - including the difficult area of sexual morality.

To modern society, Veritatis Splendor is written as a moral wake-up call, reminding people that freedom cannot be detached from truth and challenging them to make God's commandments the foundation of their daily actions.

All this is framed in a heartfelt appeal for men and women to remember that life is indeed a spiritual journey, and that the quest for moral good is linked to the promise of eternal salvation.

Published Oct. 5th, the pope's message was a long time coalescing, and it responds to trends the pontiff has followed with alarm for many years: The "systematic" questioning of church teaching among theologians and the faithful, the idea that individuals can design their own sense of right and wrong, and the widespread view that the church is showing "intransigence" (refusing to compromise) when it insists that some acts are intrinsically evil.

Veritatis Splendor does not reveal new truths so much as illuminate and insist upon old ones. It may not preach a popular lesson, but that is part of its significance, papal aids believe.

"The pope is trying to call a secularized society - and a church influenced by a secularized society - back to the essentials of moral theology. I think this document opens a very difficult dialogue .... and may mark a turning point for the pope," said one Vatican official.

The difficult dialogue involves, first and foremost, theologians. The encyclical repeatedly cites schools of theological thought to illustrate how skepticism and relativism have seeped into Catholic theology, even into the church's own seminaries.

"This relativism becomes, in the field of theology, lack of trust in the wisdom of God," the pope states. He expounds on the theological errors, such as "so-called pastoral solutions contrary to the teaching of the magisterium," and of "a false dichotomy between morality and faith."

The pope is himself a moral theologian, and his language here is at times a highly specialized one that borrows from Scripture, Thomistic writings and the documents of the Second Vatican Council. As the pope points out, it marks the first time such arguments have been assembled in such an authoritative way. For these reasons, theologians may well comprise the main readership of the encyclical.

But "Veritatis Splendor" is addressed specifically to bishops, and the pope is no less concerned about their role in stemming what he calls "a genuine crisis" with grave pastoral implications.

"We have the duty, as bishops, to be vigilant that the word of God is faithfully taught," particularly in seminaries, theological faculties and Catholic schools, he states. It's a point he has been making all year long to U.S. bishops during their "ad limina" visits.

But Pope John Paul's message is not just nay-saying. As he tells the bishops, "it is not enough just to warn the faithful about the errors and dangers of ethical theories - people must first be shown the splendor of that truth which is Jesus Christ himself."

The average reader, in fact, will find in Veritatis Splendor a passionately argued invitation to embark on "a moral and spiritual journey toward perfection." The pope confidently appeals to the "yearning for absolute truth" in every human heart.

Yet he insists on the church's guiding role, and here Catholics will find a concentrated version of what the pope has been saying for years about doubt and dissent; that morality is not determined by consensus; that the conscience is not autonomous; and the church's moral teaching requires obedience. (My comment: Souls are lost without the Church's inerrant moral teaching.)

"Opposition to the teaching of the church's pastors cannot be seen as a legitimate expression either of Christian freedom or of the diversity of the spirit's gifts," he says.

The pope extends this argument in discussing the church's duty to make its teaching known and to influence social policies in every age, in every society.

Far from demeaning human nature, he says, the church's firmness on moral norms is a service to human freedom. It contrasts with the worrisome "decline or obscuring of the moral sense" in modern society.

Although the encyclical is deliberately general in theme, the pope does cite some examples of what he means by "intrinsically evil" acts, ranging from murder and abortion to prostitution, and contraception in marriage.

There are "no privileges or exceptions" for the moral norms prohibiting such acts, he states.

Veritatis Splendor is certainly a comprehensive defense of the church's teaching authority. But the pope recognizes that, in the end, authority alone will not carry the day. Thus, toward the end of the document, he emphasizes that the "life of holiness" is the best way to teach the church's evangelizing message. To lead people toward morally good behavior, the pope says, the church needs to offer not only the "word proclaimed" but the "word lived." >

Enigma: Historical research shows that a civilized society remains civilized only when a majority of its members conform their lives to a moral standard of right behavior. The life of Jesus Christ is the best example of this standard and the best example of obedience the Divine Justice of God demands.

We are accountable for the way we use our God-given free will, our conscience and our talents. It is irrational to live as though freedom is intended for self-indulgence, even self-destruction; or, to neglect the education of conscience; or, to willfully oppose the moral guidance within our conscience.

"The Catholic Church is by the will of Christ the teacher of (inerrant) truth. Her charge is to announce and teach authentically and for all time that truth which is Christ, and at the same time with her authority to declare and confirm the principles of the moral order which derive from human nature itself." (#14 of Declaration on Religious Freedom). It is nonsense to believe that the Son of God can't accomplish whatever He wills.

My stupidity is recognizable through testing (as noted in my Jan. 29, 2003 letter in the Preface): "If tests are designed authoritatively, the procedure followed exactly, etc., the result is true and verifiable."

The authority for the test I propose is the Son of God who, when asked: "Teacher, which commandment of the law is the greatest," He answered, "You shall love the Lord your God with your whole heart, with your whole soul, with your whole mind and all of your strength. This is the greatest and the first commandment." (Mt 22 36-38)

The test is easy and very practical. The only instrument I need is my conscience.

Randomly throughout the day, I ask myself, "Is God in this thing I am doing?" Or later, "Was God in that TV program I watched?" "Did my heart, soul and mind willfully respond to God's love at any time today?" "Have I demonstrated for even one hour this week that I love my Lord and master in the manner he commanded?"

No one is at liberty to act against the dictates of their conscience without trembling at the consequences. I tremble at my answers.

Post Modern Man holds the future in his hands, as did his ancestors - a future subject to human folly, and to God's wrath. Post Modern Man also holds a future of God's love - wherein peace reigns everywhere, i.e. "Thy will be done on earth as it is in heaven."

I ask, is failure worthy of human beings created in God's image and likeness? Or, is this the best mankind can do at this junction/ juncture in time? Are dignity and "freedom of religion" no more than words?

CHAPTER 6

WORDS ARE IMPORTANT TOOLS

The God of Abraham is real. We know from historical records that He communicated directly to His people as when He spoke from the cloud saying the words, "This is My Son in whom I am well pleased." He is the Great Communicator. He speaks using familiar words. We know that He communicated through selected individuals - Moses, Elijah, Miriam, Samuel, John the Baptist, to name a few, and through His Angels, through Mary and more recently through His Saints, Bernadette of Lourds, Therese of Lisieux and others. And we know from their actions that each knew who spoke.

God is Perfect are very important words. His Words and the meaning of His commands will never change, because being perfect God will never be other than what He has always been. Men and women change His tools for uncovering Truth and Wisdom so as to invalidate their usefulness. In doing so man's words convey an attitude of arrogance.

Next to "I AM WHO AM" spoken to Moses, the most useful words in the history of mankind are "One in Being," the homo-ousios proclaimed in the Creed of Nicaea by the power and authority of the Holy Spirit (using the language and voices of sinful Bishops). God's tool planted for all time the truth that Jesus is One in Being with God the Father (and with God the Holy Spirit). Jesus is God. His Words are truly genuine Words of God. God's power on earth is awesome. Unending punishment is His wrath, unbearable for those who live in denial.

God cannot deceive nor be deceived. Through the intercession of the Holy Spirit, the true meaning of His message has survived two thousand years of manipulation.

God permits us to deny His wrath, even His very existence, as well as our moral duty to seek Truth. However, His perfect Justice severely punishes those who deny or manipulate His Moral Law without remorse.

Heretic is another useful word long used to describe those who deny that God exists or, who fashion Catholic doctrine to their liking.

Others more learned than I have written books about God's Truth, asking a basic question: "Can it be recognized?" Joseph Cardinal Ratzinger, a respected theologian, author and recently elected Pope Benedict XVI, asked in his book Truth and Tolerance -

"If we recognize truth, and know it, are we permitted to hide it in the name of Tolerance?".

He wrote about truths in general and Moral Truth in particular. Truth and Tolerance was published in 2004 by Ignatius Press, San Francisco.

Basic questions demand intelligent research framed in words and ideas others can understand and accept. The history and reality of One Church established by the Son of God to declare the existence of God the Father, God the Son and God the Holy Spirit is readily available but not universally accepted. This is Western civilization's sacred tradition. Yet, as Cardinal Ratzinger points out, to declare the unity and salvific universality of Jesus Christ and One Church causes a cry of Arrogance from modern society and from non-Christian cultures.

"Enlightened" leaders say the declaration has no place in modern reality. In God's reality it is such leaders who are arrogant. Denial of redemptive history to the extent that it is erased from history books and excluded from Public Schools (by court order) is a stupid choice, one of many indicators that Modern Man is reverting to paganism.

Arrogant celebrities write books and TV programs filled with the same stupidity condemned as Gnostic heresy by the Apostles and their immediate successors. Rebirth of such primitive comments is hailed as progress.

Modern men and women are building a senseless tradition from the idea that he and she are clever enough to make their own reality. It is a tradition of sophisticated incompetence that neglects and violates the laws of God. It is without a keystone. The beliefs of our ancestors, their ideas, their customs and their institutions must continue to be the foundation upon which Western civilization rests.

Important tools as words are easily subverted for evil purposes by Satan's helpers, as in slander, or by equating lust with love or making infanticide into an act of loving concern, or making man alone the benevolent provider of sustenance and happiness world-wide.

Important tools as God's message recorded in the Old Testament in which a timeless demonstration is given of His almighty power: "Did anything so great ever happen before? Was it ever heard of? Did any god venture to go and take a nation for Himself from the midst of another nation, by testings, by signs and wonders, by war, with His strong hand and outstretched arm, and by great terrors, all of which the Lord, your God, did for you in Egypt before your very eyes? All of this you were allowed to see that you might know the Lord is God and there is no other." (Dt 4, 32-35) "This is why you now must know, and fix in your heart, that the Lord is God in the heavens above and on earth below, and that there is no other. You must keep His statutes and commandments which I enjoin on you today, that you and your children after you may prosper, and that you may have long life on the land which the Lord, your God, is giving you forever." (Dt 4, 39-40)

Western Man is back in the sixteenth century with de Montaingne who declared, "Man is the measure of all things." Today the twisted tool is Globalism, i.e. world-wide imposition of economic power and the power of Technology exercised by a few influential and egotistic men and women.

Technology, according to Webster's second definition, is the totality of the means employed to provide everything necessary for human sustenance and comfort. Modern technology is the energy that powers man's new reality. Economic control over this global venture would be centralized and would operate without interference from world governments. The individuals in charge would have absolute authority to act for the material welfare of all mankind. Their aim is to implement a bogus freedom of choice.

Globalism

Globalism seeks to replace old-world Humanitarianism attuned to God's will with Secular Humanitarianism attuned to the will of a few well placed men and women. It dictates non-judgmentalism and freedom of choice in the pretence of championing diversity. Its strategy is to subvert sacred truth about God's gift of diversity and His eternal judgment.

Globalism will move us backward into antiquity to "embrace a pagan life of comfort and pleasure" as fourteenth century Humanist Man did (see Homework). Twenty-first century Humanism manufactures its own welfare.

Words Are Important Tools - Part 2

The existence of parallel universes is associated with science fiction. The idea is useful here as a tool for communicating the magnitude of the problem addressed in my treatise, i.e. restoring life to this culture of death and, claiming the unity and salvific universality of Jesus Christ and One Church" (True Reality) will solve the problem.

I began chapter 2 with the statement: "The two views of reality are right side up and upside down." A prerequisite for parallel universes is that one cannot know the other.

It is one thing to contrast reality that enlivened the thirteenth century, i.e. unity and salvific universality of Whole Man, with Modern Man's reality, i.e. polarization of Christ and chaos. It is quite another to convince those who hold a secular view of the universe that their culture of death (today's reality), as it pertains to saving one's soul, is foreboding. The modern words Success and Failure have been stripped of their finality.

Just as going from hell to heaven is impossible, going from a culture of death to salvific universality in the One Church Jesus instituted is impossible. This (I believe) is the magnitude of the problem as we start the second decade of the twenty-first century.

Jonah 3, 4-10 offers the only solution for a problem of this magnitude.

Contrast the choice of the word love for the word lust in most of today's TV programs, or the word dignity as it is used in the capitalist's world, or the word marriage in the oxymoron "same sex marriage" with the New Testament's treatment of these words.

Over the course of two thousand years the Church has come to see (in the Holy Trinity) God the Father as the lover, the Son as the One loved and the Holy Ghost as the consummation of Divine Love. Logically, the Church relates the mystery of God's design of love to the vocation of marriage in the sense that a sanctified marriage incorporates the same mutual "gift of self" humanly expressed in the sexual union of husband and wife. God willing, a new human person, God's greatest possible gift, is co-created out of Human Love. (Whether from love or lust know that the child bears the physical likeness of his/her parents and the sacred image and likeness of God.)

Logically, every child ought to be the personification of Human Love and unity as the Holy Spirit is the personification of Divine Love and unity.

Without love a child often becomes the screwed-up coupling of male and female fittings. Where in this is dignity owed to the child? Without a permanent Husband/Wife bond where is the dignity owed to God's Design for the procreation, Christian education and flowering sacredness of children?

Love, dignity, marriage, etc., as viewed in thirteenth century Europe, seem to be as distant from their fraudulent counterparts in twenty-first century Europe and America as in parallel universes.

"Apart from Me you can do nothing." (Jn 15, 5) "Apart from My Truth you can do nothing" carries the same meaning. In that the Catholic Church has preserved and handed-down God's Truth (in Latin words safe from manipulation) it follows that, "Apart from My Church you can do nothing." This too seems to be a view from some distant parallel universe.

Words Are Important - Part 3 (Christian Freedom)

The true meaning of Christian Freedom is derived from, "By His death and resurrection He has set you free." By faith in these words Christians believe that God opened the gate to Heaven closed by the original sin of Adam and Eve. Divine Justice was satisfied for all time by the suffering and death of Jesus.

All men and women who have faith in the truth of redemption must live the life Jesus showed them by His example, "Do unto others as I have done unto you," i.e. we must live not for ourselves but for God, for our children and for our neighbors.

Logical thinking applied to rules, i.e. the Ten Commandments given to Moses, discovers that Christian freedom casts these rules in a new light first revealed by St. Paul as he taught the Thessalonians and

Corinthians. St. Paul together with the apostles possessed the fullness of God's Truth. They were given to understand that it is not man but God who controls human destiny throughout time and eternity.

God gave us a free will. He gave us control of our collective destiny. Live by His rules and prosper as a civilized nation; or, disobey His rules and suffer as a nation.

The Pharisees used God's rules to showcase their "goodness" just as the majority of modern Christians do. Other Old Testament Jews saw God's Commandments as a guide to Common Good. Paul understood that this new "freedom" made possible by the crucifixion of God's only Son on a cross was in fact mankind's gift - salvation; God's infinite love.

St. Paul understood that genuine Christian freedom is much more than a guide to Common Good. He understood that the cost of genuine Christian freedom is very high. Paul suffered threats to his life, persecution and hardships of many kinds not in order to be saved, but because of his faith and thankfulness that he was saved by God's love. As he said: "For you (and I) were called to freedom, brethren; only do not use your freedom as an opportunity for the flesh, but through love for God be servants of one another" (Gal 5:13).

As Stanley Marrow wrote in Paul, His Letters and His Theology: "The freedom Christ won for us is not a freedom from all responsibility and for one's ends. It is a freedom conferred upon Christians so that they can be more free to give of themselves in the loving service of others." (Marrow's book was published in 1986 by Paulist Press, Mahwah, NJ.)

Our purpose on earth is to live out this moral potential God ordained for mankind. In the end God judges each one only on success or failure in this mission.

We are back to sinful men and women and their motives and excuses for changing, without authorization, the sacred words of God. I ask, "What can I do about the problem?" The answer is always the same, "Pray and do penance as the people in ancient Nineveh did."

I do pray. A still voice deep inside me says, for my penance write an analytical treatise that methodically examines an ailing social order in the only universe I know.

CHAPTER 7

PERSUASION - THE SCIENTIFIC METHOD

Man will never fully understand the reality of God. However, God has revealed enough about Himself for man to know objectively that it is a fatal mistake of one's soul to pretend He is not real. We know He is real from genuine knowledge gained through the science of God, i.e. theology and through reason applied to a scientific study of Creation.

A systematic plan, faith, prayer, objectivity and logical deductions, are essential for understanding and obtaining agreement that God is real. It is sometimes arguable but never impossible to obtain agreement about the reality of a collapsed bridge. Admittedly, agreement about the realty of God is a bit more difficult, because man's sinful nature gets in the way.

Indirect proof for the existence of God can be inferred from the Incompleteness Theorems of Kurt Godel published in 1931. Godel worked with Albert Einstein. These two are said to have possessed the greatest depth of scientific knowledge in the twentieth century. Godel's Theorems deal with the lodestar of mathematics - a routine way of combining all mathematical truth about the physical universe into one "perfect" mathematical equation.

Using scrupulously accurate mathematics, Godel demonstrated that such an equation, by its nature, is impossible for mankind to prove. His conclusion is accepted as scientific fact.

Godel said it is reasonable to assume that; since man by his (imperfect) nature is incapable of deriving a Unified Theory to perfectly describe this tangible universe; and, since scientific studies have demonstrated that the operation of the universe is in fact guided by perfectly intelligible principles; then, there exists an intelligent being capable of combining all mathematical truth about this physical universe we see everywhere we look.

God's existence gives meaning to our intelligibility and purpose

- in fact, to our finite existence. We are called by God to glorify Him through the imitation of Jesus, His Son.

My treatise claims that perfection, i.e. peace everywhere on earth, will follow when men and women everywhere fulfill their purpose. Corruption of man's will is also real and is as certain as the law of gravity commanding the ebb and flow of the oceans.

Dutiful and diligent study ("homework" I called it), objectivity and logical deduction are the other components of my treatise offering two observations: Nations prosper where most of the citizens obey God; and, nations fail that habitually defy God.

Homework begins with verification of the premise from which the treatise unfolds. Theology includes eschatology, a branch dealing with final events or the ultimate destiny of mankind. Eschatology can answer the question, is peace in nations everywhere on earth the ultimate destiny of mankind?

We find that the intention for which we pray to our heavenly Father, "Thy kingdom come on earth as it is in heaven" (greater perfection) is not our ultimate end on earth. Rather, the reverse is true. Moral decay and damnation are man's final destiny on earth. The final events in man's history include deception, men and women glorifying themselves instead of glorifying God, self-indulgence, persecution (of those who believe in God) and validation of "all that God spoke by the mouth of His holy prophets of old" (Acts 3:19-21) and taught by the apostles, Saint Paul and their legitimate successors.

Unrestrained immorality in nations everywhere is prophesied for the "End Times." We learn through God's Words that men and women at the end of time suppress their will to glorify God and thereby frustrated His design for an earthly peace.

Yet, man does have the means to influence when time ends, since peace (on earth) will surely follow (as God promised) when men and women everywhere put all "Strange Gods" aside. Distributive justice, dignity and peace flow from people who live by God's rules. History records that progress toward morality grew at times described in the Old Testament and flowered in the century of excellence. Solidarity and obedience made fertile soil.

The best men and women can expect on earth comes when sinful people trust sinful people and selfish people trust God's promise in the Lord's Prayer.

We need to find it within ourselves to defeat Atheism and self-indulgence if we hope to prevent immorality from making the twenty-first century the worst since the twenty-first century BC.

It is our Christian duty to persuade those who reject the truth about God to put aside their hatred and listen to the voice of God we call conscience. Those who participate in Satan's folly, calling good bad and bad good, depreciate freedom of speech. They must learn that complying with God's rules benefits everyone.

Facts about self-indulgence and moral decay are presented below, along with a logical solution for immoral garbage.

Many proud "scientific minds" today are so arrogant that they will not honor the truth they believe in their hearts and in their minds.

Professor Stanley Jaki, a renowned authority on the history of Science, asked (in an article titled On Whose Side Is History? published in National Review on Aug. 23, 1985), "Is there in Science something that would play an active role for the better, as mankind heads into an increasingly scientific future, from which there is no turning back?" It is Jaki's hope that "Science may provide a better future, which will see history coming down not on this side or that side, but on all sides - on the side of mankind as a whole."

Science, Jaki fervently hopes, will again lend support to dogmatic Christianity as it did centuries ago (which the history of Western Science clearly shows). Scientists and early Greek philosophers once accepted the fact that every event/discovery has a natural starting point emanating from God-given physical laws. They knew there was a point in time when all motion started by an intentional act. It was from this certitude about a Divine origin and intelligible design that the genius of early scientists and "giants" of philosophy sprang.

This certitude gave Isaac Newton and other seventeenth century scientists reasoned optimism that the design they discovered, and were able to verify, was not accidental. It was intended. From their optimism came the effort for greater discoveries.

Twenty-first century Science teaches that the starting point for the universe was an unintended "Big Bang" and then proceeds to avoid Divine origin and withhold tribute for a perfect design that provides mankind unlimited opportunity for discovery. A universe in motion, fully knowable and readily predictable, is any scientist's dream.

Better that Science proceed to restore optimism by persuasion, using its reputation, its models for discovering natural and unnatural patterns and its practices, namely problem definition, objective research and testing, statistical probability, and deductive reasoning to investigate the important qualities that define the other half of intelligent life - the unseen spiritual half.

A concern of Science should be to study the effect on the Common Good of a statistically significant number of people (the Philippine nation saving itself from tyranny in 1986 for example) who pray for a Just God to intervene in secular affairs.

Analytical models have nothing useful to say about human desires, because to understand the fickle desires of humans, models must deal with the unpredictable behavior of rational beings who choose to be irrational.

Analytical models do offer a tried and true format for contrasting and analyzing propitious behavior in mathematical detail and deriving relevant equations to predict the effects on societies.

Socrates, Pascal and others believed that only by transcending himself does man perfect his spiritual side. Science can help by carefully gathering information on love, and other marks of human perfection that, by their nature, do not behave in a random manner. I believe the hallmark of Science (dispassionate sorting of evidence) will show the transcendence of life in the human spirit is the Unified Theory Einstein and Godel searched for (unsuccessfully).

How would the tools of Science help us to better understand the cause-and-effect relationship of love and the Common Good, which is part of the internal aspect of creation? I asked this question in a letter to the editor titled, "Americans need God," published in the Goshen News.

December 10, 1994

Dear Editor:

A scientist studies cause and effect and uses deductive reasoning to correlate the two. We have no control over the basic forces that act throughout the universe (gravity, magnetism, radiation, etc.). However, we "observe" the mechanics, the heat, the magnetic field, etc., and put to practical use the information gained from observation. So, we are able to safely navigate in orbit around planet Earth due to our understanding of gravity, a basic force.

It is time for scientists to turn their training and their tools to the most basic of all forces, God. It is time to study God and love (or no God and tyranny) - cause and effect, and use deductive reasoning to correlate each pair, then put to practical use what is learned from repeated studies.

We become aware of the fundamental importance of the social institution of marriage by studying the harmful effects of divorce. We observe that love often makes its home in a marriage. Where God's gift of love is present all manner of desirable behavior follows. Husband, wife, children, neighbors and community live more in harmony than in discord.

Today Americans need to understand, accept and apply God's love more than at any time before. History will record that discord was the principal characteristic of American society in the last quarter of the 20th century. Hate and discord are cause-and-effect opposites to love and harmony. >

Call it Scientific Evangelism - Science helping to spread the Word, or call it application of the tools of Science to the unseen forces within human nature. "It," being the movement wherein scientists turn their attention, and their tools, toward proving the dependence of Common Good on Divine Intervention in the lives of selfless men and women who willfully serve their "neighbors."

Note: An outstanding economist, E.F. Schumacher, argued for distributism in his book Small is Beautiful published by Blond & Briggs, London in 1973. He recognized from empirical evidence that economic expansionism, separated from God, can only result in frustration and dehumanization. Schumacher argued that it is in man's nature to love and serve both God and his neighbor.

Selfless love is the foundation of Common Good, as opposed to Individualism ("I'm Number One") which, by definition, stands against Common Good. The scientific community must again proclaim its ties to God, and once again accept (as Newton did) Divine Intervention as part of its standard practice, not to defend faith in God, but to defend the rationality of His Divine plan. Thus, Science would lend a hand to persuade individuals so that they might take the first small step into faith formation. Serving others out of selfless love (the Common Good) lies down that path.

Selfless love in practice, with God's help, becomes service to mankind. Mother Teresa and the lives of many Saints are the embodiment of selfless love with God's help. They demonstrated dying to one's self to live in God. On the other hand, Individualism separated from God (living primarily for one's self) is a perverted self-love. Joseph Stalin, Adolf Hitler and Saddam Hussein are the embodiment of perverted self-love common in tyrants. A tool of pure Science (mathematics) will fashion a credible equation to show that living in God favors Common Good, and inversely, separation from God, as in self-indulgence, minimizes Common Good.

The equation is derived as follows -

Selfless love : devotion in service to mankind :: dying to one's self : living in God

Note: The characters : and :: are used in mathematics. The character : means "is to," and :: means "as." For example, 8: X :: 40 : 10. Then, X = (8)(10)/40 and, X = 2

Proof for this expression lies in identifying a statistically significant number of people who have accomplished this difficult task (i.e., allowing God to take control of their lives), and recording their contribution to the Common Good. And -

Individualism : neglect of service to mankind :: living for one's self : separation from God

Proof for this expression is indelibly stamped on the history of the twentieth century. We are living witnesses to the persecution of Jews and Christians by a statistically significant number of tyrannical nations. Persecution is a technique for separating mankind from God and neighbor.

Service to mankind (the Common Good) appears in both expressions. The mathematical form of the first expression is -

$$\text{Common Good} = \frac{(\text{Selfless love})(\text{living in God})}{\text{dying to one's self}}$$

The equation shows that Common Good increases as "self" decreases.

The second expression in mathematical form is -

$$\text{Common Good} = \frac{(\text{Individualism})(\text{separation from God})}{\text{living for one's self}}$$

Common Good decreases, or is minimized, as self-indulgence increases.

In the first expression the terms Selfless love and dying to one's self cancel one another because they are identical. And, in the second expression Individualism and living for one's self are identical and cancel one another. The result shows that quantity (and quality) of Common Good depends on Divine Intervention, i.e. living in God -

$$\text{"quantity" of Common Good} = \frac{\text{living in God}}{\text{separation from God}}$$

Has mathematics (a tool of Science) given expression to a law "within" humanity and made it self-evident? If so, where did the law originate?

Joining religion with Science is nonsense today. This wasn't the case in the early 18th century when Isaac Newton's religion (faith in God) gave mankind a mathematical formula for gravity. Newton was convinced that the hand of God has been present in nature from the beginning of time. He reasoned that nature's laws are intelligible and predictable, because they exist to serve God's purpose. Newton proved the test of understanding is predictability based on observation of the divine plan at work.

Many will choose to believe the deceptive teaching of modern Science that God is a fictitious product of feeling, faith and intuition, not of scientific deduction. They believe it is fruitless to put religion into the language of Science in order to persuade hearts. They are wrong. God is eminently knowable in the language of pure Science as in all languages.

Remember, objectivity (a most difficult task) is the very heart of Science. An objective scientist (who is open to God's graces) will conclude from identification of a statistically significant number of people living totally in God, in service to man, that there is more energy in the universe than the amount known to exist within atoms and molecules.

Consider this: The universe is designed or organized to move throughout time in a predictable manner. Total energy of an isolated system within the universe will be constant, disappearing in one form reappearing in another. However, the total energy of the physical universe (over fifteen billion years) is slowly decreasing. Ultimately, the universe will become completely disorganized. Science calls this process Entropy.

Man is unique in God's plan with respect to predictability and Entropy. We are the channel for spiritual energy which decreases only by our collective choice. Man alone is free to choose whether or not to obey his Creator. If obedience is man's choice, at his end will be energy gained (God's kingdom on earth). Entropy will prevail if man's choice is disobedience. At his end will be total disorganization. We are now moving toward disorder as described in the prophetic message of St. John recorded in the New Testament Book of Revelation.

Transcendental or visionary algebra opens another path to lost (discredited) knowledge about how peace everywhere on earth works. Would an atheist who left God out of his/her view of reality be interested if mathematics threw open a curtain showing him/her the Creator as the First Cause and ordering force for the "Big Bang" and all that followed?

Would unbelievers be persuaded to wonder at the scientific community once again proclaiming as fact that God-given energy to change the world really is found within the heart, mind and in the prayers of mankind?

If so, I believe the Creator would then, in some way, satisfy that (collective) wonderment, perhaps with "gratuitous gifts" of spiritual energy beginning with Faith and ending with peace on earth; and, delay the end of time.

It is said, "The longest journey begins with the first step." But, it is a step travelers must choose to take. The journey toward salvation also begins with the first step.

God gave us love to anchor the pillars of civilized societies by maintaining order and peace instead of confusion and war in the "universe within our hearts and minds." These pillars, not unlike gravity, are gifts essential to human existence and perfection on earth. Reality is, God provides for His children.

I believe the problems we face today must be solved quickly for the good of our children. We must understand, and be convinced, that we are living in "a moral stone age." (Note: This quote is taken from a paper titled, Are we living in a Moral Stone Age? The paper was presented in October, 1997 at the 15th anniversary of the Shavano Institute for National Leadership. The author was Christina H. Sommers, professor of Philosophy at Clark University.

––––––––––––

Post Modern cultures have forgotten what we can't permit them to forget. Within "humanness" there exists a core of ethical and moral values (honesty, respect for life, self-sacrifice, integrity, human dignity, courage, and the most valuable, the wonder of love) which we know through reasoning of the heart. History and reason show that successful religions and thriving nations owe their success to and are products of collective commitment to these pillars of strength; and, to Divine Intervention.

Care must be taken to mentally separate the reasoning of Science from heartfelt reasoning. An Essay in Aid of a Grammar of Assent published in 1870, written by John Henry Newman provides much help.

Newman separated scientific deduction "formal reasoning" from informal or "cumulative reasoning," i.e. piling together disconnected (heartfelt) reasons for "assent" to the spirit persuasive by their cumulative force.

To assent is to agree to something after thoughtful consideration. The key is commitment. One's commitment to the spirit, or to other honorable human values such as life itself, determines whether the assent is real or merely based on a whim, i.e. "Notional Assent."

Christians today give notional assent to abortion without thoughtful consideration just as pre-Civil War Christians gave notional assent to slavery. Eventually the by-products of these evil practices pile together with cumulative weight to smother the heart. The heart must then "persuade" the will to choose ways to unite with others against the practice of evil.

Speaking of Science playing a meaningful role in generating optimism, as I do here, know that we are capable of (and God holds us responsible for) generating our own optimism and commitment through our own efforts. True, God needs us to do the work. He gives us hope in times of danger - a hope that opens pure hearts and minds to prayer and to a plan of attack.

Harry Disston writes in Beginning the Rest of Your Life: "Express your views in agreement or disagreement. Where your views are strongly in favor of or opposed to what you have heard or read, and it is an important issue, you can and should write to the author, or to the editor of your local newspaper expressing your views. This applies whether the particular issue is discussed in a sermon, a speech, news and comment on radio or TV, while attending a play, or reading a book." Disston continues, "Think about what you have heard and seen, and make a summary and then a judgment; then express your views." (Disston's book was published by Arlington House, Westport, CT.)

We each possess the ability to recognize Truth. We need only make the effort to find it and accept it. Books containing praise-worthy ideas of famous people are available today, in some cases thousands of years later, because ordinary people recognized (or, in good conscience, thought they recognized) value in these ideas, and made a commitment to preserve them.

Consider the large number of people who were totally committed, unto suffering and death, to preserve, persuade and spread valuable ideas of Jesus Christ and His Church so that the world would believe and find favor in the sight of God.

Without optimism the battle to break the "habit of denial" will fail.

My letter about maintaining an optimistic long-range outlook, and about getting involved, titled A Piece of the Puzzle was published on April 2, 1977 in The Republic, Columbus, IN -

Dear Editor:

Shakespeare wrote, "Life is a stage on which we play our roles." On this stage there is a puzzle, or more precisely, interlocking pieces of a puzzle; and, our roles are to fit pieces of the puzzle in the right places.

We are each endowed with special talents needed to help complete the puzzle, which says life is important, and you are important. Our purpose, if you will, is to fit a few of the pieces together, for in doing so we become part of the whole. If I work a lifetime to fit correctly one piece I will have made a valuable contribution.

Let's not become discouraged on learning that the puzzle won't be completed in our lifetime (otherwise it would be complete already). Rather be thankful that you have a role to play, and a purpose.

There are pieces lying on the stage that appear to be parts of the puzzle, but there is no place to fit them. These need to be set aside. There are other pieces, set aside by earlier generations of players that fit correctly now.

How do we know when pieces fit correctly? We know the same way we know pieces of any puzzle fit. No one is excused from the task.

We have seen players who, in their frustration, scatter pieces and parts of the puzzle that were completed. This is unjust. Not only does it waste our efforts, but it wastes the good work of earlier generations as well.

Can the puzzle be completed? Yes. We would be fools to believe otherwise. In fact, the progress of our predecessors shows a clear outline of the finished puzzle.

Is there more than one puzzle? No, because there is only one God.

A Member of the Cast

This analogy gives me an optimistic outlook on life. It is comforting to believe that everything I see and hear and smell fits together. We know from observation and from Science that all things exist in harmony. All men can Be in Harmony, we believe from the Spirit. The apostle Paul said to the people of Corinth, "To each is given the manifestation of the Spirit for the common good. To one is given through the Spirit the utterance of wisdom, to another the utterance of knowledge according to the same Spirit, to another faith by the same Spirit, to another gifts of healing by the one Spirit, to another the working of miracles, to another prophecy, to another the ability to distinguish between spirits, to another various kinds of tongues, to another the interpretation of tongues. All these are inspired by one and the same Spirit, who apportions to each one individually as He wills." (1 Corinthians 12:4-11)

Life is a puzzle for everyone. We are able to solve puzzles because each is made from pieces designed from the beginning to fit together. Success starts with an orderly plan.

Moreover, the pieces are interlocking which gives a lasting quality to the work. Those who insist on reshaping pieces made by God into squares find that in time their part of the puzzle comes apart. The injustice is to themselves.

My professional life was devoted to research (much like working puzzles). I discovered that "togetherness" waiting to be discovered in plastics is quite clever. For example, rubber-like plastics are flexible because they are composed of long chains of carbon atoms where each chain is "loosely" bound to adjacent chains. It is reasonable to expect that a material having this "elastomeric" character will be soft and flexible. Whereas, rigid plastics are usually composed of short chains of carbon atoms with each chain tightly "cross-linked" to adjacent chains.

The fact that there is a verifiable answer waiting to be discovered for each of the hundreds of billions of components scattered throughout both the physical and the spiritual universe is indisputable proof that the hand of God is present in the puzzle.

The universe is custom-made and really quite clever as Isaac Newton understood. Where there is universal harmony of order, simplicity and purpose on an awe-inspiring scale, there must also be our awe-inspiring God. Since intelligence favors, in fact demands, that there be agreeably related parts, one could ask: Is denial of truth ensconced in modern Science?

Yahweh is a generous and a patient Father. The puzzle is not made with square pieces for child's play. He created a real challenge and sound reason to trust and hope.

We trust puzzle-makers, why not trust God?

The picture, when completed and viewed from above, is beautiful as Love. The view from the wrong side is terrifying.

The Enlightenment Movement and French Revolution in the 1700's are examples of square pieces (wild ideas) associated with the seeming injustice of human nature. Men and women chose to deny their duty by killing the Boss. The puzzle came apart. After a time the world fell apart. Europe went to war. Later, two world wars were fought, followed by fear of mutual assured destruction of life on earth (MAD) - a satanic domain.

As Pope Leo XIII foresaw, "Satan roamed the twentieth century seeking the ruin of souls."

Untruth cannot impose itself where truth belongs. From time to time frustrated players appear on the stage who scatter Truths of earlier generations in their quest for power. These pseudo intellectuals are of one mind. They detest God and deny His Justice and His ability to delegate authority to prescribe morality on earth. With Satan's help they are able to persuade others to join their nearsighted hedonistic religion.

We have a responsibility and every right to ask, together with Pascal the mathematician, Jaki the historian of Science and Schumacher the economist: What's going on when intelligent men and women choose to work on the wrong side of the puzzle?

What's going on when intelligent men and women waste time on more studies aimed at understanding the truth about the importance of the traditional family unit, when truth in this instance is self-evident.

The family is the primary tool for character formation. Our ancestors established schools to help them in their labor of love. Naturally, their standard of excellence was not confined merely to earthly existence.

Our ancestors knew that children who grow up with the guidance of both loving parents receive gifts found nowhere else. The gifts mothers give by virtue of their gender are mother's love, compassion, tenderness and mercy. This is part of God's Plan for Creation, as is the Truth that the gifts a father gives by virtue of his gender naturally complement mother's gifts. Strength, justice, independence, leadership, to name a few, these are the components of a father's gift of love to his children. The threads mother and father weave work together as warp and woof giving strength and beauty to the fabric of their children's lives.

Truth is: God forbids adultery because adultery sets divorce in motion; and, divorce destroys families and deprives children of character-shaping gifts of both genders that God intended children to have. Divorce robs children of a vitally important teaching aid, namely, mother and father in love. All one needs for understanding is common sense and reasoning from the heart.

Time-honored wisdom that needs repeating: Traditional families are the keystone of civilized society. The family unit (father, mother, children) is the seat of learning.

Stay at home mothers are the keystone of traditional families. From the beginning it is woman (mother) who creates the family. She makes a home for her family and carries each of her children into it. She lives and works at home growing the family's fruits. Her happiness comes from always giving (and expecting nothing in return). God crowns her merits by endowing motherhood with such satisfaction of self-fulfillment on earth that fatherhood can never merit.

What's going on when Betty Friedan and our culture of death encourage women to desert their God-ordered purpose? Friedan mocked the life of a mother and homemaker. She said women who choose to be full-time mothers live comfortable, empty, purposeless days. They forgo any possibility to grow and realize their full potential. Friedan (and her crowd) believe marriage and children are enemies of self-fulfillment.

The Feminist Movement was laid-out in a book titled The Second Sex, by Simone de Beauvoir published in 1949. The author insisted that women must be as self-assertive, self-indulgent and independent as men. The quality of "manliness," sought after for leadership in government and industry, ought to be accepted as a feminine quality too, since society must become gender neutral. This is twisted self-fulfillment of Individualism.

De Beauvoir and Friedan glossed over the fact that most women hold it to be self-evident that manly qualities are unnatural in a woman, therefore weird. They know society never was and never will be gender neutral as long as common sense remains. Those who allow themselves to be deceived by this lie suffer the consequences, particularly the self-depreciation experienced in sexual liberation Feminists promote.

If God had intended for women to be as promiscuous in sexual behavior as sinful men are, women would not contract sexually-transmitted diseases in far greater numbers and greater severity than men, as studies show.

I read a poem which says trust in God and perseverance are the warp and woof in the fabric of a mothers life -

> My life is but a weaving between my God and me;
> I may not choose the colors, He knows what they should be.
> For He can view the pattern upon the upper side,
> while I can see it only on this, the under side.
> Sometimes He weaveth sorrow, which seemeth strange to me.
> But I will trust His judgment, and work on faithfully.
> Tis He who fills the shuttle, He knows just what is best;
> so I shall weave in earnest, and leave Him the rest.
> At last, when life is ended, with Him I shall abide.
> Then I may view the pattern upon the other side.
> Then I shall know the reason, why pain with joy entwined,
> was woven in the fabric of life that God designed.

The poem was included in "Best Loved Poems" from The Salesian Collection, New Rochelle, NY, edited by Sara Tarascio. The author was not identified.

Persuasion - The Scientific Method - Part 2

Part I dealt with use of the tools of Science and Mathematics to persuade unbelievers that it is eminently reasonable to expect Common Good to increase as "self" decreases in service to God and neighbor. Nations prosper that obey God; and, nations fail that habitually defy God. Three things are required of unbelievers. Put aside your pride, do the math and pray for God's merciful assistance.

Part 2 advances my hypothesis, namely: Those who believe, yet choose their own version of God's Truth must accept a large share of the responsibility (and punishment) for moral apathy that let loose Satan in the guise of the Enlightenment Movement. They, too, must put aside their pride, do their homework and pray for God's mercy.

I could not persuade others to consider my hypothesis without doing my homework. I learned that unity of hearts (Solidarity) and moral courage were strongest in the thirteenth century resting on the "Rock". Apathy was not a problem in a (Western) world filled with faith in the power of God to preserve the moral authority of the Catholic Church.

St. Paul and the apostles taught all that had been revealed by God. This "Good News" was explained and defended in the following centuries by St. Clement, St. Ignatius, St. Polycarp, St Augustine, St. Jerome, St. Gregory the Great and others who were "New Testament prophets." These men, together with other saintly messengers, were commended by Jesus when He said, "He that heareth you heareth Me."

Faith in the Holy Spirit's infinite power permits the scientist in me to assume that the message of the Son of God is Truth that remains uncorrupted for all time in St. Jerome's Latin Vulgate Bible.

I learned that faith of early sixteenth century Catholics was put to the test. Moral authority of the Church was undermined in protest against its actual and its imagined abuses. Five hundred years of men and women "Re-forming" Divine traditions followed.

"Cafeteria Catholicism" gained momentum with the revolt of Martin Luther in Germany and the arrogance of Henry VIII in England against the fount of Solidarity instituted by Jesus. Luther was a Catholic monk ordained in The Order of Augustine in 1507. He was a professor of philosophy.

Henry VIII was a Catholic king.

Anglicanism was founded in 1534 to appease the conscience of King Henry VIII whose lust for Anne Boleyn was thwarted by Pope Clement VII. Later, in 1560, Queen Elizabeth I (Henry's daughter) ruled that the church her father started would be the Church of England. She bound her subjects, Catholics, Lutherans and Presbyterians, to this Anglican Religion under a penalty of death. This was Queen Elizabeth's "Good News".

Critical historians cite the period from 1517 to about 1560 AD as a time of extreme agitation in the Western Empire due to badly needed Church reform. Ambiguous, undisciplined, heretical, bold, unfaithful, and corrupt are adjectives used in historical accounts of abuses in the Catholic Church and in the actions of a philosophy professor and a daughter of England's King Henry VIII. Whether agitation was by the hand of God or Satan, is the subject of heated arguments then and now.

Arguments to the present day are hampered by conflicting historical documents describing Martin Luther's beliefs and his involvement in Church reform. Documents dealing with diabolic corruption within the Catholic Church of that time, and Luther's "95 points," tend to dismiss infallible teaching authority, particularly in the areas of good works and salvation; areas that disturbed Luther deeply.

No one denies that, at this period in history, the Catholic Church, although One, Universal (i.e. Catholic) and Apostolic, was troublesome due to sinfulness of its Bishops. The Church was not Holy in ways that concerned (and alienated) many priests and the laity. Sinful acts of some Bishops and even some Popes needed fixing. But trashing Catholicism completely missed the mark.

Pope Leo X (1513-1521) also missed the mark by failing to recognize the magnitude of the alienation and revolution within the Church.

Martin Luther, King Henry, Queen Elizabeth and others made the great mistake of refusing to meet with Church authorities to resolve the problems. Luther threw the Pope's (Leo X) list of forty-one charges (against Sola fides and other doctrinal disputes) into the fire and joined with other reformers; becoming their hero. Thus, "The plea for reform within the Church became a demand for existence without" (See page 364 in Great Religions of the World, copyright 1978, National Geographic Society).

Note: The Council of Trent, assembled December 13, 1545 by pope Paul III, corrected abuses within the Catholic Church. The mending Martin Luther and others tried to do by themselves took the Council eighteen years to complete. The Council closed December 4, 1563 during the rule of pope Pius IV.

The Council of Trent prepared the way for Catholic revival including (among many changes) formalizing the learning process and establishing Seminaries throughout the Western world to better prepare men to become Catholic Priests; and, commissioning Scriptural scholars to separate heretical versions from the one authentic (genuine) Bible.

Martin Luther was thoroughly convinced that mankind was depraved in it's every act. He believed even man's acts of piety are seen by God as Mortal sins. He said men and women are saved from damnation only by their faith (Sola fides) that God will grant them pardon. Luther neglected to include the other half of God's reality - the fact that God's forgiveness of man's sins does not absolve them from their Christian duty to live in loving service to one another.

Luther taught that the faithful enjoyed immediate access to God, claiming a "priesthood of all believers." (See page 367 in Great Religions of the World). He discounted the sacred history and sacred symbols of the conversion process ongoing throughout the previous fifteen hundred years saying, "If your Catholic history annoys you with the word "alone" (added to Rom 3:28), say that Dr. Martin Luther will have it so. Luther is a teacher above all the doctors in Popedom." (See also A Catholic response to Sola Fide by Bryan J.P. Gesinger published in the September 2007 issue of New Oxford Review.)

Martin Luther condemned Catholic Tradition as man-made to support Catholic doctrine. He neglected to mention that his own German translation of the Bible contained suppressions of and changes (corruption) to the genuine Biblical manuscript, made to support his disputed doctrines.

It is not surprising that Luther would disregard his own depravity by offering his followers a German Bible without first proving authenticity. Or, that the most widely used Protestant Bible today (the first in English) namely, The St. James Bible (after James I of England) would ignore the teaching of the Apostle James, the first Bishop of Jerusalem: "My brothers, what good is it to profess faith without practicing it?" (2:14). St. James added, "Do you want proof, you ignoramus, that without works faith is idle?" (2:20) <u>"You must perceive that a person is justified by his works and not by faith alone"</u> (2:24).

Lutheran Tradition became a living shoot (appendage) off of the tree that is the Body of Christ, minus Apostolic authority and other blessed symbols (fruits).

Martin Luther's "Priesthood of all believers" closed universities founded by and run by monks. They did away with celibate priests and nuns. They retained the Sacrament of Baptism but abandoned other Sacraments. The bread and fruit juice served for communion were secular facsimiles of the Last Supper.

Martin Luther was excommunicated for heresy.

Martin Luther, Queen Elizabeth and other anxious zealots threw Catholicism into confusion and lawlessness, i.e. disagreement over and disregard of God's Law. These were "reformed Catholics." Their Re-forming Tradition, in effect and in centuries that followed, became a fallible choice over the thorns in God's One, Holy, Apostolic and Catholic Body, the Latin Vulgate Bible and the Latin language.

> John Calvin and his followers discarded parts of Luther's theology, as well as parts of authentic Catholic dogma. They founded the Presbyterian church in 1536.

Fifteen autonomous, quarrelsome Religions took root throughout Europe, and slowly spread to the New World. All are Christian religions. All believed that Jesus Christ, through the Incarnation, took human form to suffer and be crucified for the sins of mankind. Also, most incorporated the Holy Trinity into their dogma. Each branch denied infallibility of the Catholic Pope, and other parts of authentic Catholic dogma found to be uncomfortable (marriage law, and confessing sins to a priest are two of many examples).

Today men claim ownership of this or that piece of the Body of

Christ: Martin Luther (Lutheran), King Henry VIII (Anglican and Episcopal), John Smythe (Baptist), John Calvin (Presbyterian), Joseph Smith (Mormon) and so on. (See listing of Christian religions on pages 380-81 in Great Religions of the World.)

Each of these men sanctioned his own dogma, on his own authority. Personal freedom to interpret God's message followed naturally. The number of distinguishable Protestant versions of the "Good News" (Bibles) in current use is nine and counting.

Comment: The Good News of the apostles is from the owner of a perfect Will that cannot deceive nor be deceived and from a mind indivisible.

History has come full circle. Five hundred years ago the One Infallible Scriptural Authority and his seat of office (the Holy See) were renounced. Also, five hundred years ago St. Jeromes Vulgate Bible was declared authentic by the Council of Trent.

Today, one man, made infallible by God in matters of faith and morals, is abandoned by Protestants; and, nine (or more) other bibles are disposed to suit the whims of fallible men and women.

The havoc of religious terror intensified. Christian men, women and children were put to death by Christians over belief in one or another version of God's Words; "in churches blind and evil" - churches built on both sand and rock.

Sixteenth century Protestants (called Anabaptists) were persecuted and murdered by Protestants and Catholics alike, because Anabaptist dogma specified that adults baptized as infants must be baptized again. Their Bible mandated Adult baptism of new members who convert (as in the time of John the Baptist).

The "infamous" Catholic Inquisition in Spain paled in comparison with the Anglican Inquisition of Queen Elizabeth I. She murdered thousands of Catholics, Anabaptists and other non-Anglican Christians, burning many tied to a stake.

Today, Muslim men, women and children are blown to pieces by Muslim terrorists misled by belief in one or another interpretation of the Koran.

I ask: Was the deception, conspiracy and manipulation in the struggle for power in the Catholic priesthood any different than the deception, conspiracy and manipulation in the struggle for power in the Protestant priesthood or among the caliphs of Islam?

How could this happen? How could God the Holy Spirit acting through the Church God the Son instituted be manipulated? How could Western Man turn away the beauty and fullness of God's Word or reject the intimacy of Jesus Christ Himself received in the Eucharist?

"Amen, amen, I say to you: Unless you eat the flesh of the Son of man, and drink His blood, you shall not have life in you. He that eateth my flesh, and drinketh my blood, hath everlasting life, and I will raise him up at the last day." (Jn 6:53-54)

It is time to ask of history: Did the Son of man intend that the Western world be united in One Body in order to defeat Satan? Did He forget that without a universally accepted papacy to preserve and interpret His Words modern Christian souls could not attain Solidarity?

Without Solidarity Christians must tolerate civil laws enabling heretics to confuse right and wrong. With Solidarity in One Body under One Head, as the Son of God instructed, the possessions of heretics would be "instantly thrown from the wagon." (See the Preface for my letter of December 28, 2005).

The Church founded for all time by God's Son can neither deceive nor be deceived. Furthermore, the Church founded by God's Son cannot (for long) hide it's light under a basket.

Without the will to fight and win over those who seek to (as in Isaiah) "call evil good and good evil," the twenty-first century (as in the words of C. S. Lewis) "will be the worst since the twenty-first century BC before the call of Abraham and the founding of Judaism."

Start with what we know about choices. Tolerance of evil choices, under the mantle of freedom, causes much suffering. This must not be confused with common sense tolerance of freedom to make good choices.

Freedom works best when everyone chooses to obey the rules. Simplistic examples are traffic control rules. City planners use sophisticated instruments for traffic control, i.e. traffic lights, timers and sensors to detect the volume and location of cars. The rule: <u>Do</u>

what the traffic light instructs you to do. The point here is not that the light cares whether a motorist stops when it turns red. The point is, the efforts of city planners to further the Common Good are frustrated when motorists habitually choose to disobey the light.

We know what happens to freedom of choice in this example.

We know the light continues to instruct, whether we misuse it or not, just as our conscience continues to instruct whether we misuse it or not.

We know what happens to other motorists who, out of their habit of obedience and their common sense, choose to obey the light. They suffer. And we know guilt for choosing to disobey a rule and legitimate authority for the common good.

Substitute God's Plan for city planners and one begins to understand the nature of man's insult to common sense. We are not free to act against the object of God's Plan, i.e. Common Good. A society fails that habitually defies not only a plan for its betterment, but the also the authority for the plan.

We are back to sinful men and women and their politically correct motives and excuses for denying personal responsibility.

Secularism's intolerable tolerance is a Culture of Death strategy used effectively in the face of moral apathy that has been building for hundreds of years. Valueless values, free love and other of Secularism's strategies are now the norm.

Many believers at this critical juncture in time manipulate and minimize knowledge God has revealed about His Plan for our salvation. We find a comfortable place for His Word in our own plans instead of centering our plans in His Word. We are conscious of our guilt and our weakness. We succumb to the temptation to fill our minds and bodies with enjoyable distractions and leave the attention our souls demand for later.

What is in our will that overpowers both mind and heart? Why do those who know in their hearts that the universe is ours by design not by accident harden their hearts? Why do those who argue that miracles violate scientific laws not recognize that each law Science formulates is in fact proof of a miracle? Why do (many) physicists refuse to acknowledge that the laws of Physics they use to postulate a "Big Bang" did not come out of nothingness to cause all that happened in that amazing (first) micro-second of time.

And, why do those who know that God painstakingly prepared a universe for His children's bodies not know that He would show even greater concern for their souls?

CHAPTER 8

"WHY INDEED?"

The odds against intelligent life in this vast universe, not as some small meaningless part, but as the central part bringing every other part together for a common purpose, are impossible to imagine. This fact taken together with order and purpose observed throughout the universe argues convincingly against the human race being an accident uncaused. Yet, men and women persist in believing the unbelievable. Their religion is Atheism.

Atheism is defended by attacking anyone or any organization that believes in a Creator, i.e. it attacks other religions, particularly Christianity. The newest plan of attack is sophisticated and disciplined. It uses techniques that are part of a one hundred year-old science - the science of mind and behavior known as Psychoanalysis. Broadly speaking psychoanalysis is a method for studying and treating disordered behavior by having patients talk about their early childhood experiences and their dreams. The Will to Believe, by William James, a psychologist, is an excellent example of the mental effort required for Psychological Man to undermine Christianity.

Allow an ex-atheist and professor of Psychology at New York University, Professor Paul C. Vitz, to provide information supporting the assumption that, "psychological concepts used quite effectively to interpret and attack religion are two-edged swords that can also be used to interpret atheism." (See his book titled Faith of the Fatherless: The Psychology of Atheism published by Spence Publishing Company, Dallas, TX.)

An assumption is necessary: "The major barriers to belief in God are not rational but, in a general sense, can be called psychological," and/or in the state of one's will.

Commitment to God requires a change of lifestyle, otherwise commitment is not intellectually honest.

Professor Vitz recounted his fall into atheism: "The ultimate issue is one of the will and our sinful nature. Through reflection on my own college experiences it is now clear to me that my reasons for becoming and remaining (for 20 years) an atheist-skeptic were superficial, irrational, and largely without intellectual or moral integrity. Furthermore, I am convinced that my motives were, and still are commonplace today among intellectuals, especially social scientists."

Professor Vitz gives three factors that were involved in his choice: "General Socialization - Desire to be comfortable in the new, exciting secular world of psychology at Stanford and later at New York University. Specific Socialization - Desire to be accepted by the powerful and influential scientists in the field of psychology who seemed to be united in only two things; their intense career ambition and their rejection of religion. And, Personal Convenience - In today's powerful secular and neo-pagan world it is quite inconvenient to be a serious believer. Besides, camaraderie and sexual freedom were too much to resist. There may be other factors as well, perhaps neuroses, which influence one's decision to choose atheism."

He adds, "I can't but assume that such are the shallow reasons behind many an unbeliever's position."

The two-edged sword Professor Vitz referred to is the psychological concept of an Oedipus complex that some psychoanalysts use very effectively to criticize the "religious experience." Freud believed and taught that belief in God is a neurotic wish-fulfilling experience derived from childish needs for protection and security or, from other natural causes. Freud postulated a universal Oedipus complex as the origin of all our anxieties.

Webster's definition for Oedipus complex is: "Positive libidinal feelings that a child develops toward the parent (usually) of the opposite sex, and may be a source of adult personality disorder when unresolved." Rebellion of son against father for any of a number of reasons (deserting the family is quite common) naturally produces a strong desire for a "real" father. Psychoanalysts call this "Oedipal wish fulfillment."

Vitz emphasizes two points: 1) "Although the Oedipus complex is valid for some, the theory is far from being a universal representation of unconscious motivation." 2) "Freud's critical reaction to and rejection of religion is clearly rooted in his personal bias - he hated his father." Objective comparison of personality disorders must conclude that Freud's neurotic act of rejecting God the Father was "Oedipal wish fulfillment."

The irony here, according to Professor Vitz, is that Freud and other influential psychologists provide, by way of the Oedipal theory, a powerful and equally effective tool for understanding the neurotic basis for rejecting God.

The main obstacle preventing men and women from living together in harmony on earth, and living in perfect happiness in heaven, is in the state of their wills, not in the state of their minds. To quote Professor Vitz again, "The ultimate issue is one of the will and our sinful nature."

This is the answer to the question "Why?" We know through experience that order demands an orderer, and we know from history that men and women are sinners by nature and saints by choice. The philosopher George Santayana said, "Those who cannot remember the past are condemned to repeat it."

We can deny man's sinful nature but we cannot change it.

Is it a coincidence that last evening I should read Harry's letter in Sunday's South Bend Tribune?

Dear Editor:

I can sum up how we have gotten to the point where we are in this society.

Madelyn Murray O'Hair complained that she did not want any prayer in our schools. We said OK.

Then someone said, "You had better not read the Bible in school." The Bible that says thou shalt not kill, thou shalt not steal and love your neighbor as yourself. We said OK.

Dr. Benjamin Spock said we should not spank our children when they misbehave, their little personalities would be warped. We said OK. Then someone said teachers and administrators better not discipline our children when they misbehave. We said OK.

Then someone said, let our daughters have abortions if they want, and we will not have to tell their parents. We said OK. Then someone said, let's give our sons and daughters all the condoms they want so they can have all the fun they desire, and they will not have to tell their parents. We said OK.

And then some of our top officials said that it does not matter what we do in private as long as we do our jobs. We said as long as I have a job and the economy is good, it does not matter to me what anyone does in private, it is nobody's business. We said OK.

So now we are asking ourselves why our children have no conscience. Why they do not know right from wrong. Why it does not bother them to kill. Probably, if we think about it long and hard enough, we can figure it out. I think it has a great deal to do with Galatians 6:7, "A man reaps what he sows." >

The decisions people of faith make - to believe selected parts of God's revealed Word and dismiss other inconvenient parts, is in "the state of their will, not in the state of their mind."

Professor Vitz gave three reasons why he chose to reject God. I think rejecting God and His commandments is all about ego - a "peculiarity" of mankind alone among all life-forms. I find no way around the fact that my existence is either about me, or it is about God.

The "Good News" about God becomes bad news for those who enjoy/prefer a self-indulgent lifestyle.

Existentialists say mankind lives alone in a universe of such complexity and vastness as to be incomprehensible. Christians and other devout believers learn that they can find their way through this smoke: The universe celebrates the power of God - a God who told us He loves us as our Father. He will be with us always. I am alone by choice.

Existentialists say that, while we must assume full responsibility for our behavior and our acts of free-will, mankind is without certain knowledge about good and bad, or, about "fair play." Jews and Christians will answer that God's Words revealed in both the Old and New Testaments - the Torah and the Bible, teach good and bad, right and wrong. Devout Muslims look to the Koran and agree that Abraham's God taught them all they know about right and wrong behavior.

What about the morality of modern contraceptives? Biblical Interpretation of God's Words applied to this moral choice involves "reading between the lines," which the Catholic Church (based on two thousand years of "on the job training") is most qualified to do. Some will "read" that the practice of contraception is both good and practical, i.e. it is sexual pleasure freed from the purpose God intended. Some will accept Church teaching on Human Life (Humanae Vitae) that contraceptives frustrate God's Plan, therefore contraceptives are evil. Some married couples won't take the time to learn that "Natural Family Planning" is both good and a practical use of the cycle of fertility God designed.

How can man-made morality be acceptable to a God who is Justice personified; a Father who cannot deceive nor be deceived?

"What is truth? said jesting Pilate, and would not stay for the answer." This quote from Of Truth, an essay of the same name by Francis Bacon (1561-1626), is for existential operators who sneer at homework saying: "Statements about God are as numerous as the stars; it is impossible to know the Truth."

Again, the problem comes back to sinful human nature and free will. Since the "fall" it has been necessary to overcome, in a manner of speaking, the nature of our very being in order to love God with our whole self and to embrace the authority He established on earth.

Modern man no longer fears Divine justice and the wrath of God, which for nearly four millennia served as a strong motivator to lead a moral life in accordance with His Commandments.

CHAPTER 9

VATICAN COUNCIL II SYNDROME

Syndrome is a pattern of signs or an easily identified pattern of behavior - contempt, insubordination, etc. - that characterizes a particular social condition; in this case, Catholics who put Divine Justice aside by rejecting some forms of legitimate moral behavior and picking others, much as one satisfies his or her appetite in a cafeteria.

Proof of carelessness about Divine Justice is found in the increase in immorality of Roman Catholics in Western nations, the U.S. in particular, following the close in 1965 of Vatican Council II. Vatican Council II is an Ecumenical (worldwide) Council called by Pope John XXIII.

Ecumenical Councils are a means for exercising the teaching authority of St. Peter's successor, the Pope, in union with the College of Bishops; all governed through the grace of the Holy Spirit. This gift of Divine Guardianship enables the pope, with or without an assembled Ecumenical Council, to proclaim and interpret God's Words totally free from error. THIS IS AN ARTICLE OF FAITH WITHOUT WHICH REALITY AND MORAL TRUTHS, i.e., THE WORDS OF GOD, BECOME WHATEVER IMPERFECT MEN AND WOMEN CHOOSE TO MAKE THEM.

Solidarity and lasting peace everywhere is impossible without Divine Guardianship.

There have been twenty-one Ecumenical Councils of the Catholic Church. The first was the Council of Nicaea, called 300-years after the crucifixion and resurrection of Jesus. The Council was inspired through the Holy Spirit to proclaim (in words sanctioned by Pope Sylvester I): "The Son of God is consubstantial - of the same substance or nature with the Father." This divinely inspired human proclamation defeated the heresy of Arianism as described in Chapter 3. This infallible proclamation of the Ecumenical Council of Bishops at Nicaea is the keystone of all Christian communities.

Arianism was resurrected in the 17th century by Thomas Hobbes and John Locke

to promote natural religion over Revelation. Their ideas influenced the choice of
words Thomas Jefferson used in writing the Declaration of Independence.

Vatican Council II opened on October 11, 1962 and ended on
December 8, 1965. It was an Ecumenical Council called to evangelize
the world. The consistently inerrant teachings of God's Church as
they pertain to salvation in the modern world were essential.

Interpretation/clarification of long-standing teachings is essential
for salvation, particularly in this age of sophistication and prosperity.
It is more essential now, because arrogance before God is a greater
obstacle compared with the "Age of Excellence" and humility.
Salvation demands that we humble ourselves before God and (again)
accept the teaching authority He gave us.

A book published in 1999 by HarperCollins, Inc. New York, titled
Witness to Hope, records the spiritual experiences of Bishop Karol
Wojtyla at the Council told to the author, George Weigel. Following
his election as Pope on October 16, 1978 he said: "Any interpretation
of the Council that does not treat it as, first and foremost, a profound
spiritual experience - a Gift of the Spirit to enrich the faith of the
Church so that Christians might live an increasingly full participation
in divine truth - is simply going to miss what was central to the
experience of the Council itself."

What did go wrong after Vatican II? Why did priests and
members of religious orders leave the Catholic Church in the decade
immediately following this Ecumenical Council? Was it for the same
reason as when priests, Bishops and members of the laity and religious
orders left the Church five hundred years earlier? No.

Why do some Catholic theologians today substitute their own
opinions for the teaching authority of the pope expressed through
particular documents of Vatican Council II; and, a related Encyclical
of Pope Paul VI (Humanae Vitae)? Was it the same reason Martin
Luther had for substituting his opinions for the teaching authority of
the Church? Probably.

Why did so many of the laity choose to follow an easier path than
the path of self-sacrifice in observance of the teaching of Jesus, His
apostles and His Church? Was it for Luther's convenient interpretation
of Romans 3:28, wherein he inserted the word "alone" after the word

faith, i.e. "For we hold that a man is justified by faith 'alone' apart from observance of the law?" And in Romans 3:30, "It is the same God who justifies the circumcised and the uncircumcised on the basis of faith 'alone'"? Yes.

Read verse 31 in the Letter to the Romans 3, and pray for enlightenment. Would Saint Paul ask all Protestants beginning with Martin Luther, and today's "fallen away" Catholics: "Are we then abolishing the law by means of faith?"

In their obstinacy many Catholic theologians and Bishops (then as now) are not willing to work with the pope. Legitimate moral authority in the 16th century centered on "95 points of ecclesiastical abuses in the Catholic Church" set-down by Martin Luther. Legitimate moral authority in the latter half of the twentieth century centered on birth control, pederasty, abuses in the laity and poor judgement by Bishops and priests in suggesting that God's Church is a "peoples Church," with authority flowing from the bottom up opposed to the top down. (See Russell Shaw's Papal Primacy in the Third Millennium published in 2000 by Our Sunday Visitor Division, Huntington, IN.)

The outcome (then and now) casts doubt on the binding force and legitimacy of Saint Paul's teaching about Christian Freedom. See Chapter 6, page 105.

Artificial Contraception

Today, doubt centers specifically on Pope Paul VI's Encyclical Humanae Vitae (Of Human Life), published July 29, 1968, condemning artificial contraception; and to a lessor extent on the application of Canon law to modern immorality.

Pope Pius XI stated what is obvious in his 1930 Encyclical Casti Connubii -

"Since the conjugal act is destined primarily by nature for the begetting of children, those who in exercising it deliberately frustrate its natural power and purpose sin against nature and commit a deed which is shameful and intrinsically vicious."

Casti Connubii continued -

"Those who deliberately frustrate the natural power of the conjugal act to generate life are branded with the guilt of grave sin."

In Section 18 of Humanae Vitae Pope Paul VI wrote -

"The Catholic Church proclaims with humble firmness the entire moral law, both natural and evangelical. Of such laws the Church was not the author, nor consequently can she be their arbiter; she is only their depository and their interpreter, without ever being able to declare to be licit that which is not so by reason of its intimate and unchangeable opposition to the true good of man."

The "rock" of moral teaching dealing with the sexual union of a man and a woman is that it is conditional. Sexual intercourse is connubial, intended by God to unite husband and wife in love; and, it is procreative. Vatican Council II called this act "the full sense of mutual self-giving and human procreation in the context of true love. It must always remain open to the generation of new lives." (See Pastoral Constitution on the Church in the Modern World).

Conception occurs naturally as God intended. Abuse results where conception is artificially controlled by men and women. Artificial birth control is like every other sin. Its consequences are far more destructive to women than society is willing to admit. It accommodates promiscuous sex which promotes lust which harbors venereal diseases particularly severe for women; and, the act very often leads to abortion which (often) causes Post Abortion Syndrome and years of despondency; again, particularly debilitating for women's sensitive nature. In short it is a sin that turns women into outlets for plugging into; obviously not what God intended mothers to be.

Contraception is virulent in that it quickly overcomes the will. Promiscuous sexual behavior ending in abortion is malignant in that it threatens the life of one's soul leaving a permanent emotional scar on both partakers. The more "popular" promiscuity becomes, particularly with young people, the more their morality and emotional balance are corrupted.

These precepts and concerns hold good today just as much as they did yesterday and will hold true tomorrow and always, for they are expressions of Natural Law and Divine Law.

God created the universe to provide a suitable home for His children. He gave mothers/fathers the means for conceiving "new life" and He holds them accountable for giving that life back to Him.

Concern of the Catholic Church for teaching "new life" mirrors the concern God expressed in His Divine Plan. Procreation implies mutual cooperation of mother and father with God. The act itself begins a process intended to prepare the child for his/her journey back to God. Concern that the bond between mother and father must not be broken dates back before God's Son was born to a virgin to the time when Moses handed down God's Commandments.

How were the laity tricked into turning celebration of God away from this long tradition, away from Jesus on the cross, toward themselves? How were they tricked into ignoring the universal belief of medieval ancestors that salvation is man's reward for a life of obedience, and everlasting torture man's punishment for resolute disobedience? Why do Catholics today, in large numbers, favor and convert to the newer Protestant tradition, i.e. salvation (pure and simple) is God's gift of infinite mercy? All are saved who have faith. Not to worry about confession to God's appointed agent for a life of disobedience and indifference to the Pope and to the teaching of Ecumenical Councils.

"In My Father's house are many mansions" (Jn. 14:2) is often used to defend or explain the fact that the Church founded by the Son of God consists of many diverse elements. Whether it is valid in the sight of God to split Christ's "Rock" into individual (smaller) pieces will be made known to each of us at the Last Judgment, where God will seal our eternal destiny.

The answers to "Why?" and "How?" fit the observation of Professors Vitz and Adler: "The ultimate issue is one of the will and sinful nature;" and fits Harry's observations as well.

Vatican Council II and Humanae Vitae did not soften Catholic teaching to suit powerful theologians, bishops and the laity. In no way was deliberate prevention of conception or impregnation not a mortal sin.

I see pragmatism, pride and convenience behind false teaching. And I see collegiality; something far more sinister.

National Conferences of Catholic Bishops were organized in the liberated (free-thinking) Western world of the 1970's. Conference organizers saw this as a door to a collegiate church guided by the Holy Spirit. The relationship or "collegiality" of Bishops in a national Conference, they said, allows that nation's Catholic Bishops to function in communion with the papal office. Political power exercised when their Conference agreed unanimously on a specific papal teaching was equivalent to papal power.

The collegiate Church satisfied the need of rebel Bishops to add weight to their declarations.

Conference members agreed that "Whoever honestly chooses to act in accord with what seems right to him, in good conscience, is not culpable."

An old door opened in the 1980's. A door to a cafeteria offering choices opposed to the bitter, immovable, salvific teaching of the Church. Today, salvific food is served with a choice of icings.

A powerful pro-choice culture now runs the cafeteria. Catholics, "in good conscience," see no problem with divorce followed by another marriage (and another). Many Catholic women believe, "in good conscience," that they have an equal right with men to wield ecclesial power.

The absolute jurisdiction, i.e. power to apply the law of St. Peter's successors, is being undermined to serve/satisfy a "cafeteria conscience." (The 500 year-old squabble over ownership of God's Church continues.)

Vatican II is the most important interchange of ideas on the impact infallible Catholic teaching has had since the Council of Trent in 1545. Rehashing of Council proceedings is expected to continue for at least a hundred years more. In this area sacred history is as predictable as sunrise. Rehashing will have no impact because what is finally proclaimed is the Will of the Holy Spirit. The time for theological arguments, democratic sharing and shaping a consensus is in the years before a Council is convened and during Council sessions, prior to the final draft of Council documents. It stands to reason that the Pope, as God's Overseer, must be the sole and the final moral authority in order for God's Truth about Salvation to remain inerrant.

Twenty-eight years after the close of Vatican II the then Bishop of the Catholic Church in Rome was asked: "For what does the Pope pray?" His answer -

> "The subject of the Pope's prayer is the phrase that begins the last document of the Second Vatican Council - Gospel means 'good news', and the Good News is always an invitation to joy." He explained in more detail: "The gospel is the revelation of the truth about God. God who is Creator and Father; God who 'so loved the world that He gave His only Son, so that everyone who believes in Him might not perish but might have eternal life.' Creation was entrusted to humankind as a duty, representing not a source of suffering but the foundation of creative existence in the world. The Church and the Pope pray for the people to whom this mission must be particularly entrusted."

(See Crossing the Threshold of Hope, by His Holiness John Paul II, published in 1994 by Alfred A. Knopf, New York.)

Vatican Council II defined the relationship of the Church to non-Christian religions in a document that begins with the words Nostra Aetate (In our time). This document speaks of unity in a pragmatic sense, and links it with the current trend to bring humanity closer together through the resources available to our civilization.

> "There is only one community and it consists of all peoples. They have only one origin, since God inhabited the entire earth with the whole human race. And they have one ultimate destiny, God, whose providence, goodness and plan for salvation extend to all.... Men turn to various religions to solve mysteries of the human condition, which today, as in earlier times, burdens people's hearts. From ancient times up to today all the various peoples have shared and continue to share an awareness of that absolute though enigmatic power that is present throughout the course of things and throughout the events of human life, and, in which, at times, even the Supreme Divinity of the Father is recognizable. This awareness and recognition imbue life with an intimate religious sense. Religions that are tied up with cultural progress strive to solve these issues with more refined concepts and a more precise language." (Nostra Aetate 1-2)

In 1995 the Vatican published an Encyclical of John Paul II titled

Ut Unum Sint (That They May Be One) wherein he points to the "full communion" Jesus desired for all peoples (made easier in this age of one close-knit community linked together by the Internet). As One Community, with One Origin and One Ultimate Destiny we must pray for strength to resist postmodern doubt that religious truths not only can be known but (of necessity) the foundation and authority for those truths must reside in One Man.

Pope John Paul II cited a passage from The Pastoral Constitution of the Second Vatican Council.

"In truth, the imbalances in the modern world are linked to a more profound imbalance found in the heart of man. Many elements conflict with each other in man's inner struggle. As a created being, he experiences his limitations in thousands of ways yet he also perceives himself to be boundless in his aspirations and destined to a higher life. *Enticed by many options* (italics added), he is continually forced to choose some and to renounce others. Furthermore, since he is weak and sinful, he often does what he detests and not what he desires."

"This causes him to suffer an inner division, which is the source of so many and such grievous disagreements in society.... With all of this, however, in face of the modern world's development, there is an ever-increasing number of people who ask themselves or who feel more keenly the most essential questions: What is man? What is the meaning of suffering, of evil, of death, which persist despite all progress? What are these victories, purchased at so high a cost, really worth? What can man offer to society and what can he expect from it? What will there be after this life? The Church believes that Christ, who died and was resurrected for the sake of all, continuously gives to man through His Spirit the light and the strength to respond to his higher destiny. Nor is there any other name under heaven given to the human race by which we are to be saved. The Church also believes that the key, the center, and the purpose of all human history, is found in its Lord and Master."

Devout Catholics, by the gift of Faith from the Holy Spirit ("ask and you shall be rewarded"), and trusting in their 2000-year Divine

Tradition of proclaiming God's infallible Words free of error, accept the mission spelled out in the documents of Vatican II.

"What can man offer to society and what can he expect from it?"

It is a fact that "enticed by many options" is what we can expect from thoroughly materialistic societies, a fact easy to prove. Consider a day in the life of a typical American (yesterday for example) -

This American was on the road and needed to use a rest-room. He stopped at a large shopping mall in Kalamazoo. Walking back to the car he overheard a girl, 9 or 10 years old, say to her mother, "I want to go to the shoe department first. They have some brown shoes I want." Typical? The thought came immediately to mind - "age 10 and already a savvy shopper." His conclusion: The girl's mother, whether knowingly or not, has impressed one so young with the ease of getting what she wants.

I can't say this proves much. It does however get us into a large mall - one of about half-dozen very large malls in Kalamazoo - where businesses (and credit cards) entice us to buy "goods" we want, but may not need and, in too many instances we can't afford. As though this is not distraction enough from our "life of obedience," add the vast effort by advertisers to sell the idea that the sole or chief good in life is one's own pleasure. This hedonistic idea anesthetizes one's conscience causing overextended credit now and payment due in eternity.

Western society exists in a Grand Mal wherein nervous systems are relentlessly enticed and subconsciously disturbed with satellite television, a hundred other audio/visual products (IPods, games, mp3 players), cell-phones, and on and on. And sex. It is as John Paul II said, "We do what we detest and not what we desire." In our hearts we desire eternal happiness. In our consciousness we dread God's wrath.

Our personal problems (and society's problem) is that doing often what we subconsciously detest soon becomes habit forming, even neurotic wish-fulfilling.

If we desire to approach this "life of obedience" determined to please God we must work on changing worthless habits starting with the most basic habit I call irresponsible excitement, including the sexual variety.

Every argument advanced in my letters and my comments is integrated into a single assertion: God is real. The ability to identify social problems with absolute certainty, and the right to call slavery, child molesting and child killing injustices presupposes an unerring method for defining, judging and dealing with injustice. God's gifts of a Divine Standard for Justice, one infallible judge; and, solidarity deep-rooted in one obedient universal Body, stand to reason.

Those who seek the Truth prayerfully and do their homework with an open mind, find that; 1) The traditional Catholic Church holds a core of settled convictions in total agreement with scripture and in agreement with beliefs Christian Churches everywhere hold in common; 2) Devout Church members, together with Jesus, say to the Father, "Not my will but thy will be done." They express this relationship with God the Father as Jesus did, through love, trust, prayer, compassion, and forgiveness; 3) the Church is charged by Christ to preserve, defend and teach God's Word throughout time, authoritatively. It has nurtured, defended and transmitted God's Word unchanged for two millennia; 4) as an institution for learning, for trustworthiness in the midst of sin and for length of service she has no equal; 5) her teachers include the Holy Spirit, Popes, saints and other learned men and women, supported by a library holding original manuscripts dating back more than two thousand years.

Those who seek Truth prayerfully and do their homework with an open mind often receive more from the Holy Spirit than conviction about becoming Catholic. Many converts are given, in addition, the zeal to challenge from within each and every Catholic Bishop who does not teach the Word of God fearlessly.

Success in halting the runaway regression of morality depends equally on strong leadership and on committed followers who vote in accord with their Christian heritage.

Name another church, headed by and staffed by sinful human beings, more qualified by reason, by history and through Faith to claim infallibility through the Holy Spirit in all matters of faith and morals. I believe it will be converts who turn the tide in perhaps our last great battle.

A Troubling Time

Following in Pascal's footsteps I offer my thoughts, as he did, attempting to fit the Christian Worldview into a systematic and reasonable whole. Aided by the tools of science and logical thinking, I conclude that living and voting the genuine Catholic ideal is the solution for reversing the Western world's ever increasing bad ideas.

CHAPTER 10

EVOLUTION AND CREATION

C.S. Lewis said the twenty-first century will be very good or very bad. He hoped it is good. I do too.

The issue discussed here, Evolution and Creation vs. Evolution or Creation, must be resolved for Common Good to triumph. Modern Science must be persuaded to return its view of Creation to that of Isaac Newton, because goodness will not come about until Science acknowledges that the design they find throughout nature is not accidental.

Scientific discoveries clearly show that each and every form of life, particularly human life, is a highly organized assembly of parts working together in close union with their neighbors. The scientific name is Symbiosis.

Symbiosis is far more complex than Darwin's blind process of evolution allows. Moreover, Science must acknowledge that the spiritual realm (the unseen part of the assembly of human parts) is beyond evolution's reach as humans work together selflessly with other humans creating goodness.

Science must reject two inventions promoted by twentieth century Secularism. 1) "Man, the supreme ruler of the universe, defines "Goodness." 2) "There cannot be a rational approach to God."

 Scientists must be persuaded to take-up the call for what Nancy Pearcey and Charles Colson call Total Truth in their book of that title.

Total Truth - Liberating Christianity from its cultural captivity (Published in 2005 by Crossway, Wheaton, IL) examines two views of truth. Truth with a capital T, denotes "factual" truth that is objective and rational, i.e. consistent with what Science calls public knowledge. This is the branch of truth zealously proclaimed by Secularism. Modern scientists own the patent.

Spiritual truth, with a small case t, denotes "emotional," private truth "perceived" as factual, but not provable by scientific experiments.

This is the branch of truth secularists and atheists reject because it is truth revealed by God about God. Science calls it "religious truth." I call it Whole Man's truth (truth with a capital "T").

The claim of modern Science is that cultural progress is achieved by making Whole Man's Truth irrelevant. The strategy is to remove God the Creator from Public Schools and from the Public Square. Love in families, and other moral values, humility for example, are discreetly underrated in the process. This is progress?

Modern Man's heart is burdened with what Pope John Paul II called "the mystery of the human condition," as it relates to cultural progress. God in the family and in schools provides insight for solving this mystery. "What does it mean to be human" becomes a basic question. Divine origin and purpose (or no purpose), success in eternity (or failure), hope (or despair), even sanity (or insanity) hinges on the choice between Creation revealed by God, or blind chance zealously promoted by Atheism rooted in modern Science.

I believe a close examination of the faithlessness Michael Denton called the Darwinian Revolution is essential for understanding the vicious attack on God's Plan by modern Science. In his 1986 book Evolution: A theory in crisis, published by Adler & Adler, Bethesda, MD, Denton makes the case against the heresy of "social Darwinism." He claims that the social and political currents that have swept the Western world would have been impossible without the legitimization Darwin's theory provided.

I say the demonic inhumanity released during the twentieth century would be incomprehensible without this so-called "social Darwinism."

Arguments for and against orthodox, or scientific Darwinism are burdened with egoism, i.e. man's every conscious action is motivated by self-interest - the active ingredient in controversy. Egoism affects theologians and scientists alike. Egoism is the key to understanding the Ideology of Denial surrounding Darwin's Theory of Evolution.

Evolution is claimed by Godless Science to be truth (with the "t" capitalized) about the early development of life forms on earth (including Homo-sapiens). "Truth" about Homo-sapiens is - they are merely the next step up from Homo-erectus, who were the next step in an accidental, self-starting, natural selection and mutation process. Neither God nor Satan is part of the transformation.

Evolution was first advanced as a supposition (hypothesis) in 1859 by Charles Darwin. His book On the Origin of Species proposed that human development is patterned on the process he discovered by which early life forms seem to evolve, develop and mutate (or adapt) naturally in order to survive in the local environment.

Letters, other resource material and my comments are presented here which discuss Darwinian Evolution, and the supernatural side of the human development issue arising from Intelligent Design. They explain why secular news about man's origin is incomplete. For example, microbiologists have shown that changes in genetic constitution, "mutation" within species, occurs through sexual reproduction. Numerous advances in Science (particularly Genome Mapping) have occurred since 1986 that diminish the crisis Darwin inspired and strengthen the case for Intelligent Design.

Also discussed is the fact that students in Public schools are receiving out-dated information about the origin of mankind - information that lags behind discoveries in Molecular Biology of the past two decades.

A claim made in my treatise: The rivalry of Modern Man with Whole Man affects the well-being of the human race. The focal point in this struggle is "wisdom." Modern Man is educated (at public expense) to accept wisdom called Science, i.e. all Truth worth knowing about our welfare and well-being is knowable by the application of scientific laws. Whole Man is educated to accept wisdom called God in all things, i.e. all Truth worth knowing about our welfare, particularly our well-being, is knowable through the Holy Spirit.

An article in the Sept. 24, 2005 Goshen newspaper, by the Rev. Daniel Haifley, said it best -

Give students all the options in Science class

Euclid of Alexandria wrote 13 books called "The Elements" around 300 BC. These books laid the foundation for geometry. They were assumed as axioms, without proof. Deb Russell, in her basic geometry course, makes the statement, "Not everything is proved in geometry, thus we use some postulates which are basic assumptions or unproved general statements that we accept."

Math and science are like that. To determine an unknown you must begin with a known. To measure a distance you must begin with a fixed point. This is commonly known in all scientific fields, which is why I am surprised by a statement made by a scientist about belief in God.

Here's what happened as reported by the New York Times in the Aug. 23, 2005 edition. There was a scientific conference at City College of New York. A student in the audience rose to ask the panelists an unexpected question: "Can you be a good scientist and believe in God?" The reaction by Herbert A. Hauptman, a Nobel laureate, was quick and sharp. "No!" he declared. "This kind of belief is damaging to the well-being of the human race." He also stated that belief in the supernatural, especially belief in God, is incompatible with good science.

This is the kind of unscientific opinion that excludes the theory of Intelligent Design from our public school classrooms.

The debate is not raging over what is "true" science and what is not. No indeed! The debate is where you fix your starting point.

Evolutionary scientists begin their study with the belief that there is no God, therefore everything that exists is entirely accidental. They reason that because they cannot see God anywhere then He must not exist.

The Intelligent Design scientists begin their study with an Intelligent Designer. They reason that because our world is full of specific design, it is rational to conclude that there was a force much smarter than man who designed it.

Can you see how both of these theories must begin with a fixed point?

I believe that a school education should not be about indoctrination of one idea or another (my comment: Evolution or Creation). Education should be about exposing the students to the ideas and philosophies of the world (Evolution and Creation). Let the students see the differences. Let them draw their own conclusions from the facts in front of them.

What some of these pseudo-scientists are afraid of is that a thinking person will naturally come to the fixed point of Intelligent Design. And that, by the way, brings with it some responsibility (my comment: Add intense discomfort). >

Not only are students indoctrinated in public school Science classrooms, Modern Man's "judicial wisdom" mandates compliance with various laws that sets him against God's wisdom.

At this juncture in time pseudo-scientists, secular judges, secular news managers and others of the mini-minority are winning in the rivalry over the well-being of the human race. Whole Man was winning in the thirteenth century. My treatise suggests that God will call "Time Out" if pseudo-scientists and secularists win this war in the twenty-first century.

December 20, 1996

The South Bend Tribune
South Bend, IN

Intelligent Design and Evolution are opposing battle flags

Dear Editor:

Before we argue over which theory, Evolution or Creation, is best to teach our children, we must be certain that the definition of mankind held by an evolutionist is the same as that held by a creationist. They are not the same.

Natural Evolution is scientific knowledge about the development of early forms of plants and animals into more complex forms by hereditary transmission of DNA/RNA "building blocks" in successive generations. The short-coming of natural evolution is that the theory cannot explain how mankind came to be, unless of course we are willing to accept the secular definition of mankind - an accident of no consequence.

The argument is similar to dialogue between a Communist and a Christian over the meaning of humans. A Communist sees men and women as ancient pagans did. They are little more than matter that has organized itself. Isn't this the same definition an evolutionist uses for mankind? The meaning of "future" for Communists and evolutionists alike excludes eternity, which is a world apart from the Judeo-Christian meaning.

The materialistic concept of man, i.e. natural evolution theory, has no place for spiritual values. This means the evolutionist starting point does not and cannot account for the existence of that which distinguishes mankind from all other animals, the human soul.

It may be surprising to learn that 2400 years ago Plato wrote in a book titled The Republic: "The soul, like the eye and the ear, has a work or function to perform, and possesses a virtue by which, alone, it can be enabled to perform that work. This virtue of the soul is Justice." Ask the ACLU which ape Justice evolved from.

Harm can be avoided by accepting the proof for the existence in each person of a soul created by God, and saying so.

Robert Jefferson

If we are truly concerned about being successful (or failing) in life, or about cultural progress, it matters which of the two prevalent starting points of thought best measures success (or failure) i.e., which best affects total well-being.

Darwin's Theory of Evolution has been a subject of controversy for more than a hundred years. Arguments between scientists and theologians a hundred years ago centered on the discovery by Anthropologists that "mankind" inhabited this planet for nearly a million years; whereas, the appearance of the first man (Adam), projected from information taken literally from the Bible, occurred about five thousand years ago.

Publicity surrounding the 1925 Scopes "Monkey Trial" shifted the focus of dispute from When? to How? Inherit the Wind (a 1960 movie) left the viewers with the impression that naming God as Creator of the world and all of it's creatures, as the Bible does, is irreconcilable with fossil records suggesting macro-evolution as the process whereby species evolved by descent from preexisting species through adaptation during the aeon since life first appeared on earth.

Fact: The ACLU used the Monkey Trial to oppose a ruling (the Butler Act) by the state of Tennessee sanctioning the teaching of Creationism in Public Schools. The plaintiff, John Scopes was enlisted as their witness.

The argument about when and how human beings appeared on earth has been on-going for more than two thousand years. Judeo-

Christian ideas of God's creation prevailed into the 19th century. At that point "enlightened" atheists, trusting in their "new" Science, revealed that "God is dead" and Christianity is ridiculous. Darwinism offered mankind religion without revelation.

Twentieth century Science took the mystery and the miraculous out of nature and insisted that Public Schools teach atheistic naturalism. Modern discoveries of irreducibly complex biological adaptations readmits a designer God into the argument and (we hope) back into Public Schools.

My recommended resources (homework) for understanding the one hundred year-old Evolution/Creation controversy are -

Darwin's Black Box by Michael J Behe. Published in 1996 by New York Free Press.

Toward a New Philosophy of Biology: Observations of an Evolutionist by Ernst Mayr. Published in 1988 by the Harvard University Press.

Evolution: A theory in crisis by Michael Denton. Published in 1986 by Adler & Adler.

The Blind Watchmaker: Why the Evidence of Evolution Reveals a Universe Without Design by Richard Dawkins. Published in 1996 by W.W. Norton & Company.

The Evolution-Creation Struggle by Michael Ruse. Published in 2005 by Harvard University Press, Cambridge, Massachusetts.

The Language of God by Francis Collins. Published in 2006 by Free Press, New York.

Message to the Pontifical Academy of Sciences on Evolution by Pope John Paul II. Published on November 14, 1996 in Origins, Volume 26.

The Creation Hypothesis by J.P. Moreland. Published in 1994 by InterVarsity Press

Reading these books, one comes away with additional evidence that self-interest, that "peculiarity" which separates mankind from all other life forms, is alive and well. Self-interest corrupts scientific fact as well as theological fact. Fortunately, true knowledge is also alive and well.

Education is valued as a duty and a privilege for everyone who believes that true knowledge gives direction and meaning to life. Consequently, if we are to understand the relationship between natural Evolution of human and other life forms and their supernatural Creation, historicity and objectivity must be maintained.

Who but God could reveal whether or not Evolution's process of natural selection and mutation over time was incorporated in His Plan, together with His own guarantee that each fertilized egg beginning with the sexual union of the parents of mankind would receive a life-giving soul formed in His image?

ITEST is a better organization to turn to than most in order to learn from the controversy over human origin - whether the universe and mankind began as "blind chance" would have it begin; or, whether the universe and mankind were created on purpose in accordance with an intelligent plan.

"Intelligent design" is a reasonable explanation for the recent discovery that living cells follow an irreducibly complex path in the performance of their functions of manufacture and maintenance.

ITEST is short for Institute for Theological Encounter with Science and Technology, organized and incorporated in 1968 by Robert Brungs, S.J. Membership now stands at about 600, comprised of people from thirty nations engaged in all major professions; Medicine, Biology, Law, Physics, Theology, Philosophy and etceteras. The Institute is located at the Cardinal Rigali Center, 20 Archbishop May Drive, St. Louis, MO 63119. ITEST can be contacted by calling (314)-792-7220.

In my biased opinion ITEST is a learning resource which honors the facts. ITEST is a sounding board for leaders in the sense that its members include scientists who first established "those proven scientific facts." Dr. Lazarus W. Macior, Distinguished Professor of Biology at the University of Akron (Ohio) said, "What better way to seek the biological/historical/theological underpinnings of the theory or fact of Evolution and the doctrine of Creation than to have all aspects of the question be addressed by those with expertise in their respective fields and that none presume to knowledge not professionally acquired." Members and guests listen.

I attended an ITEST Workshop held October 17-19, 1997 in St. Louis, on "Evolution and Creation." Dr. Macior presented a paper titled Critical Scientific Concepts in the Creation/Evolution Controversy.

I learned that Evolution, as Charles Darwin theorized, really is "a grand sequence of events" nearly impossible to comprehend. Darwin said, "Our minds refuse to accept as fact that evolution is the result of blind chance."

I add: Evolution, as an accomplishment of Science, does explains how all forms of life change and adapt. It is left to Theology to explain why.

Creationism describes mankind as the work of the Will of One God who is the uncaused cause for the universe and its occupants. When Moses asked His name He said, "I AM WHO AM." ("I am He who created space and time.")

Creationism does not challenge natural evolution; or, the first law of thermodynamics, i.e. matter can neither be created nor destroyed. Evolution (as credible scientific knowledge) does explain the complex chemical process by which a given species at its "micro stage" of development receives its genetic constitution through sexual reproduction, thereby becoming a unique individual.

Thermodynamics and all other laws of Physics came out of a single act of God's will simultaneous with creation of space and time.

Science cannot spontaneously generate life from lifeless chemical compounds or change nature's force expressed in the formula for gravity, nor can Science isolate in a laboratory the major intermediate stage of spirituality vital to human development. The chemical process we call Evolution is not a credible explanation applied to Adam and Eve at their "macro stage" of infinitely complex cellular and spiritual development.

Note that Darwin did not have instruments capable of quantifying on the molecular level the many changes he observed. In order to fully grasp the limits of his theory he needed to "see" inside the process of Evolution and identify its many stages, all involving multiple reactions of amino acids.

It is reasonable to assume from scientific research into the birth and development of stars, the discovery of numerical constants for fundamental physical forces, from biochemistry, etc., that all around us is a totality of chemical, physical and biotic items in one busy factory of infinite complexity.

Numerical values for Nuclear Forces are precisely that required for celestial ovens to bake hydrogen, the raw material of the "Big Bang," into the ingredients for God's bread.

Examples: The exact value for asymmetry between matter and antimatter at the next instant after the "Big Bang" occurred has profound significance for the existence of the universe itself.

All living things need a "spark of life" to begin that is beyond our understanding.

Physicists have proven that the strength of the universal gravitational constant is the precise value necessary to assure that the stability of this expanding universe would continue (for fourteen billion years) to allow all of the dramatic events to occur for producing chemical elements that compose and sustain living organisms. (See The Anthropic Cosmological Principle by Barrow and Tipler, published by Oxford University Press.)

After cooling for ten billion years nuclear fusion in neighboring suns had manufactured the carbon, oxygen, nitrogen, potassium, sodium, iron, iodine, magnesium, copper, silicon, etc, essential for rocks and cellular organisms. Our sun and its orbiting celestial bodies were formed out of these and other related atoms.

My comments (outside the Workshop): 1) We are a product of intelligent design as undeniably as is any vacuum cleaner. Human beings are many times more complex; yet, as a designed system of fabricated parts each properly shaped and properly placed, we are products of a Super-intelligent Being as clearly as vacuum cleaners are manufactured using fabricated parts of man-made design. 2) Living beings are capable of reproducing themselves. One male, one female and God is required. God is the source of life; and, He gave to each person an eternal soul and command of his or her actions.

It is as absurd for atheists to declare (and attempt to persuade Public School students to believe) that living cells perform their various functions by natural selection of accidents, as for a mechanic to declare that he/she can throw the pieces of a brake assembly in the air and have them fall fully assembled in their proper place on the rear axle of a 1941 Ford.

Francis Collins in The Language of God provides metaphysical evidence to prove that human beings are unique in ways that defy accidental macro-evolution.   Humans embrace a Moral Law that provides certain knowledge of right and wrong. Throughout history humans searched for God. The fact that this search was successful highlights another faculty not derivable from the genetic code. We possess wills that are free to deny God.

Question: Do human cells have an ignition button? Theologians are better equipped to answer this question than scientists. Their answer is "Yes." It is logical that the initial embryonic cell possessed God's breath of life otherwise cellular development could not continue. Theologians call this vital step in cellular development ensoulment. Where twins are conceived ensoulment probably occurs within a few days after conception.

(End of comments outside the Workshop.)

ITEST invited Professor Michael Behe, Department of Biology at Lehigh University, to discuss his paper titled Darwinism and Design. He described complex biomolecular cells (heart cells, brain cells, liver cells etc.) and explained that the removal of any one of their essential chemicals, i.e. amino acids, prevents them from performing their individual function.

Each cell is preordained by design to join like cells and grow a particular organ.   The order of events involved in growth is unmistakable. Other cells are organized to do the work of maintaining a particular organ. Again, specific chemical elements are properly shaped and correctly placed in particular molecules needed to perform their specific tasks.

Professor Behe presented analytical data showing that cells of different types vary widely in their molecular make-up and in the ordered assembly of their components. This wonderful variation is dictated by the work each cell does.

He diagrammed the arrangement of organic molecules to make a cilium work. A cilium is a biological system designed to perform an essential bodily function. Cilia are hair-like structures attached to surfaces of specific cells. Their job is to move fluid over the cell's surface, or to "row" single cells through a fluid. Cells lining the respiratory tract for example, have about 200 cilia each. These cilia beat in unison in order to sweep mucus toward the throat for elimination.

He said: "A cilium consists of a bundle of hair-like structures called an axoneme. An axoneme contains a ring of 9 double "microtubules" surrounding two central single microtubules. Each outer doublet consists of a ring of 13 filaments fused to an assembly of 10 filaments. The filaments of the microtubules are composed of two proteins called alpha and beta tubulin. The microtubules forming an axoneme are held together by three types of connectors: Subfibers A are joined to the central microtubules by radial spokes; adjacent outer doublets are joined by linkers to a highly elastic protein called nexin; and central microtubules are joined by a connecting bridge. Finally, every subfiber A bears two arms, an inner arm and an outer arm, both containing a protein called dynein."

He continued: "The ciliary motion results from chemically-powered "walking" of the dynein arms on one microtubule up a second microtubule. The two microtubules slide past each other. The crosslinks of the protein molecules are short, allowing microtubules to slide only a short distance relative to a neighboring microtubule. Consequently, the entire axoneme is held together and is able to function as a self-moving, self-motivated broom would function."

Cilium contain their own motor. Their hair-like filaments resemble flexible bristles designed to move in a manner which produces the unique motion we recognize as "sweeping."

Discovering how the body's respiratory tract eliminates mucus really is like working a puzzle. The molecular pieces need to be put together, but first the features of each piece must be studied (for example puzzle pieces with one straight side make-up the puzzles perimeter - two adjacent straight sides are "corner pieces," etceteras. Trial and error helps puzzle workers and Molecular Biologists fit the pieces together.

My comment: Imagine a battery-powered automatic Sweeper

able to perform in a cilium-like manner. How many parts would this appliance and battery contain? If the parts were in a disordered pile within reach of half a dozen monkeys, how many aeons would the monkeys require to assemble them in the correct order? The monkeys had only their lifetimes to complete the job, because "blind chance" was still fumbling with the critical parts of their reproductive systems.

More to my point, who was smart enough to make the pile of molecular parts of an axoneme and who did in fact assemble them in the correct order? Atheists choose to believe the unbelievable. All of this was accidental.

––––––––––––

Biology courses in most modern universities teach that humans start life as a single-cell embryo, the product of the union of a complete human genome and the programming cytoplasm of a human egg. Fertilization occurs at the point in time where union is complete. Not mentioned is the stroke of luck. Nuclear Forces were precisely the values consistent with the Anthropic coincidences for nuclear fusion and molecular kinetics to manufacture the component parts of each living cell - the ingredients for God's bread.

It is self-evident that the initial living cell of each human being must possess "life" and be "ordered" and equipped to grow other cells to produce and sustain in turn each vital organ of a fetus. Then, when it's gestation period is completed, to "deliver on order" a unique child unlike any other child. This fantastic blueprint didn't "just happen."

Nowhere are we told what mechanism Modern Science proposes to explain how that first cell with the capability to "clot" blood originated. Or, as Charles Darwin wondered, how the eye, "an organ of extreme perfection and complication," comes to life?

Living things are too incredible, too beautifully "designed" and too complex to have come into existence by chance. Modern scientific discoveries in physics, from ecological studies of symbiosis and from evidence in a dozen other fields prove "the book of nature and the book of Scripture were written by the same author" (quotation from St. Augustine).

I cannot repeat Mortimer Adler's statement too often: "The choice whether or not to believe in God is in the state of one's will, not in the state of one's mind." Atheism sacrifices dignity to hold onto its absurd choice to deny an almighty Creator.

Someone asked Dr. Behe: "How has the scientific community dealt with the many examples of "irreducible complexity" discovered through biochemical analysis?" And, "How does modern Science reconcile mutation (of species) in response to their environment by simply calling it Natural Selection?"

There were three parts to his answer -

- Many examples representing biological systems, the origin of which cannot be explained by Darwinian evolution, are found in the latest generation of college Biochemistry textbooks. No listing is given for "Evolution" or "Natural Selection" in their indices.

- The Journal of Molecular Evolution was founded to record and discuss the results of biochemical investigations dealing with microevolution, i.e. evolution on the molecular scale. It is edited by respected molecular biologists. Speculation about the origin of "Evolved Molecules" is conspicuous by its absence.

- Students learn from Biology textbooks that only a living cell has the capacity to produce another living cell. They are not told how.

My comment: Students are familiar with the reaction of a pregnant woman's body when her fetus ceases to develop. She suffers a miscarriage.

Behe did not offer a scientific explanation for how such complexity arises. He merely offered his observation of what is.

Scientific tests aimed at spontaneous generation of living organisms directly from non-living matter are aptly called "giggle tests."

The acronym ITEST reveals that the other half of the learning experience at the Evolution and Creation Workshop centered on theology.

Monsignor Paul Langsfeld, Professor of Theology at Mount St. Mary's Seminary, Emmitsburg, MD. presented a paper titled The Theology of Creation and Evolution. Msgr. Langsfeld emphasized that human beings are set apart from all other life forms in ways that science may observe and rationalize on the experimental level, and philosophers may study. Such gifts as self-reflection, freedom, moral conscience, metaphysical knowledge (we are able to "put the universe in our heads") and aesthetic and religious experiences are found only in human beings. This uniqueness of human beings is attributable to the spiritual soul each possesses, and to free will.

Msgr. Langsfeld said, "John Paul II in his Message to the Pontifical Academy of Sciences on Evolution recognizes that modern science must be faithful to it's own methods and criteria of truth; and, he calls for a 'trustful dialogue between the church and science.'" But, Langsfeld said, "denial of evolution as a fact amounts to denying the interconnectedness of all life, past and present in the face of irrefutable scientific evidence showing that chromosomes and genes are the codes that regulate the development of all life, from bacteria through human life and including the oldest known fossils." This "material sameness" of DNA and RNA building blocks in all living beings is the foundation for Science's belief that Evolution is a proven theory not an unproven hypothesis.

My comment (outside the Workshop): During the Enlightenment period the title "the only true source of knowledge" was bestowed on Science. This period, which is at its peak today, is marked by an emphasis on Science's ideology of Naturalism, i.e. scientific laws are adequate to account for everything. We see this peculiarity in the behavior of a scientific community which demands that Science be permitted to dictate the terms for any debate with theology by establishing the criteria of Truth (identified earlier as scientific truth with a capital T).

In his Workshop presentation titled Darwin's Dangerous Idea ... And St. Paul's, the Rev. Dr. Steven Kuhl restated text from St. Paul, who is by far the most articulate communicator on this issue:

"The defining feature of the natural world as we know it, the human and non-human parts working together, is not the awe inspiring design and complexity (Rom 1:20; Rom 8:18-23: etc.), though that is certainly an important aspect of the creation, but the 'Wrath of God,' i.e. Divine Justice, that rests upon it (Rom 1:18;

3:23; etc.), giving the world a dubious, ambiguous, meaningless character. Moreover, and this is the most important for Paul, the (theo)logical counterpoint to this wrath is the 'mercy of God.' This mercy which is the basis for a truly meaningful (justified) existence in the world does not exist naturally, but was established historically in the life, death and resurrection of Jesus Christ (Rom 3:25; 5:6-11; etc.), is presently being made available to all humanity through the Word (Rom 10:8-17) and is appropriated by humanity personally through faith." (Rom 1:17b; 3:25; 4:5; etc.).

"Modern Theism places its emphasis on the Mercy of God." God exists to guarantee consolation and meaning in our lives regardless of circumstances. For St. Paul, before God can be seen as the focus of our consolation, that very same God must first be satisfied (obeyed) in order to remove the ultimate threat to our existence. If this idea sounds strange, it only underscores just how systematically misunderstood, distorted or avoided Paul's dangerous idea about God has been in today's Christian theology and in America's secular culture." >

(End of Evolution & Creation Workshop.)

The traditional reading of St. Paul's text predates the period of Enlightenment, even the Protestant Reformation, and in a way accounts for the rise and growing popularity of both. Man's reason and his conscience recognize the Hand of God in Creation (i.e. God's intelligible Plan); and, both faculties recognize that God must be obeyed lest man invites endless punishment. The traditional reading is discarded by enlightened atheists and softened by Christians because the kind of selfless love God demands causes intense discomfort. Atheists and others choose to anesthetize their consciences to quiet fears of God's wrath.

St. Paul emphasized that God's gift of Love enacted through giving of self on the cross requires that we show our love by giving of self to God and our neighbors. St. Paul told the Galatians to do all things not in order to be saved, but precisely because you have been saved.

Twenty-first century Science has far advanced our understanding of "Creation" over eighteenth century Science, a time when scientists openly praised God for the wonders they were able to discover - knowledge they gained in humble recognition of God's will that man should discover His Works. Example: God invites our wonderment at His blueprint for microevolution –

The Works of God in Nature

"Next, I will remind you of the works of the Lord, and tell you what I have seen.

By the words of the Lord his works come into being and all creation obeys his will.

As the sun in shining looks on all things, so the work of the Lord is full of his glory.

The Lord has not granted to the holy ones to tell of all his marvels which the almighty Lord has solidly constructed for the universe to stand firm in his glory.

He has fathomed the deep and the heart, and seen into their devious ways; for the Most High knows all the knowledge there is, and has observed the signs of the times.

He declares what is past and what will be, and uncovers the traces of hidden things.

Not a thought escapes him, nor a single word is hidden from him.

He has imposed an order on the magnificent works of his wisdom, he is from everlasting to everlasting, nothing can add to him, nothing taken away, he needs no one's advice. How desirable are his works, how dazzling to the eye!

They all live and last forever, whatever the circumstances all obey him.

All things go in pairs, by opposites, and he has made nothing defective; and one consolidates the excellence of the other, who could ever be sated with gazing at his glory. (Sirach 42:15-26)

The Book of Sirach was written by Ben Sira about 180 BC. It is no surprise that faith preceded (even decreed) the success of eighteenth century scientists and others of our ancestors. Indeed, "who could ever be sated with gazing at all of the marvels in the universe He has solidly constructed to stand firm in His glory."

Today, knowledge of nature/Creation (the Genome Project is an excellent example) is persuading reasonable scientists to admit that their success is dependent upon intelligibility of God's ways. St. Augustine said it best: "I believe so that I may understand and I understand so that I may believe."

Consider the teaching of the Catholic Church that "God's love is uniquely fitted to each person." How then is faith in this singularity possible unless no two are alike. The Human Genome Project provides scientific proof that no two persons were, are, or ever will be alike. "Who could ever be sated with gazing at His glory?" Man succeeded in sequencing his own genome. (I add: Such is the love and gifts God bequeaths to mankind.)

The Human Genome study Francis Collins managed was completed in 2003.

This scientific study of but a single facet of micro-evolution provides mankind with what I choose to call God's unique physical specifications for cellular development in each and every Human being (along with all other living organisms). God's design contains more than three billion variables. As far as Collins and his team were able to determine an infinite number of unique individuals are encompassed in the Genome Code.

The wonderful part of God's gift of Faith is that in time Science will provide the means to better understand His ways. Until that time those "of little faith" should recall the words of Jesus to St. Thomas: "Blessed are those who believe without seeing."

The latest textbook for assembling living things begins with DNA/RNA as the genetic code for living cells, with the initial cell having methodology and purpose, i.e. to develop into a wonderful child of God.

The code contains twenty specific amino acids complete with messenger nucleic acid, transfer nucleic acid and ribose plus nucleic acid to build proteins. These molecular parts form a network of four different groupings to form genes and chromosomes, i.e. "Genomes." A Genome packages the building blocks for tissue and organs that, through a process called fertilization, develops into a unique child loved individually by God.

Time will tell whether future editions of the DNA textbook for assembling living things, particularly a sinful human with a soul that possesses both God-like and Satan-like behavior, will make a believer of modern Science.

———————

A dream of Robert Brungs, the father of ITEST, was to broaden our thinking about God, using His Creation as a tool. He thought of ways an all-loving God would communicate love to the "children" He created and he became convinced that (in addition to the "Revealed Word") God does communicate His love to us through His Creation.

God gave us the ability to fathom "the order He has imposed on the magnificent works of His wisdom" (Sirach). Would not God then expect us to use Biology to probe goodness in His plan for constructing all living things, or Astronomy to probe wisdom in the way He constructed the universe?

Consider the biological study of another of the many facets of micro-manipulation and cooperativity designed by God to sustain human and animal life on earth -

God's creatures need oxygen and nourishment to survive. So, He specified that one-fifth of earth's atmosphere will be oxygen. Respiration in humans (on the molecular level) uses an amazing protein called hemoglobin in red blood cells to transport oxygen, in air we inhale, from the lungs to brain tissue, heart tissue and etceteras. In addition, molecules of carbon dioxide (the waste material from metabolism) are transported to the lungs by hemoglobin where they are released in the air we exhale.

Nourishment comes from God's plants and trees by a process biology students know as photosynthesis. Chlorophyll in leaves, enzymes and energy from our sun are the means God's nature employs to convert carbon dioxide in the air we exhaled and water in plants and trees into sugar and other carbohydrates.

Yesterday I listened to a speaker add to this cooperative relationship. He discussed the chemical reactions involved in the production of maple syrup by The Sugar Process: Six molecules of water (from a maple tree) and six molecules of carbon dioxide (from the breath we exhaled) combine to produce one molecule of maple syrup (gathered from the tree) and six molecules of oxygen given back to the air we may inhale.

God made nature self-supporting and intelligible. Science conveys that intelligibility using symmetry principles (symbiosis at one end of the spectrum of interests and $2 + 2 = 4$ at the other).

For those of us who find God present in everyday life, Science offers a way to get to know Him better.

Robert Brungs wanted to start early. He and his co-workers developed "Education Modules" to teach children in K - 12 how they can learn about God's plan by studying (through the eyes of Science) the way all things in nature cooperate, thereby making Science a tool to shape a better world as God intended. (Information about Educational Modules can be downloaded from the ITEST website www.creationlens.org)

A contribution of theology to these modules deals with the teacher's presentation of "pitfalls." The key is God's Command to respect the dignity of atheists who would forbid mixing God with Science and using the mixture to teach children about God. They are our neighbors.

Two years before his death on May 8, 2006 Bob Brungs had gathered a small group of teachers, scientists and theologians (and a sponsor) in order to bring his dream to fruition.

I attended an ITEST Workshop titled Education for the Faith/ Science Ministry held October 19-21, 2006 in Belleville, IL. The purpose of the Workshop was to review two years of group effort developing "Education Modules," to critique the work and to get on with making his dream real.

Thomas P. Sheahen presented a paper titled The complementary roles of science and religion. Dr. Sheahen earned his PhD in Physics from MIT in 1966. He is Vice Director of ITEST.

It should be obvious, he said, teaching Science courses that fit together well with religion is no longer simple (or easy). In times past even small children knew that God is smarter than anyone's wildest imagination. Sheahen said: "Without being asked to spell epistemology, we want students to be able to recognize when they actually know that something is true." He pointed to Godel's Theorem (see Chap. 7) showing mathematically that "faith statements" are often known to be true with certainty. They need no proof; moreover (as Godel discovered), no proof is possible.

Dr. Sheahen pointed to symmetry principles in the way students intuitively understand God through things they see in nature.

Where to begin but in the beginning. "In the beginning God created the heavens and the earth." As early as the fifth century AD St. Augustine wrote: "The world was made, not in time, but simultaneous with time. Time is a measure of change and motion; time needs an agent (the created world) through which to act." (See St. Augustine's book titled The City of God.)

Fifteen hundred years later Albert Einstein used mathematics to prove that we live in a spatio-temporal universe tuned to make life probable. One hundred years later most scientists realized that the laws by which our spatio-temporal universe operate are intelligible because they are orderly. The relationship of one law to another and (collectively) the conditions the laws of nature permit are precisely the relationship and conditions that cause us to consider human beings as the most significant entity of the universe (anthropocentricity). Order is so precise that had one law or another varied from what it is by an infinitesimal amount we would not exist.

Everything starts with discovering God. As Einstein said, "I shall never believe that God plays dice with the World." This quote is found in Philipp Frank's book Einstein, His Life and Times.

A young student is not expected to understand space-time coordinates, anthropocentricity or Godel's Theorem, but he or she knows intuitively that for God to create time He must be timeless; so, we are able to believe without proof that we receive everlasting life (timelessness) from God, who has everlasting life to give.

As a child is taught to use reason to recognize truth, he/she grasps the simple truth that God does not keep company with nonsense; so, they appreciate why all of nature they see around them makes sense.

They learn later the blueprint for making a flower from a small seed and the blueprint for making a child from a small seed. They learn some of the details for making a billion planets (including the "blue Marble").

Dr. Sheahen emphasized:

"A key point to remember when interpreting Science or Scripture is that man's ability to absorb what God wants to reveal is limited. Conflicts, whether over faith in the interpretation of Genesis, or faith in Einstein's concept of Gravity or in Darwin's concept of natural evolution, usually need deeper interpretation."

Einstein discovered that the force of Gravity is constant. Its force is the same, he said, whether exerted on a moon or on a cotton ball. Physicists half century later are seeking ways to verify his statement.

Theologians four millennia later are arguing over the six-day story of Creation in Genesis. Fourth century teachers of Genesis doubted a six-day span for Creation based on scientific knowledge available to them.

Sixteen centuries later Fundamentalists swear that Creation of the world occurred in six of our days in spite of scientific evidence that fusing and cooling the elements used to make the world took fourteen billions years.

Teachers must be made aware of limitations of faith both in religious knowledge and scientific knowledge. Where there is doubt (as in the examples above) a deeper interpretation, together with reason, is needed to advance knowledge and faith.

Example: Biology teachers should emphasize that modernized Darwinian Evolution is a theory that describes "nomogenesis," i.e. the natural development of species (over eons of time) determined by a DNA/RNA code. Nomogenesis does not explain the origin of the code nor the process by which mankind acquired (in Plato's words) "the virtue of the soul called Justice."

Micro-evolution understood as a self-organizing molecular system may one day lead us to accept the faith statement, "Eve was made from a rib taken from Adam" as a supernatural event.

Micro-evolution may one day reveal a genetic pattern specific to females associated with their gender's obvious capacity for identifying the needs of children and others, and the humility to surrender themselves to those needs. Scientists will, as they always do, wonder why. Those who know that God is love will know the answer.

Dr. Sheahen reviewed the advancement of scientific and religious knowledge and faith from where they stood four hundred years ago when nearly everyone thought the earth marked the center of their world. His point is; mankind's ability to absorb what God wants to reveal is obstructed by the tremendous amount of work involved and by our own weaknesses. Even when we get it right we must continually overcome those who prefer piles of garbage.

This is particularly relevant when Science sets itself in opposition to all that is unseen. Beginning with the Industrial Revolution, and with Darwin's On the Origin of Species as its bible, Science turned the wrong way. To hold onto disbelief it dismissed a basic tool (logical deduction).

"God created all things seen and unseen" assures us that faith in Science and faith in Religion are essential for human knowledge to advance, not as Religion alone intends or as Science alone intends, but as God intends.

Dr. Sheahen discussed The Encyclical Faith and Reason issued in 1998 by Pope John Paul II that cautions against too much reliance on faith alone, or on reason alone -

"Truth is conformity between the intellect and objective reality." Statements that express the most basic Truth about the controlling principle in the universe cannot be proven by reason alone or by faith alone. Nevertheless, that basic Truth has withstood the test of time.

The major themes included in ITEST's Education Modules are: God made a world that makes sense. He did it in a way so clever that human efforts over thousands of years to understand God's Plan have not fully succeeded. God reveals knowledge to us on His terms, not ours. God gave mankind the ability to explain how things (including sexuality) make sense. Science is an important way of gaining knowledge, as is Religion. There is no limit to our potential for knowing God, because God has no limit. And, it is right and good to push ahead along all of the frontiers.

The goal is to develop in students, from kindergarten through high school, an appreciation of both Religion and Science, and how they fit together in a unity of knowledge.

My puzzle analogy (Chap. 7) helps me understand better why togetherness is so important. Darwin set the stage with "that grand sequence of events which our minds refuse to identify as the result of Blind Chance." Pieces of the puzzle are fitted by an actor on one side (Science) holding proofs without certainty; and fitted by an actor on the other side (Religion) holding certainty without proofs.

With actors working to complete the puzzle from opposite sides it is inevitable that helping hands pass between.

————————

The letter below came in the mail while proof reading an earlier version of Chapter 10. It fits here -

Today's Catholic, Ft. Wayne, IN
Published on June 13, 1999

Putting life into perspective

Dear Editor:

With all the ills of society today and the lack of morals and values, perhaps the following thoughts could help bring us back to a reality we've forgotten.

The world would be an infinitely better place if people could understand and accept this basic concept. Suppose you were standing on a sandy beach stretching for miles, and on the tip of your finger was one tiny speck of beach sand, almost microscopic, sparkling in the sun. That speck represents our time on this earth compared to eternal time represented by all the grains of sand on the beach and all the beaches of the earth. That's how long our life is, these few years, like the blink of an eye compared to the infinite stretches of eternity.

Why have we, and the billions who have come before us and the billions who will come after us, been given this moment of life by God? So that we can do our best to love God and love others during this moment and to spend eternity, which is our real life, with Him. And that's the only reason we've been put on our tiny planet in the vastness of space.

For the sake of each of us, for the sake of others and for the sake of the world, we must understand our reason for being here and what we're supposed to be doing here. Choosing to give up our future with God by not living as we're meant to, is to believe that one grain of sand is more important than all the vast and uncountable sands of eternity. How could anyone make that choice?

Joan C. Kelly

We exist, not by some impossible accident, but by uncountable acts of love. Consider the benefit to our children and grandchildren if we all came to understand what Joan is telling us. Life is not hopeless unless we choose to make it so.

CHAPTER 11

THE SECULAR MEDIA

Seventy five years ago Will Rogers said, "All I know is just what I read in the newspaper." I think of his words often. They explain why lately, life in the United States has not made sense. This is the reason for my letters to editors complaining about orchestration of news to malign morality and its standard bearer, with particular emphasis on making abortion an accepted custom called, "a woman's right."

It is a long story. Distortion of the facts about "free sex" and abortion began in earnest in 1973 with the Supreme Court ruling in Roe vs. Wade. Today there are tens of millions of teen-age girls from two successive generations, who are very confused about the value of their personal dignity and about the real meaning of sex in love-making. Pro choice is now an accepted custom. Pro choice, the synonym for pro abortion, is a poor choice and a dangerous custom.

My January 29, 2003 letter in the Preface, Joan's letter from the previous page and my two letters below published in the Goshen News give viewpoints on dangerous customs, harbingers of today's culture of death -

July 1, 2003

Dear Editor:

The Family Circus (June 30) had Billy asking his grandma, "Are we living in the present tense?" Grandma answered, "These days, Billy, many of us are living in the present VERY tense." (True?)

Had Billy been ten years older he might have asked, "Why?" Grandma, being perhaps seventy years older than Billy, could have told him.

Age is important because it gives perspective.

Tenseness is due to an alarming increase in confusion over norms of behavior. The perspective covering the Modern Age, from the end of World War II, allows one to "see" that world-wide confusion over good and bad behavior is increasing at an alarming rate (probably equal to the rate of increase in technology). Bad ideas about good behavior, coupled with today's weapons for war and terrorism ought to make everyone tense.

World wide confusion over good and bad behavior in business, in news-making, and in government ought be more alarming than war and terrorism, because this kind of confusion is more seductive. It can destroy a nation more surely than nuclear weapons, though not as fast.

People Grandma's age are able to see this if they choose to see. Because pain comes with bad ideas, our grandchildren will suffer greatly from current confusion.

Those who choose to make their own right and wrong must justify their choices to our grandchildren. They will do so by first denying that a fully logical universe must call for an all-powerful Creator. And they must deny that the Creator, in His infinite Justice, must demand obedience from all of creation. This is obvious in the fact that the universe He created was not given a choice but to obey the laws He set over it. Choice is meaningful for mankind who alone was created with a free will.

By denying the embodiment of infinite Justice in the Creator the way is clear for man to announce that the norm for personal behavior is not as old as mankind. It was invented "yesterday" by man. >

Billy again, in a letter dated August 12, 2004 in the Goshen News -
Dear Editor:

The Family Circus in Sunday's Goshen News (Aug. 8) had Billy and his sister standing alone on the beach looking at the ocean. His sister, with arms spread wide, says, "Nobody on the beach this morning," to which Billy, in a reflective mood, says, "Yeah, this is what it must have looked like when Columbus discovered it."

They didn't see the sand littered with cans, a hamburger box, an old shoe, bottles, a Pizza box, and a garbage can stuffed with beach umbrella, more cans and boxes, etceteras.

I wonder whether other readers saw the Cartoonist's Hidden message - we are becoming so accustomed to living in garbage that we no longer "see it" for what it is. Children are too young to see.

One of Webster's definitions for garbage is useless or inaccurate information. Too many Americans are naïve about the dangers of this kind of garbage. We know with certainty that our futures will depend on how well each one lives up to the moral potential God imprinted on his or her heart. But, we are distracted.

We live in a nation that proclaims freedom for everyone. But, the one good choice for a successful future (Joan's choice) is covered with a thousand bad choices. We are conditioned on every side to respect freedom, meaning freedom to make bad choices not freedom to make responsible choices.

We live in a nation where the list of ten instructions for living up to our God-given moral potential was removed from public view. Laws were passed by the high court to revise the fifth the third and the seventh.

Forty years ago God was all but removed from the political process. Today we are about to ship-out to Pleasure Island with Pinocchio where (if you forgot) children become donkeys. >

Will Rogers was telling us that citizens in a free nation rely heavily on their newspaper to make up their minds about fact and fiction. Recall that President Lincoln believed citizens in a free nation must rely heavily on their conscience to make up their minds. In Lincoln's day newspapers supplied ninety percent of the "brain trust" citizenship required. Judging the truth or falsity of ideas (individual, social and political) in the 1800's was generally accepted as a moral duty assigned by God. Today judging moral ideas of others is not politically correct.

Moral duty in the 1800's required U.S. citizens to judge the behavior of others (at times curbing their liberty for the good of society). Today secular news-makers and other educators tell us to act with compassion by showing (permissive) civility toward perverse forms of moral behavior.

I believe the explanation for the change lies in the fact that a majority of news-makers choose to remove God from their worldview. If Will Rogers is correct one would expect to see God's reality becoming man's plaything.

Satan's Folly

Legalized abortion is evidence of Satan's folly. Abortion has become the "litmus test" favored by the secular media (and Democrats in Congress) to screen appointees for service on the Supreme Court.

Recall the statement from Chapter 1: "There is no word in the languages of Western nations to encompass their cultural garbage as they enter the twenty-first century." Until recently, perverse forms of moral behavior were called sinful or evil. These are merely choices now.

Also recall the statement that followed: "History is not properly understood unless we humbly accept the truth - history is all about sin and grace." One in Being are the most important words to describe the graceful part of history. Satan's folly properly describes the sinful part. Together, these words cover the spectrum from success to failure toward accomplishing the task God has given mankind.

As corrosion "eats away" the usefulness of unprotected iron bridges, "permissive civility" eats away the usefulness of unprotected words and ideas. As with the bridge, the rate of corrosion is important. The rate at which the English language is undermined is easily determined by comparing ideas defined in two dictionaries - a recent edition vs a forty-year old edition.

Look up definitions of Mother and Motherhood in a Dictionary printed before 1960 and one printed after 1990. You will find that properties such as nurturing, dignity and authority traditionally belonging to mothers have been expunged from modern dictionaries.

You will find that value, relations and justice were properties formerly associated with Judgment. These are expunged from modern definitions of Judgment.

Modern definitions of Garbage include inaccurate and worthless ideas; whereas, the traditional definition was trash, offal or waste from a kitchen or a store.

Everyone suffers in time and in eternity when significant numbers of men and women are persuaded to refuse the truth about Satan and his power to turn them away from God. They are devastated, and their nations crumble from within. The difficulty in accepting this chaos is as great as the difficulty in accepting Saint Paul's teaching on Christian Freedom (a great paradox of Reality). We act "not like the God who creates everything out of nothing; instead, the 'man-god' creates nothing out of everything." (This quote appeared in an excellent article titled, "How Much Freedom Can Our Culture Stand?" published in the February 2000 issue of New Oxford Review, pages 40-42. The author is Tom Martin, Professor of Philosophy at the University of Nebraska at Kearney.)

Chaos is predictable.

The twentieth century showed many faces of tyranny. The news-making profession became a tool for molding minds to conform with its Godless religion of Secularism.

My letters reprinted below are dated from 1973 into the twenty-first century. They deal with both sides of a problem which young adults might believe is of recent origin, namely, trustworthiness of words and ideas in the Secular Media -

February 18, 1973

Robert P. Clark, Editor
Courier Journal & Louisville Times
Louisville, KY

Dear Editor:

Your "Letters From the Editors" article in last Sunday's paper raised a few points which deserve comment.

I believe there is real cause for concern that newsmen's writing and handling of news can become tainted by their personal involvement. Newsmen are neither more nor less frail than other workers - they are naturally prejudiced. Involvement simply makes them more prejudiced.

Your conflict-of-interest policy, while it is certainly commendable, can effectively control those unwanted activities which occur at the conscious level, i.e. those which are premeditated. The current situation is far more complex.

Partiality is inherent in all of us. Occasionally I have reviewed my work. I have never found it to be free of partial judgments. Naturally it has occurred to me to question whether newsmen are less prejudiced than I am. I'm willing to concede that we are equally frail. Furthermore, I know for a fact that as workload or output doubles such frailties multiply.

If you believe, as I do, that America is in a state of moral decay, and you are seeking reasons, as I am, I offer the following thought for consideration: Print media reports, and in a sense controls, the reader's ideas about issues and about people. H.L. Mencken is reported to have said, "All successful newspapers are ceaselessly querulous and bellicose. They never defend anyone or anything if they can help it; if the job is forced upon them, they tackle it by denouncing someone or something else." Airing human weaknesses is an old practice and, because it gives readers a deep-rooted pleasure, it is part of the strategy for selling newspapers.

Newspapers are filled with details about poor judgments made in government, and in industry and labor organizations, and about outright dishonesty and stupidity. When a reader concludes often enough that stupidity caused this crises or that problem, his confidence must decrease; first with respect to government practices, then with business practices, and finally in his neighbor. If he doesn't know his neighbor, as few do in America, then we have the makings of a real problem.

Arguments that favor censorship to solve the problem are not looked on with favor. We are expected to believe that censorship and damnation go hand in hand. However, I don't believe that the one must follow the other.

I will chance disfavor and continue this line of thought: Your own paper can be rightfully accused of censoring - the proper phrase is censorship by selection. Subjects which are of no interest to your editors get little or no space in your newspaper. Subjects that you oppose are not carefully researched, and when they do appear in print the facts are often distorted. These are daily occurrences. Newspapers are labeled conservative or liberal for these reasons.

So, can it matter greatly whether news is censored by you, or by a central agency? A central agency might be more consistent and efficient.

If America is in a state of decay, historians will eventually piece together the causes. And, if the thoughts presented above are even partially valid, historians will then report an instance wherein damnation and freedom (of the press) walked hand in hand.

Editor Clark's answer -

Mr. Robert T. Jefferson
Columbus, IN

Dear Mr. Jefferson:

Thank you very much for your response to my Letters From the Editors.

Your comments about frailty of judgment, and the inability to avoid some prejudice, are very pertinent. All we can do is to try and avoid prejudgments and unwarranted prejudice.

I must disagree with you, of course, about censorship. It is quite true that we "censor by selection" in deciding what to use in our newspapers. I hope that our selection is based on "good" professional judgment as to what is important and interesting to our readers, but I realize that one man's view of what is news is sometimes not another's.

I would disagree that censorship by a newspaper is the equivalent of censorship by a central agency. This is because any central censorship would not allow opposing views in the various news media - whereas there are now many competing newspapers, columnists, commentators, radio and TV networks and stations, and the like. So the opportunity for various kinds of news and opinions is still manifold.

In any event I enjoyed your comments.

Sincerely yours,
Robert P. Clark

Mr. Clark was correct. There were many competing newspapers in 1973. However, in the interim between then and now the so-called mainstream media no longer competes in the traditional sense of the word. The dominant columnist, commentators, radio and TV networks and stations, as Cal Thomas wrote, "believe that God is meaningless in their intellectual, i.e. enlightened view of hard news."

It is evident from forty years of research of nearly a thousand presentations appearing on the "hard news" pages of newspapers and in the words of TV commentators I listened to that readers and listeners were indoctrinated in the false belief that God is irrelevant.

Throughout the last forty years publishers and TV networks have consolidated their hold on what Martin Esslin and President Lincoln referred to as the nations Brain Trust. I found little media interest in efforts to legally oppose the brutal killing of unborn babies; or, to report the facts relating adultery to family break-up; or, to report Catholic teaching objectively, without derision; or, to analyze Republican policy, without derision; or, in reporting the fact that those men who engage in promiscuous sodomy cause AIDS and widespread misery.

I charge national print media managers and network television of consciously controlling and moving the culture away from Christian Humanism by exaggerating the way viewers and readers perceive themselves, their peers, their teachers and their God. This is a serious charge. It will be covered in greater detail, because I believe "news-making" in print and on television is a major contributor to national disunity and apathy.

This charge is easy to prove. Look at the past forty years of "news-making" in newspapers and mass circulation magazines. Review the articles in secular newspapers and recall network television reports. Read and watch how the five "news" categories named above are reported. You will find innuendo and indoctrination, not education. You will find an agenda wherein legislation proposed by Democrats receives "good marks" and similar legislation proposed by Republicans receives "bad marks." Lies? Certainly. Garbage?

If "All I know is lies and innuendo about our legislators that I read in the newspapers"; and, if "I" represents the majority of eligible voters; and, if "Congress legislates in deference to popular demand" (poll results); then, news-makers had better get it right!

The Associated Press, the New York Times wire service, the Cleveland Plain Dealer, etc. show a solidarity of effort to subvert public morality by surgically removing sin. I call this denial of reality conscientious ignorance.

The entertainment industry is worse. It shows us the stupid things everybody's doing. In the process it demeans symbols venerated by religious people. A favorite "prop" is a crucifix worn by the bad guy.

I call this unmistakable garbage.

Television is a major contributor to America's pagan culture of death. The description "vast wasteland" was used by Newton Minnow, chairman of the Federal Communications Commission, in his May 9, 1961 speech to the National Association of TV Broadcasters (#69 on the list of best speeches). He said, "When television is bad, nothing is worse."

An article titled TV, America's Worst Disaster, by Kenneth R. Clark was published August 20, 1981 in The Republic, my local newspaper (Columbus, IN). The following are selected quotes -

"The American system of television is the biggest disaster that has happened to this country. In centuries to come, historians may very well conclude that the ruin of America was not Watergate and not Vietnam, but television." So said Martin Esslin, professor of drama at Stanford University, and the author of a book published in 1981 titled The Age of Television.

He said, "Children's cartoons are scandalous, terribly ugly, badly drawn and terribly brutal, and they are embedded in advertisements for junk food."

Esslin continued, "The well-being of any modern nation depends enormously on the cultural level of the top 10 percent. If you have an industry devoted to making people stupid, you're lost."

"The top 10-percent in America are being deprived of intellectual incentive by a very small minority of news-makers in television and the print media."

I agree with Professor Esslin and add: The danger of Television is that it presents immorality as entertainment. Immorality is habit-forming. The first signs are identifiable - personal responsibility, discipline and politeness diminish.

Others have said harsh things about news management. Following is an abridged article titled The low ethics of the press, by Father Virgil Blum published August 17, 1986 in The Harmonizer (Predecessor to Today's Catholic) -

"It is interesting to note that journalists are always shocked at the low 'honesty rating' they receive from their readers. That is probably due to the fact that they do not recognize the extent to which their own prejudices and secularist values pervert their reporting of facts."

"The Lichter-Rothman study of several years ago revealed, for example, that 90 percent of the most influential journalists in the American press approve of killing unborn babies for any reason whatever. That callous degrading of the sanctity of life strongly impacts on their reporting of incidents that have to do with the killing of unborn children."

"The impact is great; in fact, it is overwhelming. There is not a major metropolitan newspaper against abortion. There is not a secular television network against abortion. There is not a mass circulation magazine against abortion."

"While many people can be indoctrinated, manipulated and even persuaded by the media to approve the killing of unborn children, there is an increasing number of citizens who are no longer so simplistic and gullible as to accept uncritically everything the media expounds as God's truth. They think for themselves."

Father Blum gave an example showing why the American people no longer think that the media are honest and ethical: "Some years ago Congressman Henry Hyde spoke to the Pro-Life Council of California. The Fairmont Hotel in San Francisco where he spoke was picketed by 30 persons huddled across the wide street from the hotel. Looking out from the entrance of the Fairmont, it was hard to know who they were or what they were doing or even that they were there.

The next day the San Francisco Chronicle reported there were 300 (not 30) picketers and that was the whole story; what Congressman Hyde said was totally censored and suppressed.

That kind of reporting is the reason why the people rate the honesty and ethical standards of the media so low."

My letter published two years earlier (April 8, 1984) in The Republic, calls for an Affirmative Action Plan for the mainstream media -

Dear Editor:

I was sorry to learn from your April 5, (1984) editorial, Correcting The Media, that "The National News Council is folding its tent." (William Rusher served on that Council for eight years. He is a good man.)

As you said, it's good that errors in the newspaper are corrected more easily today than 10 years ago, referring to the Errata and Amplifications column in The Republic. If the National News Council and other local News Councils were instrumental in bringing about this change they deserve credit.

The kinds of errors I find addressed under Errata and Amplifications generally involve a wrong name, or some other statistical infraction. I'm not saying such errors need not be corrected. Obviously correctable errors ought to be corrected.

What bothers me about the national press and about TV News programs, and what bothered Mr. Rusher, is their conscious attitude of misrepresentation of specific issues in the news. This is a serious problem with vital issues, and one that the National News Council publicized but was not able to correct. Mr. Rusher was quoted in another article. He said, "The media have become much too powerful, too chesty, too opinionated, and too far from the mainsprings of American thought."

Recent studies show that the majority of the so-called "Media Elites" hold and promote negative values, which angers many Americans. These studies also show that 80 percent of Media Elites are secular humanists. Their faulty ideas about what is right and what is wrong are embodied in the words they use to present the daily news.

Truly professional newspaper publishers, editors and reporters suffer tarnished reputations, as does journalism itself, as a consequence of the grab for power by this influential clique.

Left-wing media elites doubt that there is a God. If God exists, they say, He should keep notions of good and bad to Himself. They are intolerant of anyone or any group that tells them about God. They shrugged-off sin twenty years ago, and for a generation they have preached a cruel-kindness (permissiveness) for everything and every life-style except one.

How dangerous is their spin on morality? The facts speak for themselves: An alarming increase in crimes committed by the generation most susceptible to their ideas. Abortion, sodomy and AIDS, socialism and self-worship have become obsessions. Young adults are targets, family ties are weak as is commitment. There are nearly as many divorces each year as there are marriages. And, child pornography, incest; and on and on. (Update: 1990-2000 census data recorded fewer than 25-percent of American families fit into the traditional mold. The failure ratio for marriages in a 2005 study was 50-percent.)

The purpose in guaranteeing Freedom of the Press under the First Amendment of the Constitution is to insure that citizens are well informed, an essential ingredient for a Representative government. When a case can be made that information printed in the mainstream media is false and consciously obstructs justice one of two things must happen: A plan must be adopted and followed by the media itself to correct its errors; or, readers and viewers must put the worst offenders out of business.

I favor an Affirmative Action Plan to obtain better balance in what today's news teaches. The Plan would require that hiring of "media elites" will be balanced not only by color and sex, but by political, religious and philosophical ideology as well. >

Editors of time-honored newspapers should encourage a grassroots movement to restore respectability to our Brain Trust.

An article written in the Spring of 1982 by Robert N. Brown publisher of the Republic (my local Brain Trust) defended the role of newspapers in guarding citizen's interests. The article, titled Newspapers Remain Chronicles of Society, is included here to recognize the dedicated efforts of editors, writers and publishers who are respected in their communities -

In 1872, The Columbus Weekly Republican, predecessor of The Republic, was founded.

This was the year the Amnesty Act finally restored civil rights to most citizens of the South, and Congress founded our first national park - Yellowstone in Wyoming.

Much of the country was still a frontier. Only three years earlier, the golden spike had joined the first transcontinental railroad at Promontory, Utah. Col. George Custer had not yet made his "last stand" in the Sioux Indian Wars.

Since its inception, as far as we can tell, this newspaper has never missed an edition. My years with it have covered nearly one-third of its 110-year existence, yet I have been preceded by three generations of my family who served either as publisher or editor.

This has been a challenging, rewarding and sometimes bittersweet experience. The most curious change I have perceived during my long professional life is that, despite the fact the citizen's interest is being guarded as never before, today's newspapers seem to be regarded with more hostility and suspicion. As I review early copies of our paper, as well as others of that period, they were blunt and outspoken. Direct attacks on the character or ability of individuals were not uncommon, and news was often written in highly opinionated form.

Yet, for all this, we seemed to be respected. Today, despite our best efforts to be fair and equitable, we seem to be attacked from the right and left, below and above, with each segment finding fault with "exaggerations" or "distortions" of the news.

This may result partly from a perception on the part of the reader that since The Republic is the only show in town it somehow follows that it must exhibit an element of irresponsibility or possess sinister motives. It seems that no one wants the spotlight shining on his own act, but is secretly yearning for a return to the old days when slight-of-hand was ignored, if not applauded, and never exposed.

Despite our frustrations in dealing with people whose ideas may be affected by emotion, we try hard to be evenhanded by presenting a general digest of ideas from which all can choose according to their likes.

But, as Sidney Harris of The Philadelphia Inquirer wrote in 1978, "It may someday be written about the press that, with all its available devices, it was unable to calm anger, to elevate discussion beyond emotion, to dispel the most elementary cliches and slogans or to defend on a positive basis its important societal role and its use of power for the public good."

Perhaps what we are seeing is no more than a transient phenomenon - a spin-off from the tensions of contemporary society, or perhaps we haven't yet learned our proper role.

In any event, today's newspaper is the only place where all the daily news can be read and reviewed in depth. It is the chronicle of our society. It has provided the only complete record of our community for the past 110 years.

Despite shrill and vituperous comment to the contrary by our local radio, the 1,760 daily newspapers in the USA now rank first as the nation's largest manufacturing employer, and the revenue from newspaper advertising exceeds radio and television revenues combined.

From its beginning, this newspaper has experienced steady growth. Circulation, now in excess of 22,500 subscribers, is at an all-time high. We are optimistic regarding the future and the continuing need for newspapers in our society.

Bartholomew County is a remarkable place in which to live - an oasis which provides a quality of life far beyond the norm. We will continue to do the best job we can within the limits of our resources to make The Republic an excellent newspaper and to play our proper role within the community. So, here is to the next 110 years. >

Publisher Brown has good reason to say, and I quote, "today's newspaper is the chronicle of our society." The Republic has provided the only chronological 110-year record of the community known as Columbus, IN.

The Republic, and many other local newspapers, provide a readily accessible resource for information dealing with vital statistics of the communities they serve, i.e. births, deaths, who is in the hospital and why, high school game scores, who is holding a meeting and about what, etc. In fact, about seventy percent of the labor involved in operating a daily newspaper is allocated to publishing local events of interest. The remainder is allocated to national and international reports supplied under contract with wire services and national newspapers.

Journalism sixty-five years ago was a welcome and respected profession in spite of the fact that it was opinionated, as all Ism's are. Descriptions of issues and events satisfied Webster's definition of Journalism: Writing characterized by a direct presentation of facts without an attempt at interpretation.

This was the case twenty-five years ago when Brown's article appeared in The Republic. Today most national and international reports no longer honor the Journalist's Code. News is a matter of secular opinion where morality and political issues are (as they say) relative. Today most news-makers pursue the politically correct Godless agenda. (Yesterday most news-makers pursued God's agenda. We live in a different world today.)

Standards of Ethics for journalists are listed in a number of college Journalism textbooks. The definitions below are those of the American Society of Newspaper Editors. Their code is as follows -

1. FREEDOM OF THE PRESS - Freedom of the press belongs to the people. It must be defended against encroachment or assault from any quarter, public or private.

2. TRUTH AND ACCURACY - Good faith with the reader (or listener) is the foundation of good journalism. Every effort must be made to assure that the news content is accurate, free from bias and in context, and that all sides (God's side too) are presented fairly.

3. RESPONSIBILITY - The primary purpose of gathering and distributing news and opinion is to serve the general welfare by informing the people and enabling them to make judgments on the issues of the time. Newspapermen and women who abuse the power of their professional role for selfish motives or unworthy purposes are faithless to that public trust. The American press was made free not just to inform or just to serve as a forum for debate but also to bring an independent scrutiny to bear on the forces of power in the society, including the conduct of official power at all levels of government.

4. IMPARTIALITY - To be impartial does not require the news media to be unquestioning or to refrain from editorial expression.

5.   INDEPENDENCE - Journalists must avoid impropriety and the appearance of impropriety, as well as any conflict of interest or the appearance of conflict.

6.   FAIR PLAY - Journalists should respect the rights of people involved in the news, observe the common standards of decency, and stand accountable for the fairness and accuracy of their news reports.   Persons publicly accused should be given the earliest opportunity to respond.   Pledges of confidentiality must be honored and, therefore, should not be given lightly.   However, unless there is clear and pressing need to maintain confidences, sources of information should be identified.

"Journalists have an obligation to serve the truth and not offend against charity in disseminating information." (Article 8, section 5 of entry #2497, Catechism of the Catholic Church.)

Morally responsible speech is much like the Christian ideal - it has been found difficult and left (mostly) untried. Never the less, God expects from the unique beings He created in His image and likeness that they strive for perfection. And, the founding fathers had faith that the people would sustain the good government they established. The destiny of the nation and of our souls depend on honest efforts.

"Ideas have consequences" is a truism worth repeating amid commercial distractions and the latest news. The print media judges (as Editor Robert Clark of the Courier Journal & Louisville Times said) "what is important and interesting to our readers." He claimed his newspaper uses "good" professional judgment. I added quotation marks to good, because some will say, "what is good for one man is not good for another." Moreover, promoting one's freedom to choose his or her own good minimizes Common Good, as proved earlier.

Others have written about the Journalist's Code charging that news-makers on television and in nationally distributed magazines and newspapers have lost their objectivity. They failed thirty years ago in their obligation to serve the truth and they fail today.

They bring shame to their profession.

Code Words of the Media, is the title of an article published in 1983 in The Republic. Reed Irvine chairman of Accuracy in Media,

Inc. is the author -

Editor and scholar Irving Kristol charged in a recent article in The Wall Street Journal that television news broadcasters are guilty of serious bias and distortion by virtue of the way they use adjectives. Kristol writes: "Thus there are 'ultraconservatives' on TV news (e.g. Cardinal Lefebvre, Senator Jesse Helms), but when was the last time you encountered an 'ultra-liberal?' Apparently there is no such species. Nor are there any 'extremists' to the left of center - only 'militants' or 'activists.' An 'extremist' is someone who passionately holds the wrong views, while the 'militant' is someone who is immoderately pursuing the 'correct' ends."

"Similarly, Ronald Reagan is a 'right-wing Republican.' But is George McGovern a 'left-wing' Democrat? There are occasionally, left-wing students. But they never 'riot,' they merely 'protest.' Only right-wing students riot."

"But the neatest ploy of them all is the selective use of the word 'controversial.' Legislation to deregulate the price of natural gas is 'controversial,' legislation to regulate the price of natural gas is not 'controversial.' Anita Bryant is 'controversial,' leaders of Gay Rights groups are not."

Irving Kristol has focused on a problem of great importance, because the advocacy journalism (secular and political bigotry) that is embodied in the adjectives that the writers and broadcasters apply can be extremely influential. The essence of effective propaganda is constant repetition (30-second sales bites are a prominent example). It is a lot easier to saturate the viewer or reader with propaganda embedded in selective adjectives than it is to repeat complicated arguments.

Not only is the repetition less obvious and more subtle, but it is also less likely to draw complaints. Who wants to write a letter of complaint about so minor a matter as the choice of an adjective? (I do.)

But with Irving Kristol leading the way, perhaps the time has come to protest the adjectival asymmetry, not only in broadcasting but in the print media as well.

Consider, for example, the article in Newsweek of July 25, headed

"Women vs. Women." This was a report on the conflict between feminist and anti-feminist women. The word feminist, either as a noun or adjective, was used 21 times in the article. The word anti-feminist was used only three times. The rest of the time they were referred to as "conservatives" (8 times) or "right-wing" (twice). Not once were the feminist referred to as "left-wing" or even "liberal." Once they were referred to as "radical" by an anti-feminist who was quoted.

In this Newsweek article, the anti-feminists practice "bloc" voting. They "bait" their opponents. They make "farfetched" charges. They use "scare" tactics and they "misrepresent" the ERA. They "lobby" legislators. The feminists, of course, do none of these nasty things. They are merely going to "analyze the political situation in each state" and "organize."

My comment: No. 5 in the American Society of Newspaper Editors code defines Independence as - "Journalists must avoid impropriety and the appearance of impropriety, as well as any conflict of interest or the appearance of conflict." Perhaps there are no journalists reporting for Newsweek.

A reader of The New York Times recently sent me a copy of a letter to the editor of that august paper in which he had jumped on this sentence: "Mr. Wellborn conceded holding 'right-wing' views, but he emphatically denied ties to the (John) Birchers."

The reader wanted to know what was so remarkable about a person's holding "right-wing" views that this had to be described as being "conceded." Was Mr. Wellborn "coming out of the closet?" he asked. Does the Times ever describe anyone "conceding" that he owns left-wing views? A person doesn't "concede" that he won the Nobel Prize. He may "concede" that he was driving while drunk. Keep an eye out for code words such as these. They are worth complaining about. >

The English language is as important to me as it is to James J. Kilpatrick. Consequently I must complain when adjectives are used to buy votes and trick unsuspecting readers/viewers into buying into the culture of death.

I agree with Reed Irvine, this is a frustrating problem made intolerable by the fact that it consciously manipulates "Popular Political Demands," thereby sabotaging lawful government. (A recent example: The impeachment trial of President Clinton was widely reported on television as the work of extremists.) And, it disrupts national unity.

The bottom line is trust.   People judge trust-worthiness of information sources by trial and error. They are alert to deception.

Trust can't be rebuilt until the object of that trust is repaired, be it bridges or New York Times editorials. Tools of science can repair a bridge, but not a liar. Tools of religion can repair a liar, but normally not a bridge. Which set of tools generates hope for building solid trust in printed or televised information and restoring unity to the nation?

Next, (more recent) excerpts from an article titled The fall of journalism's empire by Cal Thomas, in an issue of the Goshen News, dated November 19, 1998 -

"The real discrimination is over belief. Every network anchor believes the same thing. Every cable show pumps out the same ideology. America's biggest newspapers editorialize in favor of abortion rights, gay rights, big government, no tax cuts, more regulation and increased government spending. Real diversity would include not only faces of different colors, but also reporters and editors with different shadings of belief. That kind of journalism would restore the faith of the disaffected in the profession and would improve ratings and circulation."

"But don't look for it to happen any time soon because, the Left is so into denial it would rather shut the door and turn the lights off than to open up the field to beliefs other than its own."

And, from his column titled Prophets without honor in the January 21, 1999 issue of the Goshen News -

"These media people and the Democrats in Congress fear that removing Clinton from office (via Impeachment) would give Republicans a chance to grab the White House again and that the next president might reduce abortions, cut taxes, slow the gay-rights juggernaut and challenge public schools by offering freedom of choice to parents."

I find it interesting the way pertinent data appears at my fingertips when it is most useful. Half an hour ago the mail was delivered including the latest issue of Today's Catholic. The editorial echoes

Publisher Brown's sentiments. It belongs here -

Along the road to journalistic ruin

Pollsters have asked the question often over the years: What professions do you have most respect for and which ones do you find most distasteful?

Doctors and clergy usually rank up there toward the top. Somewhere at the bottom, next to lawyers and morticians, is a spot reserved for journalists.

It is a bit distressing for those of us who got into the news business for noble reasons - to inform the public on important issues and events.

News reporting got a boost in stature from the Watergate scandal, in which a couple of average reporters stumbled onto a series of crimes that brought down the Nixon presidency. Those were heady days for journalists. The book and movie All the President's Men helped many people see journalism as a higher calling.

Of course, that was then and this is now. Reporters in mainstream outlets are now seen as creatures very low in the food chain, somewhere below the earthworm. The way the mainstream media has performed the past years, it is a wonder reporters have maintained any credibility at all.

Take the O.J. Simpson trial, for example.

It is well-known journalistic practice to have two or three different sources confirm information that is vital to a big story you are covering. If you hear something unbelievable, get other people to confirm the facts before telling the world.

The Simpson trial changed that. The competition for new information was so intense that reporters were publishing and broadcasting rumors, usually from unnamed sources, instead of facts. They were rewriting the handbook on journalistic ethics as they went along.

Even worse, wire services were distributing stories full of these unconfirmed rumors. Within seconds, hundreds of newspapers and television and radio stations were presenting these stories thinking they had been checked and rechecked.

The growth of the Internet has had a large impact on the news business. It used to be that someone who presented himself or herself as a reporter knew the difference between fact and rumor. Now anyone with a little know-how and a few bucks can create a Web site that offers what looks like news but is really only that person or group's weird version of the facts.

These developments make being a news consumer more difficult. The ability to discern fact from fiction has become more vital. Unfortunately, the big, bold line between the National Enquirer and the New York Times is now a bit worn and faded.

The Catechism of the Catholic Church says: "By the very nature of their profession, journalists should strive to respect, with equal care, the nature of the facts and the limits of critical judgment concerning individuals. They should not stoop to defamation." >

These are words to live by for all journalists.

It is not Truth (capital "T") that stimulates the secular media, particularly ever-present bad television.

Abortion and the Secular Media

A few times in the history of mankind an issue develops with the potential for destroying national cultures and civilizations. Modern man faces that situation with the issue of legalized abortion. The issue is about authority to define the essence of human beings: Trusting man vs. trusting God to define "humanness;" and, it is about the consequences to the public conscience of poor judgment about unborn children and their mothers.

Judging the issue of "humanness" at every stage in its development, be it an embryo, a fetus, a handicapped infant, etc. demands verifiable sources of information. This starts with accurate reporting of scientific research, which demands adequate knowledge of God's laws, a well-formed conscience, and common sense about reality.

God exists; therefore, reality is what God says it is, not what a secular newspaper, or TV analyst, or even modern Science says it is.

Good background information (knowing the source) reduces the work. The following article is about the crucial act of ensoulment, wherein God makes an embryo into a living child. The article was published September 8, 1985 in Twin Circle Magazine. It was written by Monsignor R.G. Peters.

The article provides theological information that is considered irrelevant by many resources including Catholics for a Free Choice.

When does life begin?

Does the Church teach that every abortion, at any and every stage, is definitely taking of a human life?

And does the Church at the same time teach that the uniting of a soul to the human body or fetus does not necessarily happen immediately at conception?

That's what a booklet, The History of Abortion in the Catholic Church, says about the Church. But, it was published by Catholics for a Free Choice. Anyone who reads the news should know that's not a group that agrees with Catholic teaching on abortion.

The booklet was first published in 1981, and it's back in the news right now because Catholics for a Free Choice is planning to distribute 10,000 copies in a Spanish version in Latin America.

The purpose, of course, is to create doubts about the Church's teaching on abortion.

For a story on the plans, NC News Service interviewed Father Donald McCarthy, former director of education at the Pope John XXIII Medical-Moral Research and Education Center in St. Louis. He had criticized the booklet when it was first published.

He said: "The Church has refused to approve destroying a developing embryo or fetus, even though there is the possibility that the spiritual soul is not yet present.   The Church has maintained constant concern for the life process of every human being."

Almost every time I've heard President Reagan insist that abortion is wrong, he has used the argument that you simply cannot kill a fetus when you think there's a chance it may have human life.

It may surprise some people, the "free choice" people included, but the Church does teach that "from the moment of conception" it is wrong to take the life of the fetus, but at the same time the Church teaches that it cannot know for sure exactly when the soul is joined to the body.

In 1975, the Sacred Congregation for the Doctrine of the Faith issued a Declaration on Abortion in which it definitely declared it wrong to take life at any stage.

In so many words: "From a moral point of view, this is certain: Even if a doubt existed concerning whether the fruit of conception is already a human person, it is objectively a grave sin to dare to risk murder."

And, says the Declaration, doubt can exist: "This Declaration expressly leaves aside the question of the moment when the spiritual soul is infused. There is not a unanimous tradition on this point and authors are as yet in disagreement."

I point out all this because people like the Free Choice group seize upon such a situation to imply that the Church is being inconsistent and that you would agree with the Free Choice teaching if you only knew what the facts are.

The Church is not inconsistent, the Free Choice people are revealing nothing new about the morality of abortion; and, the forbidding of murder - or the chance of murder - is still a strong teaching (particularly for the mother).

The rather foolish thing is the period of uncertainty they're talking about. You may think the Church, and others, are saying there can be an uncertainty about the presence of the soul through the first three months or some such long period.

No such thing. Moralists are talking about there being a possibility of the absence of a human soul for the first two to at most three weeks. That's a period determined mainly by the fact that twinning - the division of the ovum into "identical twins" - has been shown to happen as late as this in the development of the embryo.

After the fact, you'd say this proves that in this particular case there was no human soul until there were finally two embryos. But how could you have known that, and is it true in every case?

So, don't get your information about abortion from a source like the Free Choice booklet. Get it from the official documents of the Church. They don't deny the possibility of a "late" ensoulment, but they insist the possibility of an immediate ensoulment makes an abortion immoral even from the first moment on (i.e. in the embryonic stage). >

Information on Catholic doctrine available from Catholics for a Free Choice looks and smells like garbage.

Discovering that a specific organization is not a reputable resource for the truth about abortion is not a problem. As editor Robert Clark reminded us, there are many ethical resources. But, there is a problem where a powerful resource, namely the print and broadcast News media, cannot be trusted to tell the truth about events surrounding the "termination" of unwanted or defective persons, babies or adults.

I believe such is also the case with reporting in the secular media about other ethical issues, where Truth is excluded by minds set on excluding Catholic doctrine and other spiritual considerations.

"Godless enlightenment" rejects traditional social, religious and political ideas developed from God's Word. "Man alone, with reason and experience, is capable of solving moral problems" is the keystone of Secularism. It follows from this idea that popular judgment in an "enlightened" society would properly allow adultery, sodomy, euthanasia - and allow a mother to kill her child or allow care takers to kill everyone who does not meet their "quality of life" standard. Such conditions favor immorality, broken homes, mercy killing, AIDS and STD's and Post Abortion Syndrome - killing the baby has a traumatic effect on the mother.

I said it once and I will say it again and again: "Instead of informing their readers and viewers impartially on vital issues to enable them to make accurate and proper judgments, two generations of news-makers have abused their power by promoting a culture of death."

———————

Democratic countries will have a serious problem if large segments of their populations are blinded to Moral Law. If then, the mainstream media totally rejected it's honored keystone, objectivity, i.e. the media threw all of it's weight against the author of Moral Law; now the Will Rogers syndrome and Newman's "notional assent" clash. Reason, together with common sense, gives way to "feelings" and civil war.

Responsible and objective reporting about abortion, infanticide, euthanasia and other immoral acts must start with one central premise: Only one earthly court can hold absolute authority for Moral Law.

CHAPTER 12

ABORTION RIGHTS THE SECULAR AGENDA

Since the first century the Catholic Church has affirmed the moral evil of every procured abortion. This teaching has not changed and remains unchangeable. Abortion willed either as an end or a means, is gravely contrary to the moral law God infused into mankind: #2271 of the Catechism of the Catholic Church -

"You shall not kill the embryo by abortion nor cause the newborn to perish."

"God, the Lord of life, has entrusted to men the noble mission of safeguarding life, and men must carry it out in a manner worthy of themselves. Life must be protected with the utmost care from the moment of conception: Abortion and infanticide are abominable crimes."

Abortion Rights is key to understanding what the past two generations have been all about. It truly is the banner that identifies an army of barbarians on God's battlefield.

I carried a platoon banner in boot camp during the Korean war - Company A, 3rd Armored Division, U.S. Army. The banner identifies opposing armies. In war the leaders on both sides claim their cause is justified. Historians decide later which side was right. But, how does a historian know? This is an interesting question today, because those who follow the Abortion Rights banner deny absolute standards of right and wrong judgment.

The historian deals in just causes each side fought for. Judgments are measured according to a set of ideal values, or "Standards" the human race has tried to honor.

I am reminded of Paul Vitz's book Faith of the Fatherless: The Psychology of Atheism (Chapter 8) describing "educational conditions thirty-five years ago at Stanford University's Graduate School of

Education: The preoccupation of the Stanford teachers was to question Judeo-Christian values. When asked what they would put in place of Standard Values their answer was: We have no agenda, we just want to hold all values up to the light of reason. If they are valid they should be retained. If not, perhaps there are values that would better serve society's needs."

The light of reason has already been applied by past and present civilizations, and by more than 2000 years of people's suffering. Stanford teachers and other secular humanists seek to scrap testimony which has served mankind admirably. Will they force us to relearn history? The answer to that old question is up for grabs, as it has been many times before for other civilizations.

This conflict/war isn't about misinformation, a strategy used by the secular media and others for gaining recruits. It is about the damage legalization to murder unwanted babies does to the souls of mothers, and to the public concept of proper moral conduct.

A maternal instinct is given to higher animals, including Homo sapiens, in order to protect and preserve the species. Yet the nation's highest court encourages a mother to commit a most irresponsible act - killing her child - a momentous injustice that future historians will rank ahead of the Holocaust as the most damnable of the 20th century. It makes a mockery of God's commandment, "Thou shall not kill" and sends a message to students who kill their peers.

The legality of Abortion is the green light for sexual promiscuity and self-gratification - two factors that are proven to deliver mother and child into poverty. Yet, a diverse bloc of power made up of the mainstream media, much of commercial television, Planned Parenthood, the ACLU, the Democratic party, Americans for Separation of Church and State, Catholics for a Free Choice, the National Organization for Women, the American Pediatric Association, the movie-making industry and a majority of Supreme Court justices has united under the Abortion Rights banner to defend the Court's shameful ruling in Roe vs. Wade.

The "right" an owner had over his slaves was the dividing and defining issue during the years preceding the Civil War, so too the "right" a mother now has to kill her child was the dividing and defining issue of the 1970's and remains so. The fact that civil rights for Negroes were not protected for more than 100 years after that war ended prompts me to warn my children and grandchildren that they will be persecuted throughout the 21st century for their religion by the army that flies the Abortion Rights banner.

Conditional limits on Right to Life were immorally altered in 1973 to exclude innocent infants in order for abortion to be legalized. "Limits" were redefined so as to deny viability to infants midway through gestation. This error established a precedent that imperiled the lives of future Americans. It is more than an error. It is a crime unequaled since the slaughter of the Holy Innocents - the evil deed of King Herod Antipas (21BC-39AD). Both violated the prime directive, "The end can never justify the means."

Scientific evidence proves that infants throughout their entire fetal development are viable human beings. Moreover, from the beginning each is in the image and likeness of God.

I wrote the following letter five years after the Supreme Court's "Roe vs. Wade" -

May 11, 1978

Dr. Mildred F. Jefferson
President, National Right to Life

Dear Dr. Jefferson:

The greatest need today is to have a person who is articulate, composed, confident and able to speak with authority about abortion. You have demonstrated those qualities.

We, too, feel sad over the 5,000,000 lives ended by abortion for the reasons you gave in your letter; and for other reasons: "Holocaust" is a reminder of an outrageous event in 20th century world history. Today in America we count as many innocent babies who have suffered and died in an operation legalized by the U.S. government. Are we, a free people, guiltier than German citizens 35-years ago under a vicious dictator?

I am saddened to think that roughly half of our adult population have closed their minds to reality.

It is a simple matter to prove conclusively that a fetus is alive. If the fetus is dead the mother's body will eliminate it naturally.

Nine years after Roe vs. Wade a young woman challenged my position on abortion. The date was April 2, 1982. The title of my letter was Abortion Rights. It was published in the Columbus, IN newspaper, the Republic -

Dear Editor:

What motivates a person to be pro-abortion? It can't be devotion to reason, because the arguments advocating abortion are clearly against reason. Take as an example the Editorial in the March 25th Republic titled "A Rule on Reproduction." The opening paragraph uses "unfortunate" in reference to a recent Indiana law requiring doctors to notify parents before an abortion is performed on their unwed teen-ager.

This law deals with parents rights vs. rights of their children, specifically pregnant unwed children. The ruling recognizes the duty and the right parents have to care for (guide) their minor children, helping them to make the right decisions. Examples can be found of parents who abuse their children and in other ways fail in their duty. This is no reason to question the right and the duty all parents have to protect their children. The pro-abortion media will not tolerate anyone or anything standing in the way of an abortion, not parental duty, not anything. This law goes against reason and common sense.

During the past two decades cultural license has made it easier for children to experiment with sex. When minors become pregnant, their mistake is compounded by self-centered pro-abortionists. The gall to argue that parents should be kept in the dark about a medical procedure which could ruin their child's future is worse than unreasonable, it's straight out of hell.

Would you have me believe that a pregnant, unwed minor possesses greater wisdom than her parents? >

The challenge was published on April 7th in The Republic -

Dear Editor:

In a letter to the Editor, R.T. Jefferson asked what motivates a person to be pro-abortion. The letter proceeds to show such unreasonable attitudes and ideas that it pretty well answers itself. ...

Is it unreasonable to call everyone a pro-abortionist because they believe in some freedom of choice? Isn't pro-choice the better word?

I think pro-choice is the better answer for a good citizen in a democratic society.

Who knows their parents better than teen-age girls? They know if they have good rapport with their parents, that the parents are intelligent and really reasonable. The girls also know if their parents are tyrants, or radical anti-abortionists under any circumstances.

So what choice does the minor pregnant girls have in Indiana come Sept. 1? Not much I'm afraid.

The new Indiana law, passed by the Republican majority under the influence of Moral Majority, will try to force the morals of some on the others. This is a supposedly democratic society!

Jefferson said in his letter that when young girls become pregnant, pro abortionists compound the mistake by making it easy to obtain an abortion. He indicates that making it difficult, if not impossible, to obtain an abortion is the simple answer. Is this reasonable?

I think the pregnant unwed minors do possess greater wisdom than that. The girl should at least have some choice; it is her life!

Any staunch anti-abortionist shows little empathy for the young pregnant woman, even if she is his or her own daughter.

The girl will usually know whether her parents will help her with her problems or merely become part of her problem.

I agree with the editorial in the March 25 issue of the Republic concerning the new law on abortion. It is unfortunate the legislature played politics with such a serious matter.

The editor shows great courage and high principle in speaking out for what he believes is right on a delicate issue. A newspaper is an important pillar of strength in the community when the editor carries a torch for the unfortunate in an imperfect society. I think the Republic has that kind of editor.

Pro-Choice

I responded to Pro-Choice in a letter dated April 13, 1982 -

Dear Editor:

"Pro-Choice" has me at a disadvantage. She knows my name, but I don't know her name. (Who but a girl would write, "the girl usually will know if her parents will help her with her problem or merely become part of her problem.")

Pro-Choice prefers that I say pro-choice instead of pro-abortion. The opening sentence of my earlier letter then reads, "What motivates a person to be pro-choice?" True, pro-choice and pro-abortion are synonymous, but it is unreasonable to make communicating more difficult.

I also wrote in that letter, "When young (minor) girls become pregnant, their mistake is compounded by pro-abortionists (read pro-choicers) making it easy to obtain an abortion." When a word expresses a meaning as clearly and as unequivocally as pro-abortionist does, it is unreasonable to look for a substitute.

You proved my point Pro-Choice. It can't be devotion to reason that motivates a person to be pro-abortion.

Call me a radical anti-abortionist if you like. I am a radical when it comes to my rights as a parent. I love my kids and I will fight anyone or anything that tries to come between us.

If some of these people who keep pushing for abortion (or the choice to have one) had to experience their daughters going behind their backs to have an abortion they would think differently.

Imagine; it could be my grandson or granddaughter lying dead, murdered by choice (read abortion), rather than cuddled in my arms. My choice is a live baby.

I pray that God has mercy on all of us; those who favor abortion for convenience sake. >

Abortion is murder. Murder is a serious sin before God that causes nightmares in any mother (minor or adult) who pays attention to her conscience. The guilt resulting from an abortion can be (and for hundreds of thousands of mothers has been) devastating, according to expert witnesses, i.e. mothers who have had an abortion. Let them tell you about their experiences, experiences mainstream media censors deny us our right to know.

When The Mothers Found Their Voice

By Olivia Gans, Director of American Victims of Abortion

In many people's minds the presence of women in the pro-life movement who have had abortions and now regret them seems natural. It is in fact a relatively new phenomenon.

The story of our involvement began with a little known event that took place over 15 years ago in a hotel in New Jersey at the 1982 National Right To Life Convention. It changed the course of my life and I believe hundreds of thousands of other women.

I had attended the convention that year along with hundreds of others just curious to see what was going on. I did, however, have a secret concern. I wanted to hear what, if anything, was being said about women who, like myself, had had an abortion. I had not yet told anyone, not even my parents, about my own experience.

To my great delight 1982 marked the year of Dr. Vincent Rue's first speaking appearance at an NRLC convention. The importance of that lecture on the psychological effects of abortion can not be overstated. Dr. Rue was among the very first to identify the symptoms of a condition which continues to affect the lives of thousands of women around the world.

At the conclusion of his workshop Dr. Rue was surrounded by enthusiastic questioners. As the crowd thinned, three other women and I remained. We eagerly quizzed him about his theories as they fit with our own stories. I realized that I had found what I was looking for; confirmation that I was not alone and the assurance that someone seemed to understand what I was feeling.

Later that evening, sitting with those same women in another part of the hotel, the first informal post-abortion support group was formed. For hours we shared the depths of our hearts and memories surrounding our children's lives and deaths by abortion. The honesty of the conversation, "Did this happen to you too?" "Have you had the same nightmares?" or, "Are you afraid of that as well?" and the commonality of the answers to each question echo in post-abortion healing programs throughout the world today.

Out of our impromptu meeting came the fragile first steps to form what became the first national post-abortion support group, Women Exploited By Abortion (WEBA). We knew that we were not the only women who'd bought the lies of pro-abortionists. We desperately wanted to help create a safe place for any woman to speak freely about her own pain and find healing and peace. Equally important to us was the need to tear away the screen of lies that were spread by every pro-abortion slogan. We had lived through the truth behind the slogans and we had stories that needed to be told.

Back at that time few people in the pro-life movement had ever had any intimate contact with women who'd had an abortion. Certainly a few knew of family members who may have had one. Some crisis pregnancy center directors had met women who'd already had one, but as a rule few if any women who'd had abortions were active in the pro-life movement. We were simply lost in a limbo of our own denial and painful secrets.

What continues to strike me all these many years after that fateful convention was the compassionate response that we met with from the mainstream pro-life movement. There was a general understanding that women who'd had abortions had survived something devastating. While nobody actually knew just how far-reaching the damage was from an abortion they did know that harm had been done.

Most importantly, pro-lifers understood how deeply women were lied to by abortionists. They realized that *the mothers of unborn children killed by abortion were themselves the second victims of abortion* (my italics).

Admittedly in the early days of our involvement women speaking negatively in public about their abortions were a bit of a curiosity to many on both sides. Certainly no one in the pro-abortion camp ever thought the mothers would find their voices. Looking back I can remember the times I agreed to debate a pro-abortion leader who literally had no comment when I disclosed that I myself had been there and done that. Those days are gone now as the pro-abortion movement has found new ways to disregard and degrade our experiences. They prove that they never did and continue now to have no real concern for the lives and well being of the women who have faced difficult pregnancies or had abortions.

By 1985 the word-of-mouth effort of that original group combined with the opportunities and support of the established pro-life movement had helped to generate a flush of interest in the aftermath of abortion. It was time to establish the post-abortion voice in the mainstream of the pro-life movement. The opportunity to make our life stories available in a powerful and effective manner was critical. We ourselves knew that it would be tough to argue with experience, but we had to find a platform. From our perspective the logical base to work from was the strength of NRLC's well-organized network. What followed was the formation of the unique outreach program called American Victims of Abortion.

Our goals have been simple from the start. We have attempted to provide the states, the media, governmental bodies, and academia with the most articulate and responsible educational speakers who can honestly address the tragedy of abortion. It is always our hope that whenever one of us speaks out someone else, who may need to find the same caring help, will be encouraged to do so.

Regularly over the years aborted women have worked side by side with grassroots pro-lifers to see protective legislation passed. They have provided the vital evidence to support the critical need for parental involvement laws and women's right to know laws. Each step brings us closer to the passage of the most protective laws possible that will respect the dignity of both the mother and her unborn child.

The post-abortion arm of the pro-life movement was absolutely created by women for women who learned too late what was really at stake in their "choice." When nobody else could hear us crying in the night we found each other and built places of sanctuary in which to heal. Now, as more and more is learned about the after-effects of abortion, we can reach out to the other family members hurt by abortion, including the fathers, grandparents, and siblings.

What began in 1982 as the passionate call of a handful of

courageous women to tell the whole truth behind the slogans has grown and developed into one of the most important aspects of pro-life activity. There are now organized post-abortion healing programs in all 50 states. Every crisis pregnancy center in America is looking at training staff people to address this issue because there have been so many repeat abortions. Churches have begun to respond to the reality that in every congregation there are people who have been touched personally by abortion and that spiritual healing is necessary. Despite the glaring reluctance of the mainstream mental health groups to acknowledge the existence of post-abortion syndrome/trauma, growing numbers of professionals in the mental health field are discussing the numbers of cases that they see in practice. All of this points to the deep need in our country to heal this national wound.

Looking for ways to discredit our statements, pro-abortion forces have often claimed that we were all manipulated puppets of the pro-life movement. It was regularly asserted that we felt as we did because pro-life attitudes made us feel guilty about our decision. Nothing could be further from the truth. After working in this area for over 16 years I can truly say that I've never spoken with any woman who honestly believes that anyone or anything other than her own heart and head has brought her to regret her abortion decision. When we lie awake alone at night with our own memories we know the awful truth of what we have done.

Over these past 17 years since my own precious child lost her life because of my foolish decision I have had extraordinary opportunities to spread the word within the USA and abroad. Still, even as I, and many other brave women and men I proudly call companions, dedicate ourselves to telling our children's stories in order to save lives, we know where our gratitude belongs. It is thanks to the steadfast efforts of the pro-life community that maintains the valiant struggle to return protection to the little ones that we found a way to heal our hurt. We, their mothers and fathers, were never rejected by the true pro-life heart. When we could not or would not remember our precious children it was the movement that continued to hold aloft a candle in remembrance until we began to find our voice.

Every abortion is a death in the family. Twenty-five years after Roe v. Wade we have only begun to feel the pain of 36 million deaths. How much longer will it have to be before our nation confronts the truth, accepts our common responsibility, and grieves for our dead? As every mother of an aborted child knows, there can be no peace until we remember and embrace them even if it can only be in our hearts.

The medical condition Dr. Rue described is PAS (Post Abortion Syndrome). This debilitating sickness begins with an aching conscience and can slowly spread to the body causing, as the author said, devastation or a "wasting away." In many cases PAS takes away the will to live.

You will find Olivia Gans's story, and news about PAS, only in publications of religious organizations, the American Life League and some conservative organizations. The article above was published in the January 1998 issue of National Right To Life News.

Concerned Americans need to search their own knowledge about this widespread medical problem affecting only mothers who have had abortions. PAS has been observed and studied by members of the medical community for more than 20 years. Their work lies buried in the Ideology of Denial.

Unconcerned Americans may be interested in how widespread the effort is to cover over this problem, and in names of powerful "morticians" representing most of our Mental Health Organizations. They continue to deny the truth about Post Abortion Syndrome.

On October 9, 2008 the American Family Council sponsored a panel discussion in Washington D.C. of a negative report issued by the American Psychological Association disclaiming scientific reports proving more than ten million American women (20 to 30 percent) suffer deep debilitating guilt long after their abortion. Dr. Vincent Rue was a panel member. An article titled The Inconvenient Truth about Post Abortion Trauma is posted at www. clmagazine.org.

If you can't recall hearing or reading about PAS you ought to question the value you receive from your "mainstream" news sources. If your sources failed you in this instance in all likelihood it was due to what Nazi propagandist Joseph Goebbels (and Robert Clark, the Courier Journal & Louisville Times editor) called news management; and, to what I call an irrational desire for a duty-free kind of personal freedom granted to those who convert to the religion of secular humanism.

The date is March 12, 1999 (as I write this). A quarter of a century has passed without resolving what Mother Teresa called, "a crime that kills not only the child but the consciences of all involved." President Reagan's booklet Abortion and the Conscience of the Nation was front page news in 1984. President Reagan said: "Abortion concerns not only the unborn child, it concerns every one of us." He got it right when he insisted that it is unacceptable to end a life when certain knowledge is lacking about whether or not life is present in the womb.

The Vatican issued a document in 1986 titled "Instruction on Respect for Human Life in Its Origin and on the Dignity of Procreation" which quotes proofs reported by the scientific community establishing definitively that an individual (new) life, distinct from both father and mother, begins when an ovum is fertilized. This Vatican document was discussed in an article by Michael Novak, published March 27, 1987 in The Indianapolis Star, titled -

The Vatican vision of when human life begins

The Catholic Church has done it again. It has dissented from the conventional wisdom of the "progressives" of our time. It has said what it thinks on the technologies of birth.

What I like best about the Catholic Church is its self-respect. In an age when most church leaders elsewhere burn to appease the cultured despisers of religion, and dread nothing so much as to be thought behind the times, the Catholic Church (and especially this pope) continues to make its own calm judgments, consistent with those it has made for 2000 years.

The Vatican's new Instruction on Respect for Human Life in Its Origin and on the Dignity of Procreation is much more intelligent, better argued and more open to counter-argument *than news reports had led me to believe* (my italics).

Leave aside particular points for a moment, on which people of good will are sure to disagree. The main thrust of this document is to defend a human right never before articulated in such detail and clarity; the human right of a child to be born to two married persons through the mutual gift of their bodily and personal love for one another.

The nub of the issue, of course, is the Catholic vision of when and how human life begins. The church is now able to follow science in affirming that "from the time an ovum is fertilized, a new life is begun which is neither that of the father nor the mother." The new life has its own independent genetic code. It is an individual. It has begun the dynamic of human growth that will not end until death.

As such, in the view of the Church, it has a right to life and to integrity of growth. It is a gift. Parents have a right to express their love "through the language of the body" and the soul, but they do not have a right to a child. As their love is a gift to one another, so the fruit of that love is a gift to them. That gift, that child, has rights which not even they, nor doctors, nor scientists, nor the state, may take away.

Many intelligent persons today do not view human reproduction as the Catholic tradition does. So it always goes in a pluralistic society. As Catholics are asked to respect the views of others, so others are requested to consider those of Catholics.

If you wish a clear statement of the Catholic vision, perhaps the clearest on record, here is the text to study. It is written with the open-minded clarity for which Cardinal Ratzinger, once considered among the "progressive" leaders of the "open church" at Vatican II, has long been praised. That his words often now stick in the craw of today's "progressives" is the measure of how far they, not he, have moved away from the tradition during the past 20 years.

From this vision, the Instruction patiently takes up two medical questions: 1. The new technologies used upon human embryos, and 2. The new technologies of artificial fertilization. A number of points are raised and distinctions made under each heading.

Not everybody agrees with each of these particular points. Still, probably everyone will agree that real problems do occur under each heading. By stating its own position with extraordinary clarity on each of these, at the very least the new Vatican Instruction will help others to clarify their points of disagreement and to state their own alternative vision.

Different persons have different visions of what is appropriate and just what to do concerning the origins of human life. Now everyone in the debate will have to be at least equally clear at each step of the moral argument.

The Vatican Instruction is especially good in pointing out that, in reaching a moral point of view, good intentions are not a sufficient criterion. It recognizes and applauds "understandable motivations," "natural impulses," and "subjectively good intentions." In the Catholic view, however, these are not sufficient criteria for respecting the right of the child to be born through "the bodily language" of the conjugal act between two loving parents.

The main worry of the church is the surrender of dominion over the origins of life to "third parties" - of commerce, science, medicine, or the state - who begin to play God.

The legitimization of third-party dominion over who shall be born, the Instruction argues, would give illegitimate power over human life to those who have no rights to such power.

Researchers and other "third parties" speak from both sides of their mouth when they say that "life begins the moment the ovum is fertilized," and later claim their right to profit from killing embryos to extract their stem cells. The mainstream media, another "third party," instructs its readers that the end justifies the means - a notorious lie.

In the normal practice of in vitro fertilization, the Instruction observes, more eggs are fertilized than are implanted in the womb. Who decides which ones will be implanted? And what human being has the right to destroy the human lives already begun in the "spare" embryos? To destroy these human lives in experimentation or to subject them to commercial trafficking would be to violate their fundamental human dignity.

The Instruction worries, as well, about the confusion that results for children born of surrogate mothers. Critics say the Catholic vision involves too narrow a definition of "natural" and too unfeeling a view of the good intentions, happiness and joy of those new parents to whom the new technologies have brought children they otherwise could not have had. These are good arguments. But the

Instruction gives clear and considered replies to them.

This field of inquiry as a whole is beyond my own expertise. I have not made medical ethics a specific field of study. So I am not able to pass judgment on specific points of disagreement between the Instruction and the critics. But I am certain that Cardinal Ratzinger and Pope John Paul II have issued a well-argued and courageous document which will prove immensely beneficial even to those who disagree with it.

Yet virtually everyone will find in this document much with which to agree. Commercial trafficking in embryos, wholly unregulated and destructive experimentation, and a "brave new world" of third party dominion over the origins of human life are not likely to be desired by many. On the more disputed points, a long and thorough public argument is in order. Our society will act more wisely if we spell out for each other our own visions of human nature and destiny, in all their variety, in civil discourse and in respect for one another.

A growing fetus demonstrates at every stage of development that he or she is alive. This is innocent life, and certainly it is not responsible for its conception. Do our pro-abortion Supreme Court justices and pro-abortion members of Congress and the pro-abortion Mainstream Media believe that a pregnant rape victim - a mother to be in this scenario, would knowingly choose to kill her innocent baby? You people have a very low opinion of motherhood.

Note: For reasons that are entirely logical rape rarely results in pregnancy. Dr. C. Everett Koop, formerly Surgeon General of the United States, presented results of Rape Trial studies which showed that none of the 5000 victims in the study became pregnant. Surprised? Consider the data: Women can become pregnant only 13 percent of the time, i.e. 3 to 5 days in each menstrual cycle; rapists are male odd-balls in that a very high percentage are incapable of producing offspring; rape victims may already be pregnant, or they may be infertile due to age or for other reasons; and, today most women of child-bearing age use contraceptives. It should not be a surprise to any of our Senators and Representatives who opposed the Hyde amendment on the grounds that, "the amendment would compel poor women to carry babies conceived by rape," to find that they stand accused of being willful liars. Or do they really want me to believe that they propose to allow more than one million babies to die so that one or two rape victims become entitled to a federally assisted abortion?

The demoralization of ideals has, over the past two generations, increased to a sorry state wherein half of American voters either lack the critical skills to know the difference between lies and the truth, or lack the intellectual honesty to admit they have been deceived.

John Ruskin (1819-1900), a famous English critic and prolific writer, offered a practical insight when he said, "The essence of lying is in deception, not in words." This quote is from Modern Painters Part 9, Vol. 5, Chapter, 7, first edition published in 1860.

One does not expect to find definitive answers in the Bible for moral choices dropped on us by molecular biologists. So, the "particular points" in the Instruction Novak elects to leave aside, "on which people of good will are sure to disagree," raise a pertinent question.

Who is the final authority today to declare the true morality of these points (and others) dealing with "moral choices" when, unfortunately, God is silent?

Hell awaits those who willfully (without remorse) choose to reject God's Moral Laws and the sole authority He instituted to interpret them.

I reject the Ideology of Denial that says Hell is make-believe. I accept as meaningful a one-word definition of worldly success, namely Heaven. I am duty-bound to find and defend that "final authority" on earth that complements the Bible, i.e. makes good sense of mankind's responsibilities in the atomic age. Why? Because I can prove by logical deduction that God exists, whereas I cannot prove that God does not exist. Hell exists because God said so. God established a mortal authority on earth for all time.

The 1990's witnessed the intrusion by President Clinton on the Right to life of unborn infants. With total disregard for gestation time and without the authorization of the Courts or of Congress, he personally caused partially delivered babies to be savagely killed. He advanced the precedent mentioned above one notch by removing the Supreme Court's viability clause in Roe vs. Wade as a necessary condition for a citizen's Right to Live.

Responsibility for mankind's second holocaust must fall on government officials, particularly on President Clinton; but, it must fall on every voter as well since, in a Constitutional Republic, it is voters who oversee the activities of Congress and the President.

On March 11, 1997, as President Clinton was beginning his second term, an editorial in the Wall Street Journal stated that (Arkansas) Governor Clinton and his cronies were notorious for their strategy of gaming or mocking Arkansas's system of laws. The editorial was not about Roe vs. Wade. It was about a dangerous philosophy that turns morality on its head. Parts of the editorial, titled "Illegal Ends," are reprinted below -

Somewhere along the line - Georgetown, Oxford, Hot Springs - Bill Clinton picked up some moral philosophy. Such as; the end justifies the means, currently being put out as a defense of the DNC fund-raising frenzies.

"I would remind you," Mr. Clinton instructed the White House press corps, "that we had a very stiff challenge. We were fighting a battle not simply for our re-election, but over the entire direction of the country for years to come, and the most historic philosophical battle we've had in America in quite a long time."
The Abortion Rights banner is prominent on that battlefield.

Public life is about mainly one thing - the rules that all consent to abide by and enforce so that life can be civil. It has been the contention of this page since its earliest editorials on the Clinton Presidency that this coterie from Little Rock came to Washington not with any recognizable purpose, but to game the system.

Gaming the system is what they'd been doing their entire lives ...all of it more are less defensible because of this "most historic philosophical battle."

In more traditional terms, the first duty of the Presidency is to see that the laws are faithfully executed. It would be naive not to recognize that nearly all presidencies have at some point seen fit to squeeze the law for some larger, often disputed purpose. But we are certainly not so naive to believe that what has been going on the past four years constitutes any recognizable interpretation of faithfully executing the laws.

It is about obligations to the spirit of the laws that up to this point all politicians, even the most imperfect, acknowledged as their primary duty. Not any more. Now, on any given day, the law is what Bill Clinton, Al Gore, Mike McCurry, Ann Lewis, Bob Bennett or, it now seems, Janet Reno wish it to be. It is a philosophy for getting by, perhaps, but not likely to work well as governance.

Among the reasons Clinton gave to justify "gaming the system," there is one that should trouble God-fearing people everywhere: "Winning the battle over the entire direction of the country for years to come." This is the end he and the Democrat Party believes justifies illegal means to retain power to win the battle for unrestricted "Rights." Clinton said, "This is the most historic philosophical battle we've had in America in quite a long time."

President Clinton is a liar. This battle has not been going on for a long time and it certainly is not about truth. Abortion Rights and Gay Rights banners were raised as a "free love" initiative. President Clinton expanded the initiative and the battlefield.

We are seeing that the King's robes of finest silk are a lie. The king is naked. Moreover, the King is merely a puppet. His strings are pulled by an unsavory cadre whose goal is insurrection.

If we learn anything from the Clinton generation it must be that the Politically Correct banner is misleading. Love is not free. True love, best exemplified in holy marriages, is a "you first" process where husband and wife each give "self", their most cherished possession, to the other. Children of such marriages, enjoy happy and fulfilling lives. (Thus, the wheel goes round.)

The other kind of love, hailed by these nutty platoons, has terminated the lives of babies numbering in the millions, broken millions of marriages, brought unimagined grief to families and deep depression, bordering on suicide, to marriage-breakers. Grief-stricken lives of aborted women, fragmented families and depression are ticking bombs.

CHAPTER 13

THE TICKING BOMB

For three years violence to students by their classmates was prominent in the news. Dates and American cities where killings were reported are: September 1999 in Fort Worth, Texas; April 1999 in Littleton, Colorado; May 1998 in Fayetteville, Tennessee; April 1998 in Edinborough, Pennsylvania; March 1998 in Jonesboro, Arkansas; December 1997 in Paducah, Kentucky; and October 1997 in Pearl, Mississippi.

Mother Teresa was right when in March 1979 she wrote, "If a mother can murder her own child what is left but for others to kill each other." Following every killing advocates of the Ideology of Denial will search for alternate realities.

He who knows not, and knows not that he knows not, is a fool; shun him

He who knows not, and knows that he knows not, is willing; teach him.

He who knows, and knows not that he knows, is asleep; awaken him.

She who knows, and knows that she knows, is wise; follow her. (A proverb, some say Arabian others say Chinese.)

Political Correctness leads the way in falsely assigning blame for children killing children to the instrument rather than to the amoral education authorized by the Nutty Platoon.

The father of Rachel Scott, a student killed in the April 1999 Columbine High School shooting, testified before the House Subcommittee on Crime. I think his statement (his opinion) shines light on the evil of moral independence that is reducing this nation to chaos. His opinion was far more convincing than the opinion, "It's guns, Stupid!" If you didn't read the Subcommittee statement here is another opportunity -

"Since the dawn of creation there have been both good and evil in the hearts of men and women. We all contain the seeds of kindness and the seeds of violence.

The death of my wonderful daughter Rachel Joy Scott, and the deaths of that heroic teacher and the other children who died, must not be in vain. Their blood cries out for answers.

The first recorded act of violence was when Cain slew his brother Abel out in the field. The villain was not the club he used. Neither was it the NCA - the National Club Association. The true killer was Cain and the reason for the murder could only be found in Cain's heart.

In the days that followed the Columbine tragedy, I was amazed at how quickly fingers began to be pointed at groups such as the NRA. I am not a member of the NRA. I am not a hunter. I do not even own a gun. I am not here to represent or defend the NRA, because I don't believe that they are responsible for my daughter's death. Therefore, I do not believe that they need to be defended. If I believed they had anything to do with Rachel's murder, I would be their strongest opponent.

I am here today to declare that Columbine was not just a tragedy - it was a spiritual event that should be forcing us to look at where the real blame lies. Much of that blame lies here in this room. Much of that blame lies behind the pointing fingers of the accusers themselves.

I wrote a poem just four nights ago that expresses my feelings the best. This was written before I knew I would be speaking here today -

Your laws ignore our deepest needs,
Your words are empty air,
You've stripped away our heritage,
You've outlawed simple prayer.
Now gunshots fill our classrooms,
And precious children die.
You seek for answers everywhere,
And ask the question, "Why?"
You regulate restrictive laws,
Through legislative creed,
And yet you fail to understand,

That God is what we need!

Men and women are three-part beings. We all consist of body, soul and spirit. When we refuse to acknowledge a third part of our makeup, we create a void that allows evil, prejudice and hatred to rush in and wreck havoc. Spiritual influences were present within our educational systems for most of our nation's history. Many of our major colleges began as theological seminaries. This is a historic fact.

What happened to us as a nation? We have refused to honor God and in doing so we open the doors to hatred and violence.

And when something as terrible as Columbine's tragedy occurs, politicians immediately look for a scapegoat such as the NRA. They immediately seek to pass more restrictive laws that continue to erode away our personal and private liberties.

We do not need more restrictive laws. Eric and Dylan would not have been stopped by metal detectors. No amount of gun laws can stop someone who spends months planning this type of massacre.

The real villain lies within our own hearts. Political posturing and restrictive legislation are not the answers.

The young people of our nation hold the key. There is a spiritual awakening taking place that will not be squelched!

We do not need more religion. We do not need more gaudy television evangelists spewing out religious garbage. We do not need more million-dollar church buildings built while people with basic needs are being ignored.

We do need a change of heart and a humble acknowledgment that this nation was founded on a principle of simple trust in God.

As my son Craig lay under that table in the school library and saw his two friends murdered before his very eyes, he did not hesitate to pray in school. I defy any law or politician to deny him that right!

I challenge every young person in America and around the world to realize that on April 20, 1999, at Columbine High School, prayer was brought back to our schools. Do not let the many prayers offered by those students be in vain.

Dare to move into the new millennium with a sacred disregard for legislation that violates your conscience and denies your God-given right to communicate with Him.

To those of you who would point your finger at the NRA, I give you a sincere challenge: Dare to examine your own heart before you cast the first stone!

My daughter's death will not be in vain. The young people of this country will not allow that to happen." >

Political posturing over the April 1999 disaster was not a matter for conjecture. It was real. "Your words are empty air," said Mr. Scott.

Members of Congress refuse to take sides fearing loss of votes.

How much evil like that of Dylan and Eric can a politically correct, secular culture dismiss and still claim to be civilized?

Rachel's father said, "The real villain lies within our own heart."

The heart is the symbol for love - the basis for understanding and correcting America's perplexing social problems. The disposition of one's heart in union with many other hearts - to love God (a move toward order), or to love sin, (a move toward disorder), holds on the one hand peace on earth or, on the other, the end of civilization.

Every individual freely decides to fashion his/her heart with love or hate. The inspiration needed to move the will to love others comes from the Holy Spirit, not from Science or public schools or from Congress. Love is God's gift, free for the asking. Prayer, reason and conscience play their part.

Faith in God is the first step at this juncture where hate and studied ignorance about God's Truth is widespread. Now may be our last chance to take that step.

It is said that change is the only thing constant in life. Along with knowledge God has revealed, we have acquired a vast amount of material knowledge, which is a great accomplishment. However, like undisciplined Humanist Man out of the 14th century Renaissance, we claim credit for the products of our mind and hands. Filled with arrogant pride, sloth and other sins, we reject or curse God as the One who forbids and the One who causes suffering. As the comic character

Pogo said: "we have met the enemy and they are us." Pogo is long gone, arrogance is not.

President Ronald Reagan called the Soviet Union an evil empire - a ticking bomb. We live in an evil time.

From other Letters to the Editor dated October 14, 2001 -

Another date becomes an American marker

Shocking, revolting, disbelief! Just three little words that struck America on Tuesday, Sept. 11, 2001.

As we memorized important dates in American history, while in school, we can now add another date to the list of important events that tell the story of our country and her up and down days.

My first reaction was of fear and a very deep anger. I wanted to destroy every Arab state in the world and send all Arab people back to their native countries. Islam also came to the top of my list as an enemy. This, of course, would have been an act of stupidity. The Islam faith does not preach violence and there are millions of Arabs born in this country who love America as I do.

Now comes the sixty-four thousand-dollar question. Why did Almighty God allow this to happen? We have spent billions of taxpayer's money and have given up the lives of millions of our men and women in defense of freedom around the world. Is this to be our thank you? The answer to the first question is very simple. He (God) didn't allow this to happen. We did.

The American people allowed this to happen by refusing to rid our entertainment industry of the filth we find on television, on the movie screen, radio and in our reading materials. We allowed this to happen when we took God out of our schools and stripped our institutions of the Ten Commandments. We aren't allowed to offer a simple prayer at a high school football game because of the fear that we might offend some pea brain who has a different thought about religion. We allowed this to happen by re-electing officials who had proven themselves unworthy of public trust.

Just five years ago America watched as one of our major political conventions met to renominate their candidate for a second term president of the United States. The wrath of that convention was brought down upon those of faith and they were called right-wing religious extremists. These were some of the same people, who three years later, turned our nation's capital and the White House into a gigantic mess. We were the laughing stock of the world.

Every time we refuse to stand up on the side of right over wrong we invoke the wrath of God and hand Satan (and the Ideology of Denial) another victory.

As I complete this, I have a vision of our flag flying high, although dirty and torn, with pride. I hear her stars and stripes cry out, "We are down on bended knee but not out!" God bless America.

R.L.S

The priorities of Western democracies, and of the United States as their showcase, have moved away from God-fearing and into the kind of risk-taking described in the letter above published in the Goshen newspaper one month after the terrorist attack in New York. Indifference to or denial of the reality God made (and apathy toward immorality) is authentic. The consequences are recorded in letters and articles throughout the chapters of this book.

Again: The Son of God gifted mankind with unity and solidarity in the Holy Spirit so we could silence ticking bombs. Solidarity is absent and depression is widespread at this historic moment in the 3rd millennium of Christ's time.

Fast-forward 5-years: I read a letter by Rev. Andrew Wollman in the "Pastor's Pen" column of the Goshen, Indiana newspaper that makes a point similar to my own -

March 17, 2007

He never promised us a rose garden

Recently the Los Angeles police received a phone call from comedian Richard Jeni's girlfriend. She screamed, "My boyfriend shot himself in the face!" He died later at a hospital. He was 49. The police think it was a suicide, although it's still under investigation.

Jeni was considered by his colleagues as one of the best in the business. He's been on The Tonight Show with Johnny and Jay, as well having appeared in several movies and sitcoms.

Let's assume for a moment that this is ruled a suicide. Do you see the irony? What would make a man who was obviously very talented at making other people laugh want to kill himself? It makes me wonder how many other funny people are out there wearing the same mask?

The statistics are staggering. According to US News and World Reports via USNews.com, "In any one year period, 9.5 percent of the population, or about 18.8 million American adults, suffer from a depressive disorder." In addition, "The economic cost of these disorders is high - some estimates put the annual workplace cost of depression in America at more than $40 billion. But the cost in terms of human suffering is incalculable.

Almost 10 percent of us are depressed. My guess is that those numbers, as staggering as they are, will only rise. The future will only bring more depression, more misery, more suffering. Not very hopeful sounding, am I? The truth is, I have a great deal of hope; just not in this world. While I'm not opposed to efforts to try to make things better - we should do all we can to make this world a pleasant place to live, love, work and play. But at the same time, I am a realist, and my realism comes from the creator of this world.

Contrary to the false teaching of the pre-millenialists, Jesus is not promising to return to rule this earth for a literal 1,000 years where there will be health, wealth and prosperity for all who stay to rule with him. On the contrary, Jesus promised that things are only going to get worse (Matt. 24:7,22). This world's sin would seep so deep in the soil, that there would be no escaping its infestation.

Ever seen kudzu? I don't think there's much of it around here; but when I lived in North Carolina in the mountains, I saw a great deal of it. It's a very green fat-leafy vine that spreads and takes over acres of land. It will cover anything that gets in its way. This is the way of sin. This is the kind of world we are to expect. This is why I'm a realist; because I trust the words of my Lord. As the old cliché goes, he never promised us a rose garden. We had a beautiful garden once, but we chose death over beauty.

And while we're not to expect the roses any more, we can expect the thorns. Imagine being handed a bouquet of rose stems, with the flowers cut off; that's what Adam has given us. And we took that bouquet of thorns, fashioned it into a crown, and shoved it upon our Lord's head as a reminder of just how sinful we have become.

Jesus made it very clear that he intends to return just once (Heb. 9:28; Matt. 25:31-32) and for one reason only. Not to hang around for another 1,000 years being an earthly ruler, trying to keep his promise to the Jews that he somehow failed to keep the first time around. This is the befuddled thinking of men, not the teaching of our Lord. Jesus never failed at anything in his life. (My comment: He didn't fail with Moses or the prophets; and, He didn't fail with Peter.)

No. He made it very clear that his kingdom was not of this world (John 18:36). He came to this sin-infested, depression-filled world to declare himself our spiritual king (1Tim. 1:17). He doesn't lead us into battle over any oppressive government, but into battle over the sin that desires to oppress and possess our hearts (Gen. 4:7; 1Cor. 10:3-5). It's a more important battle and a more important king.

Please ignore the theologically oppressed that call themselves televangelists. For most of them would have you believe that God promises health, wealth and prosperity if only you have enough faith, or if you only send them enough money. Either way it's a lie.

Jesus promised that your world would be one where depression is the norm; where sin rules the day; where troubles and afflictions cannot be avoided (Matt. 10:16; John 16:33). And the miracle is that it is in this kind of world that he willingly came to give us hope. Not hope for this world, for Adam took care of that, but hope in this world for the world to come.

As you meander through the muck and mire of sin in and around you, keep your eyes fixed on Jesus, the author and perfecter of your faith, who for the joy set before him, endured the cross, scorning its shame, and sat down at the right hand of God's throne (Heb. 12:2). For we do not have an earthly king, but a king who came to our sinful earth, enabling him to sympathize with our weaknesses.

He has been tempted in every way, just as we are, yet without sin. You can approach his throne of grace with confidence then, knowing full well that there will always be the necessary mercy and grace awaiting you there (Heb. 4:15-16 Rev. 22:20).

Unlike people who change, God (being perfect) does not change. He sympathized with His people in ancient Egypt and He sympathizes with you now as you meander through the "muck and mire of sin."

God the Father appointed Moses to deliver His people from bondage and make His Commandments known to them. Peter was appointed by God the Son to preserve, defend and teach the Commandments without error through the intercession of God the Holy Spirit.

The history and Divine Tradition of the Catholic Church leaves little doubt that, from the muck and mire of sin, an organization possessing God's authority did rise up to shepherd His people for all time.

Recall the first stanza of the Arabian/Chinese proverb: "He who knows not, and knows not that he knows not is a fool; shun him." This was a popular maxim in medieval societies during (and prior to) the thirteenth century. Today polite society treats foolish people as equals and goes them one better. Modern society blinds itself to truth (with a capital "T").

Secular societies favor the bad idea that man's earthly existence is without meaning or purpose, i.e. unplanned. Modern secular societies function as though right and wrong behavior is for government alone to control. Consequently, books on rule by Civil Law make up the largest Dewey decimal classification in the Library of Congress, because rule by man must cover loopholes too numerous to count.

The Ten Commandments were inscribed by God the Father on two stone tablets. Authentic Christian explanation of the inscriptions is so simple as to be contained in one book, the Catechism of the Catholic Church. Rule by God has no loopholes, contrary to the belief of Cafeteria Christians.

Not only does rule by man take a library of books, but man's laws are unable to (and never will) motivate citizens to love their neighbors. Love of self (Individualism) will always interfere.

Modern secular societies are best characterized in three isms,

Hedonism, Consumerism and (their keystone) Individualism. If guilt is meaningless isn't it foolish not to grab all the pleasure one can, particularly sexual pleasure, and power (political, corporate, etc.), and riches (Enron) without concern for others. Consequences of this free-for-all are depression, from AIDS and seventy other sexually transmitted diseases, from abortion, infanticide, euthanasia and on and on.

The fabric of life is woven with sins. The fabric of modern life displays a grotesque pattern of students murdering other students (and teachers).

We would do well to note that students and teachers murdered at Virginia Tech in April 2007 were twice the number murdered at Columbine High School in April 1999; and, STD's are now four times as numerous with free love as when "free love" was not listed in the dictionary (see the 3872 page Oxford English Dictionary, published in 1971).

The "Big Bang" in moral bankruptcy has sounded.

CHAPTER 14

EDUCATION IN THE UNITED STATES

On October 20, 1998 the House was preparing to vote to appropriate the $500 billion Budget Surplus (H.R. 4328). Programs were promised to repay the federal debt owed to Social Security and to cut taxes. We know about this lie. It was disclosed in a Readers Digest article titled "The Great 1999 Budget Rip-Off" (Feb. 1999 issue).

Included in the total budget was a $1.1 billion down payment President Clinton wanted for his plan to hire 100,000 additional school teachers to stem the failure of public schools. Failure of public schools to adequately educate students was documented 35- years earlier in The (James) Coleman Report, and every year thereafter by other sociologists who replicated Coleman's study. The studies showed: "Per-pupil spending and teacher/student ratio do not have a significant impact on student achievement scores." This was known in 1965 the year Congress passed the Higher Education Act enabling the federal bureaucracy to eventually control public education.

Not the least of persuasive (emotional) arguments for federal control, particularly of Higher Education, was the success in the 1960's of the Soviet Union in beating us into outer space. We won the race to outer space. The Higher Education Act was not a factor.

Cause of failure of public education was labeled Progressive Education in 1978 (and earlier). Progressive Education is an outgrowth of John Dewey's Theory of Instrumentalism, published in 1909. Public school students are given no moral code except a relative one.

Failure of today's politically correct government to improve education was discussed in a 3-part article by Max Rafferty published in 1978 in The Republic newspaper. The first article in the series is reprinted here -

The Decline and Fall of American Public Education

Rome's fall had many causes, but at the heart of it was moral bankruptcy. So it is with American public education. One cancer is central to its morbidity.

Around 1900, a psychologist named William James developed what came to be called the Pragmatic Method. It wasn't really a philosophy, but rather a critique of experience.

Briefly, it maintained that the value of anything is to be found only in terms of its "usefulness" or "actual consequences." It denied the existence of "absolutes" of any kind. It attacked any attempt to explain life in terms of the supernatural or the religious.

Here began the Decline and Fall: This was the seed.

Shortly after this a philosopher (and atheist), John Dewey, seized upon this concept and developed from it the theory of Instrumentalism, which was the parent of the malignity called Progressive Education. In my time, I watched it become "life adjustment" education, "modern education," or what you will - the name changed with the shifting winds of public opinion. The cancer remained the same.

It holds that thought is simply a method of meeting difficulties - that it arises out of a constant stream of new situations which require an infinite series of productive responses - that its goals are wider experiences and the solving of problems.

Over the years, my profession adopted this gorgon. To Dewey, knowledge equals experience. There are no self-evident truths, no universal verities of any kind.

Problem solving begins with the truth about the problem. Atheists use the Ideology of Denial as a their starting point.

To Dewey, anything in life that satisfies a want is a "good." Otherwise the word has no meaning.

The implications of all this are obvious. If one concedes that "good" and "evil" have no higher connotation than satisfying or failing to satisfy an individual "want" or "need," then it follows inexorably that there can be no positive standards for child behavior, no moral code except a relative one.

Dewey's pragmatism held the main goals of education to be: To aid the child to live the life of the "peer group" and, to enable him to "adjust" to unknown and constantly changing environmental conditions.

Nothing here, you will note, about "basic essentials" of knowledge. Nothing about culture or teaching children to use the intellectual tools which the human race, over the centuries, has always found to be indispensable in pursuit of truth. Or even simple literacy, for that matter.

I charge the American education establishment, over the decades, with buying this turkey.

I charge it with still cherishing this zombie, no matter how many kids emerge from its clutches illiterate and ignorant.

Rafferty has an M.A. in Education from UCLA, and an Ed. D. from the University of Southern California. He headed the California Educational System from 1963 to 1971, where he championed what he called Education in Depth, a system he described in his book titled, Suffer Little Children (1962).

By 1975 Student Test Standards were being lowered routinely, re- normed to avoid embarrassing public school administrators and teachers. Standards for measuring the quality of elementary education in public schools throughout America are even lower today.

Six years after The Decline and Fall of American Public Education was published I wrote the following letter, printed February 15, 1984 in the Columbus, IN newspaper, The Republic -

Dear Editor:

There are two obvious problems in lowering standards of excellence. One is it is taking us in the wrong direction. The other is the injustice it does to those who are truly excellent. There are other problems too, which are not obvious.

The Columbus North listing of honor roll students published Wednesday in The Republic is an example of lower standards of excellence.

The latest qualifications for Honor Roll are a grade point average of B-plus or better, with no grade lower than C-minus.

Forty years ago a student needed to earn A's in every subject to qualify for the Honor Roll.

It is also a fact that today A's are easier to earn with multiple choice and true/false questions, and grading on the curve.

Don't expect me to be persuaded that North is an outstanding High School by an Honor Roll containing the names of roughly one-fourth of the student body. I am more likely to question the honesty and integrity of some of the school administrators, or their intelligence.

What I see here is simply another form of permissiveness - giving students honors they have not earned.

And permissiveness, being the opposite of discipline, is not what I expect from a school system for which I am required to pay. >

The following paragraphs are taken from another of my "education" letters. It was published the same year. At the time the proposed constitutional amendment to allow organized prayer in public schools was being debated in the Senate. I wrote -

"The least I want from public schools for which I help pay, particularly those here in Columbus (IN), is that they teach truth impartially. They now offer the oxymoron 'relative morality' according to Dewey, Skinner, Freud, Kinsey, etc. I want equal time given to real morality according to Jesus, Aquinas, Augustine, etc.

They offer 'How to succeed temporarily', as a mechanic, a computer operator, a bookkeeper, etc. I want equal time for How to succeed permanently, in eternity.

Public schools teach students to use tools (microscopes, etc.) to discover wonders they never knew existed. I want them to teach students to use prayer to discover other wonders that are just as real, and much more important for useful education."

By the end of the 20th century politically correct Public Schools had indoctrinated two generations of students in a secular doctrine that denies part of Natural Law and denies that God's Word is absolute Truth; but, arrogantly adds, "if such truth exists it is unknowable." This elevates mankind above God, but does not prepare Modern Man for the painful discovery that, instead of gaining more freedom and dignity, he feels smaller and smaller. He ends in a state of low esteem and despondency. He eventually loses interest in the country, in family and (for a few) in his own life.

Our ancestors had common sense. They knew what comes from

allowing the government to do for them the duties they are responsible for doing themselves. The "Great Society" of President Lyndon B. Johnson has consumed more than $7 trillion (much of it on "life adjustment" education) in an effort to pamper voters. We are spoiled because our elected and appointed leaders forgot the wisdom and teaching of our ancestors. Government policy in the 1990's sacrificed common sense and Common Good for poll ratings.

Wisdom teaches that nations fall when a majority of the citizens choose their own truth. The reason is unbearably simple. Man cannot dictate right and wrong for himself, because he did not make himself. His maker alone has that privilege, and the final word on the manner in which he conducts his life. He must go God's way simply because that is the way God made humanity to work. For however long a nation's leaders - it's educators, journalists, intellectuals, etc. are permitted to teach our children, and to indoctrinate us with secular humanism, and to promote subjective truth, that is how long our social problems and our individual problems will continue to build. This judgment is not on the state of souls, which is in the hands of God, but on immoral actions and the suffering they cause. Tolerating moral bankruptcy imperils the nation. That which imperils the nation imperils our children and vice versa.

A review of American history shows a system of free Public Schools in many of the American colonies (as early as 1642 in Massachusetts). Virginia and the Carolinas were the exception.

When asked what course was taken in Virginia for instructing the people in the Christian religion, then Governor Berkley said, "The same that is taken in England, out of towns, every man, according to his ability, instructing his children." So far as the state of Virginia was concerned the family is responsible for the education of it's children in morality, grammar and the rudiments of elementary knowledge. (The quotaton above is from a section of the Encyclopedia Americana Vol. 22, pages 774-78 copyright 1953.)

This time-tested idea was honored by state governments until after the Civil War.

Development of a system for free elementary education in the U.S. is a complex issue. It is small wonder that histories of our Public School

System found in encyclopedias and other reference books vary widely in content. For example a book published in 1999 by Transaction Publishers, Somerset, NJ, titled, Market Education: The Unknown History, by Andrew Coulson, discusses the role philanthropic societies played in American "free" education.

Sentiment in the U.S. in 1850 was opposed to State Boards of Education and other efforts by state legislators to monopolize their power over education. Coulson quotes from the Education Subcommittee of Massachusetts 120 years ago: "The establishment of the Board of Education seems to be the commencement of a system of centralization and monopoly of power in a few hands, contrary, in every respect, to the true spirit of democratic institutions, and which unless speedily checked, may lead to unlooked-for and dangerous results."

Coulson's book documents the importance of early and continuing philanthropic support in developing the education systems, private and public, we enjoy today. The "free" schools which existed 150 years ago were not the only schools. A wide range of independent, religious, and district schools were available which met the need families had, not the need of Government, to provide a complete education for their children. Church control was willingly accepted; government control, no way! How America has changed!

District schools were spaced 2-miles apart throughout the rural areas of America. They provided free education to children of poor families funded by taxation and philanthropy.

Fees of other students were low and the quality of education was high due in part to market competition.

Literacy in the pre Civil War era was surprisingly high for both men and women. Alexis de Tocqueville (1805-1859), a well-known French statesman and author, visited the United States and wrote eloquently about his findings. The following quote describes a highly literate America: "It was rare to find a New Englander who had not received an elementary education, and who was not well-versed in the history and Constitution of the United States."

The population of North America grew from 39-million in 1850 to 106- million in 1900, the highest rate of growth of any 50 year period in American history according to the Encyclopedia Americana.

After the Civil War, funding and control of public education moved gradually from the family to local and state governments. Rapid growth in population put greater pressure on government to help. Assistance meant taxation. It was right that legislators in each state lay down the conditions with which their school districts must comply in order to enjoy financial aid. It was also natural that conditions laid down (in order to be fair) must have the following characteristics: (1) Public schools must be free to all families; (2) they must extend over all stages of education; (3) they must have what was called the "educational ladder," that is, pupils must be able to pass upward freely from one stage to the next higher; and, (4) they must be patronized by all classes of the community. Rules governing minimum number of school days per year, courses of study that must be taught, and certification of teachers in subjects prescribed by the state were also dictated by legislators in each state.

State governments continued for another 80-years to respect the needs and spiritual values of the family with regard to education. But trouble was brewing. Immigrants who arrived in the 1860's, 1870's and 1880's settled in the predominantly Protestant Northeast. They were mostly Catholics from Ireland and England who were, in culture and language, essentially similar to Northeastern Americans. Immigrants who arrived in the 1890's were mostly Catholics from Eastern and Southern Europe. They were Serbs, Hungarians, Poles and Italians. They were a different culture and were not able to speak English. Also, they were unskilled laborers arriving at a time of profound economic change.

Anti-Catholic prejudice, endemic in American culture, spread like a cancer to damage the quality of modern education in the U.S.

Support for my point, that anti-Catholic prejudice is a "cancer" in education, is found in the following report from the newspaper Today's Catholic published on March 22, 1998. The reporter is Robert Delaney -

Public schools lack moral direction, legal scholar says

Changing America's education system to accommodate parents' desire for reinforcement of their religious values may be the only way to save public schools, according to author and legal scholar Stephen L. Carter.

The greatest danger to the survival of public schools is if they lose popular support as a result of continuing to stonewall parental wishes regarding curriculum and moral instruction, Carter tells those who attend his lectures.

Author of the popularly acclaimed 1993 book, "The Culture of Disbelief," published by Anchor Books, NY, Carter wrote and currently lectures about the concerns of religious parents who have waged bitter battles over the teaching of values in public school classrooms.

His views on the public school issue were a key component of his talk opening the University of Detroit Law School's McElroy lecture series.

"A majority - a strong majority - of public school parents say they would send their children to private schools, if they could afford it," Carter told about 400 people who filled SS. Peter and Paul Church in Detroit Feb. 18 to hear the first lecture.

"Of parents who have children in private schools, 89-90 percent choose religious schools," he said. Parental wishes, however, run up against an attitude that religion is relatively unimportant, and against laws "established almost entirely from the point of view of the needs of the state," he said.

Laws established to meet the needs of the state is better expressed as laws established to satisfy the need elected officials have to be re-elected.

Carter said the needs of the family should take precedence over those of the state.

Those who resist any accommodation for religious instruction on the basis that public schools were founded upon noble ideals of nonsectarianism and that there should be a common school for all children are simply perpetuating a myth, according to Carter (and according to the Encyclopedia Americana).

The truth, he said, is that the drive to establish public schools only really got under way in the 19th century as a reaction to "immigration - substantial immigration and the fear of all these immigrants bringing over 'foreign religions,' by which was meant Roman Catholicism and Judaism."

Public support of religious schools, Carter said, was not uncommon until anti-Catholic prejudice came into play. "Only when Roman Catholic schools were established did they come up with it being unconstitutional to give public money to religious institutions," he said.

Rather than being rooted in the early days of the Republic, the idea "rests on a principle that was created out of whole cloth about a hundred years ago to destroy the Catholic schools," Carter said.

Even worse than refusing to teach what parents want their children to be taught is teaching the children things parents consider objectionable, according to Carter.

He pointed to a New York case in which the state Supreme Court ruled a child could only opt out of a sex education class if the parents agreed to teach the same material at home.

"The decision conscripts parents into raising the type of children the state wants to have," he said.

Carter, who is Episcopalian, said he and his wife send their two children to an Episcopal Church-run school "precisely because we have no intention to get into a fight with school administrators over sex ed."

Nevertheless, he said he counts himself an opponent of organized prayer in public schools because it would likely be "watered-down nonsectarian prayer."

Instead, Carter asked what would be wrong with public schools having chapels in which children of various religious backgrounds could go for prayer and instruction in their family's faith tradition?

A nation that truly values diversity ought to be able to allow space for different religions, he said (my italics).

"The United States is the only industrialized country in the world that does not have some form of support for religious schools."

Far from being elitist, Carter said, religious schools are better when it comes to educating children with behavior problems. "The Catholic schools do better than any other institution in teaching children from very weak family backgrounds. How it's done isn't clear, but that it's true is a fact."

Evidence is well-documented that private and parochial schools, Catholic schools in particular, have achieved significantly better results educating children of uncaring parents than present-day public schools, and at lower costs. The conclusion a God-fearing American draws is a take-off of Rafferty's quotation: "The seed of high quality education is affirmation of Absolutes, which is paramount to moral and mental health." This conclusion is rudely dismissed by many influential people, by some courts, by the TV industry and the mainstream media, and public school planners, those who today use the power of their representatives in Congress, and the President, to keep religion out of public education.

A hundred years ago organizations such as the Ku Klux Klan, bitterly anti-black and anti-Irish, and the American Protective Association, bitterly anti-Catholic, advocated closing Catholic schools and assimilating their students into Public schools. Popular opinion in the early 1900's was solidly against government aid to Catholic schools. The Catholic Educational Association, a voluntary organization, was founded in 1904 to safeguard the interests of Catholic education.

The protest against "Catholic" education broadened in time to separate Church from State. Dewey's Instrumentalism began to take over the thinking of a few influential public school planners in the 1920's. Whether the intellectual faction saw Instrumentalism and progressive education as opportunities to advance their ideology of denial no one on the outside can know.

Pre-Depression legislators resisted attempts to impose government control over "public" education except for narrow restrictions listed earlier. Reading, writing and arithmetic were emphasized. Schooling in morality remained a natural interest of government prior to World War II. However, a small group of secular zealots were busy choosing ways to ban morality from "public" schooling.

The attention of Americans during the 40's was on World War II, and thereafter, Americans (and the world) were intent on putting their lives back together. It is said that Americans experienced a moral let-down - an easing away from the authority and stress of war times. Television offered distractions and relaxation in abundance.

Basic discipline gave way to a more permissive attitude of teaching in the 70's and 80's. Students' attention and care, formerly required to earn high grades, gradually eased. Homework assignments were reduced. Quizzes no longer contained questions to be answered in sentences, paragraphs, or short compositions. Students were offered a wide range of alternate courses hostile to religion such as "Values Clarification" and Bioethics.

Public schools in the 80's and 90's lost much of their base of parental support enjoyed for nearly 150-years. The loss was due primarily to the refusal by public school administrators to restore the basics, to employ "good and effective discipline," and most important, to honor the system of religious values students receive from their parents.

The end of the twentieth century saw the reverse of the thirteenth century. Secularism generated peer pressure for collective evil, namely drug addiction, abortions, single-sex marriages, AIDS and young people killing young people.

Education about AIDS

There are many clever disguises public education uses to confuse students about risks existing in the secular culture. Confrontation can be melodramatic, particularly with students who are being taught to dismiss both temporal and eternal consequences of sodomy. As Harry Disston advised, "Express your views in agreement or disagreement."

AIDS is an emotional issue capable of generating closet drama -

The drama opens with a letter in the Goshen newspaper, dated January 8, from Christiana, a high school student. Her letter answered Stephen's letter. Her answer is followed by my letter responding to points Christiana raised. My comment draws input from Darla, followed by my personal letter to Darla, with added comments. Gordon follows with a letter to Darla in A Readers Point of View column in the same newspaper. The drama ends with the commentator's wrap-up, including information supplied by Dr. Robert Gallo, co-discoverer of the AIDS virus, as well as Department of Health information and statistics:

Date: January 8, 1988

Education On AIDS

Dear Editor:

In response to the letter by Stephen Miller, I would like to say that yes homosexuals have been a chief factor in the spread of AIDS, but they are not the only cause.

Scientists believe that the virus first originated in the African green monkey. It was thought to have been spread to man through animal bites and eating tainted meat. The virus was spread throughout Africa mainly by prostitutes, and carried to Europe by I.V. drug users, and to America by homosexuals and I.V. drug users.

I don't think that how or where the virus came from should be the issue now. We need to find a constructive way to fight this deadly disease. Persecution of homosexuals is not going to solve anything. AIDS can be spread to anyone, anywhere, at any time. The only way we are going to be able to fight AIDS is through education and awareness, not misinformation, persecution and ostracizing surrounding AIDS victims. People with AIDS need all the love and support they can get. There has been no reported case of anyone contracting AIDS from loving and caring for an infected person.

I am a member of the Goshen High School bioethics class, and recently we put on a two-hour convocation for the students and parents of G.H.S. We discussed the history of AIDS as well as the spread of infection, the structure of the virus and future consequences of the disease. It was so successful that the two local junior high schools, Bethany and Garrett High School, have asked us to speak to them. This is the best way we know to fight this dreadful disease. By making the public aware of AIDS and educating people in all aspects of the disease and not point the finger of blame to one particular group, we can combat and overcome AIDS.

Christiana

G.H.S. Bioethics student

Commentator: In the twenty years following these "Bioethics" letters public knowledge about "one particular group" is that they have infected hundreds of thousands of innocent women and their babies with terminal AIDS.

Date: January 14, 1988

Comment On Bioethics

Dear Editor:

What is bioethics? A letter in the Goshen News (Jan. 8) told of a Goshen High School bioethics class which sponsored a discussion on AIDS education. The letter criticized another letter because it "pointed the finger of blame" at homosexual people.

Ethics is concerned with moral duty, i.e. the study of right ideals as opposed to wrong ideals. Bio, however, refers to the physical sciences dealing with living bodies. Morality and ethics are concerned with human relationships rooted in our eternal souls, not in our bodies. Since our public high schools are God-less, they cannot and do not consider the soul a vital part of social relationships.

Commentator: Public schools are not permitted to discuss spiritual topics in a meaningful way.

Bioethics is a dangerous example of double-talk, a mixture of sense and nonsense. It is grossly misleading and a waste of taxpayers money to claim education as a product of the GHS Bioethics convocation on AIDS.

If further proof of nonsense is needed the writer said in her opening paragraph, "Yes, homosexuals have been a chief factor in the spread of AIDS." She added later, "The only way we are going to be able to fight AIDS is through education and awareness, not by ostracizing AIDS victims. By making the public aware of the disease, and not point the finger of blame to one particular group, we can combat and overcome AIDS." Nonsense.

Assume for the sake of argument you or your bioethics class have something of value to say. I am not listening. Address the "one particular group" that will cause 90-95 percent of all new cases of AIDS. Address homosexuals who have tested positive and continue to infect their sexual partners.

Robert Jefferson

A letter from Darla, Christiana's classmate
Date: January 22, 1988

That's Education

Dear Editor:

I would like to address the comments of R. Jefferson in regard to the GHS bioethics class and AIDS. Mr. Jefferson seems to feel the class is of no value or social consequence.

I, for one, laud the educators and administrators who had the wisdom and foresight to see the necessity of such a class. Education exists not only as rote memorization of formulas, dates and statistics. Facts do not exist in isolation. Education is also the evolution of a mind which, when given such facts, can process them and form an opinion, create an idea or solve a problem. This, Mr. Jefferson, is known as thinking.

In a free society such as ours, the role of educators is to inspire as well as instruct, to foster questions as well as ask them, to draw out "why's," "why not's" and "what ifs." In this premise lies the difference between education and indoctrination.

We need go no further back in history than the era of Hitler's Nazism to realize the dire consequences of an indoctrinated mob, unable to think or form opinions for themselves. How different, perhaps, the course of history might have been, had but one Nazi youth questioned "Why?" of his leader.

The bioethics student is to be commended for her level-headed attitude towards the AIDS epidemic. She exhibits a compassionate understanding of the true issues at hand, i.e. AIDS is not a "we-they" disease as some would like to think. No one "deserves" to get cancer, emphysema or diabetes.

Classes such as Bioethics are also to be commended for helping to dispel some of the fear that leads to the misunderstanding of the disease. Once this fear is conquered we may begin to reach out to find answers and cures. Hopefully, these students will come to understand AIDS victims as people who need compassion, not judgment, for even Christ walked among the lepers. While there are those in the community concerned with condemnation for many of the victim's sins, are they themselves falling prey to the sin of omission involving the greatest commandment of all? "And now abidith faith, hope, charity, these three; but the greatest of these is charity." (1 Corinthians 13:13).

Date: January 24, 1988

Dear Darla:

My first thought after reading your response to my letter on your Bioethics class is, you misunderstood my meaning. Please allow me another try. But first remove all thoughts of AIDS, which is a minor issue next to education.

Education concerns the development of minds, usually in an institution of learning. Indoctrination is a technique of repetition used to teach a principle or doctrine. It is also a useful tool for spreading propaganda. As you pointed out indoctrination can have dire consequences. I agree. In my letter I said education, specifically the technique of education called Bioethics, can have terrible consequences. AIDS education in a public school is one example. Obviously you do not agree.

Consider the discipline called ethics. What is it? It is the teaching of philosophers and theologians dealing with moral duties and obligations. Ethics deals with Right and Wrong. If God is omitted in teaching ethics, and man alone is the absolute authority for Right and Wrong, we have the potentially dangerous Situation Ethics classes taught in public schools today. Use of the modifying prefix bio, together with the locale, a public high school, tells me techniques wholly separated from religious doctrines are used to teach ethics. As I said in my letter to the Editor, "a mixture of sense and nonsense."

Think about reality this way: Reality is like a coin. It has two sides. Unlike a coin the two sides are not equal in value. The Goshen High School Bioethics class is real. And, as its name implies, it does have two sides - bodies (without souls) and ethics. If the institution of learning were to permit free discussion of the spiritual soul, wherein Right and Wrong (Ethics) acquires true meaning, the end result is education. If man exercises absolute authority over Right and Wrong (Situation Ethics in the GHS Bioethics classroom), the end result is indoctrination of the type you warned about. It is a mixture of sense and nonsense. I hope this makes clear my concerns about your public high school Bioethics class. >

Added Comments: The perception Christiana and Darla (perhaps most of the GHS Bioethics students) have of "AIDS people" obviously does not come from their own experiences. The same might be true for the teacher. The students are young and emotional, easy prey. Public school teachers are instructed about AIDS from government approved pamphlets. All of the minds (students, teachers and pamphlet writers) are passively open to AIDS propaganda delivered on TV news programs, "talk shows" sitcoms and by president Carter's Federal Agency for Public Education.

Commentator: A maxim used by the Agency for Public Education is: "There are no correct answers to controversial, i.e. moral issues. Solutions for moral issues are inherently subjective and opinion-based."

At best the maxim shows what Liberalism is all about - God's Truth matters little, Civility matters the most.

Notice the liberal-minded AIDS "messages" contained in the letters written by Christiana and Darla: (1) "AIDS victims are people who need compassion not judgment." (2) "No one deserves to get AIDS." (3) "By making the public aware of AIDS and educating people in all aspects of the disease; and, not pointing the finger of blame to one particular group, we can combat and overcome AIDS." (4) "AIDS can be spread to anyone, anywhere, at any time."

These are familiar points sanctioned by agencies of the federal government, by Gay Rights advocates, by secular media managers and by our postmodern American culture. TV viewers know and repeat "as rote memorization of formulas" (Darla's words) useless ideas for constructively fighting the AIDS epidemic.

Gordon's letter preceded mine. It presents the other side of the AIDS coin. His perception of the AIDS problem is real. It brings to mind a quotation: "In the face of this broadmindedness, what the world needs is intolerance."

Date: January 23, 1988

Another look at Bioethics

Dear Editor:

I have been reading the letters pro and con, concerning the bioethics class at GHS and can hold my peace no longer. It just plain disgusts me, as a Christian, to read something with a "love" scripture thrown in at the end, and the rest contradicts God's word. Such, I feel, is the case with the letter of Darla, dated Jan. 22.

It seems Ms. ... idea of education and mine differ greatly. She stated "facts do not exist in isolation." That statement makes absolutely no sense to me. If a person knows something to be true, he knows a fact. However, just because one person knows a fact, doesn't mean that millions of people will live their whole life and never know that fact. Also, who on this earth is God, and has all the answers? Just because man doesn't know or understand a certain thing, doesn't mean that he never will. But until he does, that fact exists in isolation for him.

Then, Ms. ..., you tried to tell the difference between education and indoctrination. You stated, "In our free society" education lies in "educators drawing out the why's and why-not's" in students and "inspiring and instructing them." I ask you, if our federal and state government (Voice: Influential men and women.) tell the educators what to answer to those "why's and why-not's," is that education or indoctrination? In the bioethics class, which you defended, how do you educate people about AIDS, which baffles even the scientific world. The dormant stage of this incurable disease can be up to 15 years. A second strain was just found, the surgeon general said he's afraid of not finding a cure, and scientists and doctors are not settled on the "fact" that condoms are a safe alternative. How do you educate without facts? You don't. You indoctrinate.

Then Ms. ..., you said, "it's not a we-they disease." You also said, "no one deserves AIDS, cancer, emphysema or diabetes." The CIA report on AIDS (Goshen News, Dec. 21, 1987) stated "the vast majority of AIDS victims are either homosexual, bisexual or IV drug users." That sounds pretty we-they to me. Just because every single victim is not one of these, doesn't throw out the "fact."

Also, if I drive around a warning sign that says "Bridge Out," I deserve to sit in the water. The side of the cigarette package says smoking causes cancer. Researchers say that AIDS can be transmitted sexually, especially in homosexual and bisexual relations, and in IV drug use. If you don't take heed to the facts, you not only deserve the consequences, you are asking for them. I agree that there are those who "don't deserve" AIDS, but they are far less in number than those who "don't deserve" to die in accidents caused by drunk drivers. But who is waving the banner in their name? Hardly anyone, because society has become use to drunkenness.

And then Ms. ..., you opened a can of worms by saying "even Jesus walked among the lepers." That is a fact and you also probably know where the lepers were. They weren't down on Main Street parading for leprosy victim rights. No ma'am! They were cast out of the city because leprosy was contagious and incurable. They even had to shout "unclean, unclean," if anyone came near to them. Nowadays, doctors can't even write AIDS on a victim's charts, so the nurses don't know for sure who has it. It infringes on "the rights of our free society" to have AIDS testing so it's no wonder people live in fear.

And when, Ms. ..., you talked about "the sin of omission of the greatest commandment," you also are omitting something. You omitted the root cause of all these problems, which is sin. Incidentally, Romans chapter I talks about these very things, and Romans is written by the same man who, inspired by God, wrote 1 Corinthians 13:13. However, all these writings by Paul were written to the churches in these places, not to the unbelievers. You see, unbelievers don't know about faith, they have no hope and they don't know God, who is love. >

Commentator: Move forward 10 years. Expensive research programs have not resulted in an AIDS vaccine. Moreover –

AIDS vaccine may be impossible goal
An Associated Press release in the Goshen News
Published on May 14, 1997
WASHINGTON - Medical science may never find a vaccine to protect against the AIDS virus because the infection poses unique problems that may be unsolvable, an expert says.

Although researchers have found vaccines for polio and other diseases, Dr. Robert Gallo, co-discoverer of the AIDS virus, said "nobody can say that we will succeed for sure" in making a vaccine against HIV, the virus that causes AIDS.

Gallo, head of the Institute of Human Virology at the University of Maryland, was a member of a panel of experts at a vaccine symposium Tuesday.

"We have to say it is a serious possibility that we will never succeed with a vaccine against HIV," Gallo said. "We have to be realistic".

Others on the panel did not specifically echo his pessimism, but Dr. Anthony Fauci, head of the National Institute of Allergy and Infectious Diseases, said lack of precise scientific knowledge about HIV is a major stumbling block preventing development of an AIDS vaccine.

Fauci, whose agency takes the lead in AIDS research at the National Institute of Health, said a "full court press" by scientists led to drugs that keep HIV in check once a person is infected. But making a vaccine to protect against the initial infection "has major stumbling blocks."

"There is still a lot of unknowns," he said.

Gallo said that the uncertainty about finding an HIV vaccine has led some people at the World Bank to consider controlling AIDS by treating all of the world's HIV patients with the new and expensive drugs that have been shown to successfully suppress HIV. >

Commentator: Where is the Associated Press evidence that proves, or even suggests that suppressing HIV will control AIDS, an incurable disease with a dormant stage of possibly 15-years?

An alternative to "treating all of the world's HIV patients with the new and expensive HIV suppressing drugs" is the HIV surveillance proposal. This proposal is being considered by the federal Centers for Disease Control and Prevention for use in all the states, as reported in the following article -

Some experts say now is the time to monitor HIV cases by name
Associated Press release by James Burke,
Published in the December 9, 1997 Goshen News.

SEATTLE - The first U.S. decline in new AIDS cases is increasing support for a proposal that was once almost too controversial to discuss: Identifying and monitoring everyone who tests positive for the virus that causes the disease.

Such a shift, now gaining momentum at the state and federal level, would mark a turnaround in public health policy.

In Washington State, public health officials now track only full-blown AIDS cases. Under the new proposal, they would monitor, by name, everyone who tests positive for HIV, the human immunodeficiency virus that causes AIDS, and try to notify their sexual or needle-sharing partners that they have been exposed and may be infected.

The federal Centers for Disease Control and Prevention are asking all states to consider the policy change. Now that new AIDS drugs are keeping people healthier longer, thereby leading to a drop in full-blown AIDS cases, such a change would enable authorities to get more HIV-positive people on the drugs sooner.

"We need to keep our policies in line with new scientific evidence that early notification saves lives," said Alonzo Plough, director of Seattle-King County Department of Public Health.

"Names reporting is the best way for us to keep track of the epidemic and to make sure individuals and infected partners have this information," he said.

This change would also mean that epidemiologists could for the first time enlist traditional public health strategies in the battle against AIDS.

For years the stigma of a disease that primarily infected gay men and injected drug abusers was so great that officials, *at the insistence of the politically powerful gay community*, relied on nontraditional methods such as anonymous testing and treatment. (My italics).

Thirty states already record the names of people who have tested positive for HIV.

In Washington state, for example, reporting by name begins when the patient has clinically defined AIDS, an AIDS related infection or other symptom, or an immune system weakened to below a certain level.

Names reporting has long been used to help contain and combat other dangerous infectious diseases. The state monitors 54 such ailments including measles, tuberculosis, whooping cough, certain types of hepatitis and several sexually transmitted diseases.

Now some health authorities say it's time to add HIV to the list.

They want the freedom to attack AIDS with the traditional tools of public health: Routine testing of large segments of the population, names reporting of those who test HIV positive, and notification of people who may have been infected so that they can get tested for HIV and seek treatment if necessary.

The CDC considers names reporting of HIV the only accurate way to "track the front end of the epidemic," said Judith Billings, Washington state's former top school official and member of the President's Advisory Council on HIV-AIDS.

Billings, who stepped down from her state post after disclosing her own AIDS diagnosis last year, also leads a subcommittee of the Governor's Advisory Council on HIV-AIDS. The group has held five public hearings on HIV names reporting and will report its findings to Governor Gary Locke next month.

Note: Judith Billings was infected with AIDS by a bisexual male. She will pass the virus to her babies.

Molecular Biologists will be the first to realize that AIDS trash a baby's unique Genome package before he/she takes his/her first breath of air. Moreover, AIDS-in-mothers-to-be will lower life expectancy as procreation of the human race runs its course.

Early intervention allows health authorities to stretch limited AIDS-prevention resources, Billings said.

But, as a person with AIDS, she said she understands concerns that it could lead to discrimination in housing, employment and medical care.

"There are plenty of people who went through 10, 12, 15 years of discrimination who are very concerned," Billings said. "And we all know too well that there are some pretty innovative (computer) hackers."

Citing such concerns, the Seattle-based Northwest AIDS Foundation is opposing the proposed change in policy.

"We think HIV surveillance is important, but we think there needs to be an alternative to a name-based system," said Steven Johnson, the foundation's public policy director and a member of the governor's advisory council.

The alternative could be some sort of unique identifier or code numbers that enable officials to track the epidemic without raising patient fears of disclosure, Johnson said.

"The CDC hasn't come down with a definitive position on what they want from the states," he said. "It's unclear if the CDC will ask states to comply with the name-based system or let states do their own surveillance."

The new push for names reporting follows some rare good news in the AIDS epidemic.

Combination-drug therapies - especially a new class of drugs known as "protease inhibitors" - have shown promise in many patients.

In September, the CDC reported the first U.S. drop in new AIDS cases. In 1996, 56,730 Americans were diagnosed with AIDS, down 6 percent from the 60,620 new cases reported in 1995. At the same time, AIDS deaths declined 23 percent, from 50,140 to 38,780.

The new anti-AIDS drugs are expensive and don't work for everyone, but supporters of names reporting say the latest developments are encouraging enough to warrant re-examining public policy.

"We can't tell you what proportion of people who have HIV infection are on effective drugs, or what proportion of those people are even in care systems, because we have no idea who they are," said Bob Wood, AIDS-control officer for the Seattle-King County Department of Public Health.

"If you want to answer those very important questions, we need to have the data," he said. >

To Bob Wood and others in the field, public health officials are negligent if they do anything less than seek out the disease and eradicate it. For them, that means notifying an HIV-positive person's sexual partners, because, "if you leave it to the person it doesn't happen," Wood said.

Wrap-up by Commentator: Moral courage is lacking in your

statement Mr. Associated Press. You reported in the article above, 1st paragraph: "Such a shift, now gaining momentum at the state and federal level, i.e. the issue of identifying and monitoring everyone who tests positive for the AIDS virus, was once "too controversial to discuss?" You omitted the fact that your propaganda made AIDS "too controversial to discuss."

A follow-up plan for the Name-based HIV Surveillance System was discussed in my letter titled, Contagious disease carriers used to be isolated. The letter was published in the Goshen News -

December 15, 1997

Dear Editor:

There are two, possibly three issues where we, as American citizens, should condemn our leaders for gross irresponsibility, i.e. selling the welfare of Americans for personal gain, i.e. votes. One is abortion, partial birth abortion in particular. Another is sodomy, and its contagion AIDS - the subject of this letter.

Refer to an article titled Some experts say now is the time to monitor HIV cases by name, published last week in the Goshen News. According to the AP writer James Burke, there is increasing support for a Centers for Disease Control and Prevention proposal "that was once almost too controversial to discuss." Identifying by name, and monitoring everyone who tests positive for the AIDS virus is being discussed.

Such a shift, according to Burke, "would mark a turn-around in public health policy."

The Associated Press lied. Such a shift simply returns the U.S. to a Health Department policy in effect for more than 100 years, prior to the 1970's.

Earlier policies of state and federal Departments of Public Health were to identify carriers of infectious diseases such as tuberculosis, typhoid fever, etc., isolate them from the public (the Health Dept. called it quarantine) and treat the disease. Where the disease did not respond to treatment, as with tuberculosis, the carrier/patient stayed in isolation. The welfare of the public came first. Moreover, controlling the spread of diseases was basic to protecting the public. (Typhoid carriers lacked assets to buy political favor. Humility would have prevented the thought of "Tc Rights" from entering their minds.)

Compassion for the disease carrier and patient is a valid concern only after the steps to control the disease are implemented. To act otherwise is unconstitutional and stupid, and as a Clinton policy, it is grossly irresponsible.

There is a fundamental difference in the way the HIV virus is spread as compared, for example, to the bacillus responsible for typhoid fever and tuberculosis. The typhoid bacillus is spread unknowingly (by accident, if you will), whereas the male HIV carrier who has been tested positive spreads the virus knowingly, which strengthens my point. >

Bob Wood, the AIDS-control officer for the Seattle-King County Department of Public Health, was quoted in the Dec. 9 AP article. He said, "...public health officials are negligent if they do anything less than seek out the disease and eradicate it." This includes notifying the partners-in-sex used by the male carrier. "If you leave it to the carrier it doesn't happen," said Mr. Wood. The compassion and understanding homosexuals demand for themselves they refuse to give to their "lovers".

I will take the word of Bob Wood for that, because he has experience trying to control sodomy practiced by irresponsible HIV carriers. There are state laws making it a serious crime to knowingly infect a sexual partner with AIDS. The least the HIV Surveillance Proposal would do is make it easier to locate, charge, convict, and hopefully isolate the criminal in a sanatorium. The "Name-Based HIV Surveillance System," plus internment of the male HIV carrier, would reduce the number of slow, expensive deaths.

Mike Huckabee, a Republican candidate nominated to run for the office of President in the November 2008 election was quoted in an article printed in the Goshen News of December 9, 2007: "It is difficult to understand the public policy towards AIDS. It is the first time in the history of civilization in which the carriers of a genuine plague have not been isolated from the general population, and in which this deadly disease for which there is no cure is being treated as a civil rights issue instead of the true health crisis it represents."

Four problems must be addressed to restore quality education in public schools. The first problem is one concerned parents have with the liberal mindset of Democrat members of Congress and a Democrat President (in 1997 and in 2009): "It's broke - we can fix it and make your children better citizens. We will increase your taxes and hire 100,000 new public school teachers to modernize the social conduct and behavior of your children. We will teach your sons and daughters about safe sex and tolerance."

Notice what is conspicuous - federal and state governments put their own needs ahead of needs of traditional families, foremost is eternal happiness for their children. Too many government officials give children of God-fearing parents (and voters) seeds for eternal punishment, namely, indoctrination classes featuring intolerant tolerance, condoms, Bioethics; in short, the religion of Secular Humanism.

The judicial branch of government gives concerned parents worthless seeds - fabricated renderings of the Constitution's Separation of Church and State clause by which courts sanction the religion of Secular Humanism and brush aside Christianity, this nation's religion and the keystone of civilizations.

Tolerance for Godless Secularism promoted by Democrats in government, the secular media, a majority of Supreme Court judges, public schools, etc. is tearing our nation apart.

The second problem deals with what the business community needs from the nation's Public schools. Everyone who applies for a job must have the ability, with minimal on-the-job training, to do the job.

The business community is mainly concerned about poor commitment and about the low quality of technical and business knowledge students receive. Their employees are expected to know how to read and comprehend written and oral instructions. Those employees working in technical positions must know the fundamental principles of physics, chemistry, mathematics, etc. Basic knowledge of accounting, economics, typing, etc. is necessary for employees in business positions. Plus, employees must be disciplined, at least in so far as he or she understands the meaning of duty, justice (a day's work for a day's pay), etc. Finally, employees must be presentable, and free of addictions. These are demands of the business community, not ideals. They are not forthcoming.

Documentation is available, for example a 25 year-old report titled A Nation at Risk: The Imperative for Educational Reform, which was commissioned by the Department of Education with approval of President Reagan. The Commission was chaired by David P. Gardner president of the University of Utah and president-elect of the University of California. The report was released on April 26, 1983.

The third problem is getting parents to unite in their efforts to persuade their representatives in Congress to provide "Vouchers" for their children's education. Allow the consumer to decide which system of values children deserve.

The fourth problem is parents despair as teens drug use grows. The following is a recent study released on August 16, 2007 by Columbia University's National Center on Addiction and Substance Abuse (published in the Goshen News) -

Washington - Teenagers say drug problems at school are getting worse, and parents express doubts about ever making such schools drug free, a new study says.

The percentage of teens who say they attend high schools with drug problems has increased from 44 percent to 61 percent since 2002, and the percentage in middle schools has increased from 19 percent to 31 percent, according to the survey released today.

Four in five teens in high school told researchers they have witnessed the use, sale or possession of illegal drugs on high school grounds, or seen someone who was drunk or high on campus.

Some 13 percent of teens say they had tried marijuana, and 4 percent say they had used it in the past month. Such survey results are often understated because respondents are hesitant to admit their drug use.

The survey also found: About six in ten parents of teens at school with a drug problem say they believe the goal of making that school drug free is unrealistic.

And, most parents, 86 percent, say drinking is a big part of the college experience, but only 29 percent think their own teens will do a lot of drinking in college.

Students who consider themselves popular were more likely to use drugs, drink or smoke than students who do not view themselves as popular.

The survey found 24 percent of teens named drugs as their number one concern, down from 32 percent who listed it as a top concern in 1995.

"It has become such a commonplace experience for teens that their concern about it has come down," said Joseph Califano, the Center's chairman and president. "We've reached a point now in America's high schools where getting high and getting drunk are so common - drugs are now imbedded in the high school experience. And *despair and denial characterizes parents' attitudes* (my italics).

The survey of 1,063 teens from 12 to 17 years old and 550 parents was conducted from April 2 to May 13, 2007 and has a margin of sampling error of plus or minus 3 percentage points for the teen sample and 4 percentage points for the parents. >

Section 2291 of the Catechism of the Catholic Church - "The use of drugs inflicts very grave damage on human health and life. The use, except on strictly therapeutic grounds, is a grave offense. Clandestine production of and trafficking in drugs are scandalous practices. They constitute direct cooperation in evil, since they encourage people to practices gravely contrary to the moral law."

Drugs were not commonplace (dare I say nonexistent) in schools I attended sixty years ago. Drugs were not commonplace in American society prior to the intrusion of Secularism, together with its bastard child Relativism, roughly forty years ago.

Constant exposure to the Ideology of Denial weakened resolve to, as Jiminy Cricket advised, "Let your conscience be your guide."

———————————

Evil is winning the battle as Pope Leo XIII said it would over 100 years ago.

CHAPTER 15

CAPITALISM (amoral?)

You may ask, what's wrong with Capitalism that we need to use a Chapter analyzing it? The heading here questions whether Capitalism lies outside the sphere to which moral judgments apply.

There is nothing wrong with Capitalism. The problem is sinful capitalists - not all, but enough to cause a good thing to become a bad thing. Bringing about and sustaining the Common Good as God wills is the good thing about Capitalism.

We begin the analysis of Capitalism from the beginning -

The design of the universe and its component parts is intended to sustain life that God produces by an act of His will. Human lives are a special case, because each is made in His incomprehensible image.

God revealed that every human life is special. Every person deserves to be treated with dignity by virtue of his/her unique gifts as a child of God, and deserves to live in a dignified manner. We have a duty to be responsible for our actions. Moreover, nations (and governments over them) and economic systems within them shall be responsible for the welfare of individuals and families they serve.

Decision-makers, capitalists in particular, must not interfere with or impede the obligation of workers to provide for their own income, health, safety, old age; and, I will add, must not interfere or impede fathers and mothers in fulfilling their Baptismal vow to educate and provide spiritual guidance for their children.

These are moral judgments involving unselfish regard for the welfare of others.

This chapter applies to Capitalism a claim made in Chapter 3, i.e. the scientific community is unwilling to study (or even admit) the spiritual component in the Common Good. Common Good is a product of the grace and love of God in the lives of selfless men and women who serve their neighbors.

We did not find altruism in modern Science. Will we find it in the economic system known as Capitalism? Does this nation's view of Capitalism contain this all-important spiritual component?

Capitalism: An economic system wherein material wealth is used to create greater wealth. Along-side other economic systems Capitalism has proven itself exceptional in accumulating great wealth for a few people.

The spiritual component in material wealth is nothing new. The Old Testament shows that God's people understood their duty to share their resources with less fortunate members in their communities. Motivation for unselfish devotion to the physical welfare of others was understood to be righteousness. The Hebrew people practiced genuine altruism as evidenced (for example) by their view of usury. Three passages in the Old Testament tell of the Lord warning Moses against doing good for profit.

The New Testament, and in fact the first millennium of Catholic history, added fullness to God's revelation about the spiritual component of material wealth we call distributive justice. The Acts of the Apostles tells how the first Jewish converts to Catholicism lived the lessons Jesus taught: "They devoted themselves to communal life to the breaking of bread and prayers (2,42). Those who believed shared all things in common (2,44); they would sell their property and goods, dividing everything on the basis of each one's need (2,45)." They were truly free.

God's gift of Freedom is often an end in itself. St. Augustine in his youth offered himself freely to be a slave of sin and discovered his soul, although physically indestructible, was spiritually dead.

Catholic scholasticism had, by the thirteenth century, laid a solid foundation for the spiritual life. Human dignity for the individual took precedence over individuals doing whatever they choose. Freedom of Choice was understood to be a gift crafted by God to serve mankind.

Comment: "Me first" is not in God's plan.

During the Renaissance man's relationship with God slowly changed into man's relationship with wealth. Wealth bought (and brought) power to shape one's own life independent of God. Wealth brought freedom from drudgery, a fact often overlooked in considering distractions from the meaning of existence. The poor find comfort and meaning in God. The rich abandon God to find pleasures and meaning in their leisure.

Adam Smith, an 18th century Scotsman and an economist, is credited with the idea from which modern Capitalism evolved. He claimed that distributive justice is properly served where prices, production and distribution of commodities are controlled by competition in a free market. But, Capitalism also makes rich men richer. Wealth exposes "me-first-ism" in sinful men and women. We know the rest of that story.

The Industrial Revolution and Capitalism painted a picture of doom a hundred years ago in England. At the time an alternative to industrial capitalism was tried in separate English communities. One such community was started by Eric Gill in 1913, in Ditchling Common south of Sussex. (Reference: The Servile State by Hilaire Belloc and Eye Witness by Belloc and Cecil Chesterton, both published in 1912).

The Ditchling community followed the Christian model wherein each member was a loving servant of all, a model of distributive justice that had been the norm prior to the Renaissance. Each family owned their own home and a small plot of land around it. The family produced its food and other family needs (clothing, etc.) from their own land. These were G.K. Chesterton's "unique human beings." Each member was a craftsman as well as farmer and seamstress.

Distributionism as a model for accumulating spiritual wealth is poverty-bound - a far cry from Distributionism as a model of an economic system for accumulating material wealth.

Eric Gill and many others in early 20th century England recognized that the way of life under Capitalism was neither normal nor human, and certainly not Christian. Capitalism was seen as an economic system based on inhumane dependency. Gill had read the 1891 encyclical of Leo XIII on industrial justice. Leo XIII's encyclical, Rerum Novarum, dealt with and offered solutions for nearly all of the practical problems and relations in industrial and social life of that time.

Eric Gill was a student of history. He recognized that Capitalism was an outgrowth stemming from Renaissance affluence.

Gill was comfortable with deductive reasoning: Order in the universe implies an orderer > The universe and everything in it is ruled in His name by His appointed authority > The religion must be a world religion, a Catholicism > The Catholic Church is the only institution that professed to rule the whole world in the name of God's instituted authority on earth.

Evidence precedes and supports his reasoning process. Gill had for evidence the "nourishing fruits of Catholicism" rooted in the history of the first millennium - 1000 years wherein success meant living up to one's moral potential in a process completed in heaven.

The book The Victory of Reason: How Christianity Led to Freedom, Capitalism, and Western Science by Rodney Stark, published in 2006 by Random House, New York, documents Christianity's "rational theology" responsible for social progress rooted in personal dignity and property rights.

The message of Jesus, "Love one another as I have loved you," certainly alluded to personal dignity and opened all manner of spiritual accomplishment in distributing goods and in every other field of endeavor. Simple reasoning shows how God's Plan benefited His children (albeit very slowly, since God left the "doing" to sinful man).

Thus, it is not only possible to trace the economic system we know today as Capitalism to medieval Catholics of fourteenth century Venice and Genoa, as professor Stark has done, but also to document Renaissance sins of pride, greed, etc. that make Capitalism the mixed bag it is.

Has Capitalism lived up to its spiritual base? If not, it has lost its value. A world-wide Capitalism, i.e. Globalism, will fail without the kind of selfless love Jesus taught.

The twentieth century witnessed benefits and harm from Capitalism due to just and unjust distribution of wealth acquired through both free enterprise and technology, particularly the $2 trillion largess in medical technology. Sinful men and women made the rules and enforced them.

In 1979 The Hoover Institute Press published The Third Century, a book of essays written by 16 prominent scholars. The editor was

Seymour Lipset. The essayists generally agreed: "We live in a society that has become profoundly lowered, at times debased, in its intellectual and cultural values." This lowering, this debasement is charged to two main causes: First, The decline of the ethic of equality to what is mere egalitarianism and leveling, with all merit going to the lowest common denominator. Second, to the immense power and influence of wealthy, i.e. powerful, people in the media (newspapers, television, motion pictures) all designed largely for the purpose of diverting, gratifying, pleasing popular taste, and at the lowest possible level of intellect. "The consequences of egalitarianism and 'mediocrity' have been, on the record, almost totally destructive of culture and civility." And spirituality.

Again, we can know what the future holds. Both faith in God and natural reason show us the zenith of man's potential - a future of justice and peace everywhere in the world. Without God - a Culture of Death.

Capitalism's strange gods promote devotion to Individualism from its Holy See - the marketplace. Some corporation heads are indifferent to love, the value that makes life truly fulfilling. They use the majority to serve the minority.

Often, but not always. I retired from Cummins Engine Company twenty-five years ago. Its management clearly recognized the value of spiritual qualities in business. Corporate responsibility was spelled out in the Charter of Cummin's Corporate Action Division. It's purpose: "Serve as an in-house resource for understanding the social and political context in which the company does business. Interpret political and social issues, proper corporate policies, and coordinate public affairs programs." Also, "Work with management at all levels to ensure that all business analyses - new plant sites, new ventures, market penetration, product development, functional planning, etc. - include corporate responsibility considerations."

The socially oriented interests of Cummins CEO and the Board of Directors are analyzed by authors Jeffrey L. Cruikshank and David B. Sicilia in their book titled The Engine That Could, published in 1997 by the Harvard Business School Press, Boston, MA.

"A Charter is merely words until the company commits adequate resources (and man-hours) to assure that goals are achieved. Cummins hired an ordained minister who had distinguished himself in the Civil Rights Movement to head the Corporate Action Division. He was appointed at the vice-presidential level and reported directly to the CEO. The division was staffed with qualified educators and other professionals. These are the resources. Evidence of man-hours committed to achieve Division goals can be found in Cummin's "Social Issues Education." Managers were selected from each division of the company and brought into the Corporate Action Division for twelve to eighteen months of training."

Mankind is sinful, but individuals are capable of heroic deeds. The paradox is played-out again and again in corporations, in governments, in wars, in economic systems, in technology, etc., throughout all of history from that of Greece and Rome through the Age of excellence to modern histories of Afghanistan, Iraq and the United States of America.

The problem is not with the economic system conceived by Adam Smith, nor is it with accepted business transactions, or government-run health care, or noble efforts to assist economic growth in third world countries (the International Monetary Fund for example). The problem is St. Augustine's "slaves of sin," in this case slaves of greed, and lust for power. Men and women find ways to misuse the economic system for personal gain. The criminal element finds ways to disguise its unlawful wealth as venture capital.

Souls spiritually dead go to hell. Along their way they create shameful cultures of debt and death.

Changes I have observed going back fifty years indicate that we are moving in the direction of enormous debt and, as discussed earlier, in the direction of wonton destruction of babies.

Years ago, in a conversation with friends, I recall saying that quality of life is declining rapidly, while our high and famous standard of living and the leisure it affords keep increasing. They all agreed.

Request for information (the date was November 10, 1980) -

Russell Kirk, Editor
The University Bookman
New York, NY

Dear Professor Kirk:

There is a favor I would ask of you. I am scheduled to give a 45-minute presentation in February to the Columbus, IN Chapter of the World Futuristic Society. I have been a member of this Chapter for two years and have noted on various occasions its worldly attitude, in spite of the fact that over half of the members are Christians. My topic is "Spiritual Values." I am a Catholic.

It is my belief that all values worthy of our trust are based in theology. Couple this with the concern we have for the welfare of our children - their proper education, and you have the essence of the presentation. I understand from a brief conversation with Msgr. Raymond Bosler, a Catholic theologian (Archdiocese of Indianapolis), that a small effort is under way to promote Christian humanism and morality in the public school curriculum.

I just read your summer 1980 issue of The University Bookman. George Murphy's article, titled Western Science, ended with: "To present Science or Capitalism in the proper context, the Judeo-Christian tradition, may be difficult today, but to ignore the challenge would be to surrender one of the most important legacies of the Christian West."

I am a faithful reader of your articles in National Review. I direct my needs to you, because the thoughts you express in (some of) these articles suggest that you may be involved in the movement Msgr. Bosler mentioned. I would appreciate any suggestion you can offer. Also, do you know anyone in the central Indiana area who might like to have lunch with members of our Chapter, and talk about Christian morality and education in a capitalistic economy dominated by Technology?

Our budget is generally limited to traveling expenses.

Thank you.

Respectfully,
Robert T. Jefferson

January 14, 1981

Dear Mr. Jefferson,

Here I am, responding so tardily to your inquiry of November 10. With my wife and daughters, I was in California for several months; and at Mecosta vast piles of delayed correspondence lie before me; this by way of apology.

The programs of "value preference education" which recently have been introduced into some public schools are in general, as you probably know, virtually useless. Being wholly separated from religious dogma and doctrine, they cannot touch upon ultimate questions. I do not know about the movement Monsignor Bosler refers to. And although I was visiting distinguished professor of history at Indiana University, Bloomington, for some months last spring, I do not know your region well enough, alas, to recommend anyone in your neighborhood as a speaker. As for Christian relationships to the natural sciences, I think the best books for you to consult are those of Stanley Jaki, of the University of Chicago, a great historian of science--who happens also to be a Catholic priest. These all are in print--some from Henry Regnery Company, or rather Regnery/Gateway, Chicago; others from the University of Chicago Press. Just conceivably you might persuade Father Jaki to speak; I do not have his address here with me, but presumably a letter addressed to the University of Chicago would reach him. The name Jaki is pronounced "Yockey".

I am sorry not to be of more help. If other ideas occur to me, I will try to remember to write to you again.

Cordially,

Russell Kirk

Godless morality is acceptable in the secular worldview. It is acclaimed by many intellectuals and educators.

We realize, as Russell Kirk pointed out, that morality opens the door of objective intelligence (reason) to religious doctrines. The National Education Agency, atheists and other power blocs know this as well. Yet they object forcefully, and will never permit that door to open for students in secular schools.

Morality set apart from God is apathetic and nonsense. Professor Kirk raised this point in reference to the uselessness of Values

Preference Education in public schools. The binding authority of God's Will gives morality it's power over man, and gives meaning to His Commandments. Men and women are submissive because these truths are instilled into their hearts. They also make sense. (This was thirty years ago.)

Arrogant pride is widespread today. It causes man to choose to deny the truth of hell hidden deep in his heart and mind.

Why should young adults care about such issues? The answer is obvious. Young adults need to understand, and appreciate that the high standard of living they enjoy was purchased by their grandparents and parents. The cost in many instances was great, measured by sacrifices, attention to duty and frugality. These three qualities suffer from inattention when life becomes one long vacation.

Wealth corrupts the religion of the marketplace as it corrupts other religions. Leaders of Democratic governments possess neither incentive nor ability to resist (media managed) voter pressure driving companies to grow, patients pressure to get well at any cost, and market pressure encouraging consumers to consume. Tougher laws are enacted where CEO's game accounting systems and the nation's President games civil law. Man-made punishment of those who are guilty is inconsistent.

The Religion of the Marketplace

Three basic dogmas in the religion of the marketplace, are given in an article titled The Religion of the Marketplace, by Joseph Tussman Professor Emeritus of Philosophy at the University of California at Berkeley. They are: "The primacy of desire; Creative and saving energy of competition; and, The tolerant inclusiveness of 'Non-judgmentalism'." Professor Tussman's article was published in the September 1999 issue of New Oxford Review.

"Tolerant non-judgmentalism is peace keeping."

"Non-judgmentalism of Marketism rejects the appropriateness of the three great normative categories of Christianity: true/false, good/evil, right/wrong."

The Christian ideal of perfect happiness - the Beatific vision, is replaced by (in Tussman's words) "one great shopping mall with each of us, regardless of color, creed, or sexual preference, a happy shopper holding universally accepted credit cards backed by indulgent bankruptcy laws. Credit becomes a device for nullifying the pangs of suffering due to postponed gratification. Liberal bankruptcy laws forgive debts and shift the suffering from the debtor to the one owed."

"Pursuit of happiness guaranteed in the U.S. Constitution is confused with the pursuit of pleasure. Good is freed from the judgment of reason. Good is merely an object of whimsy."

"Marketism is an act of theological daring." It frees the pursuit of "the satisfaction of desires" from sinfulness. It gives this pursuit legitimacy and "transforms envy and greed into virtues." In an interesting alliance with Individualism, "the religion of Marketism holds not only that the individual is the center of significance, but also that if each person pursues his or her own interests the Common Good of society will surely follow."

The religion of Marketism throws reason out the window. Quoting one of its saints, the 18th century Scottish philosopher David Hume: "Reason is and ought to be the slave to passions, not their judge."

Advertising is secular evangelism. The advertising industry is committed to satiating our sinful natures. Its tools are enticement and seduction. Its gospels are arguments used to deceive. They are arguments that shake the foundation on which freedom of speech rests by claiming an unlimited right to promote Me First ism - again Hume's idea; individual self-interest ought to motivate every conscious act.

"The world is a global marketplace" where primacy of desire for the laity and primacy of profit for the clergy are powerful fuels for avarice - the engine that drives lust for wealth for clergy and hedonism for the laity. Enthusiasm matches that of an old fashioned tent revival. The speaker's platform is occupied by a huckster.

Convenience

Who will deny that generations of Americans are sold on a life of convenience by peddlers hawking their wares day and night in living rooms and mail boxes of practically every home? The Culture of Debt is now at its highest point ($2.43 trillion in the 1990's) and destined to go higher as planet earth becomes a vast sales room accessible via the internet - at best a habit, at worst willful folly, i.e. a distraction from the reality of God.

Perhaps both C.S. Lewis, and G.K. Chesterton had that thought in mind. Lewis likened the potential of the third millennium AD to the reality of the 21st century BC before God revealed himself to Abraham. Chesterton said: "The difference between those who worshipped one God and those who worshipped many gods is not as great as the difference between those who worship and those who don't."

The natural appetite of civilized man is to desire truth, affection, dignity, justice and other qualities under the control of reason. Forget it! Man's journey of the last 700-years brought us to a shabby landmark: It's all about convenience, stupid!

In his book Man Is Moral Choice Albert Hobbs implied that morality, or the lack thereof, is the measure of man's actions for or against Common Good. "A society that makes it easy to be bad is a bad society." His book was published in 1979 by Arlington House, Norwalk, CT.

The 1990's tragedies of Enron and other crooked corporations made front-page news. Tens of thousands of employees lost their jobs and their pensions. We know the stress, but not the whole slowly unfolding story. Such events in no way constitute advances toward distributive justice and peace.

Corporate leaders and lenders, with approval of the Congress, find unjust ways to ensure the growth of the corporation's "bottom line," which in turn satisfies its stockholders and in some cases stimulates employment. However, economic options available to ensure a healthy bottom line, namely, diversification, jobs (and pensions) lost in mergers with or buying-out companies, lowering labor costs by moving plants to Mexico; in the case of Enron's top management, crooked bookkeeping, etc., serve the will and economic well-being of entrepreneurs and upper management, not the worker's or retiree's well-being, nor God's will.

The "bottom line" for retirees is a savings account sufficient to live the remainder of their lives with dignity. Loss of pensions dooms many to poverty.

Retirees who invested in the Stock Market expected long-term benefits. Again, many are doomed to poverty. The market has become a casino where all manner of "games" are played. The odds favor those rich enough that losing does not affect their dignity; and, skilled enough to hedge their bets.

Again, "A society that makes it easy to be bad is a bad society.

The laborer's "bottom line" is a dependable job. Instead they receive untold hardship and broken families, in particular where American jobs are moved to Mexico. When such job transfers become common practice within specific segments of industry, for example large appliance manufacture, lost jobs (blue, and white-collar) is not the only blow to their dignity. Acquiring a new home can be a fatal blow in that homes of the majority of workers are mortgaged, many with subprime loans.

Fact: blue and white-collar workers in America, as in other affluent nations, have a history of paying off home mortgages one month at a time (or remortgaging) simply because they can't afford multiple payments. Moreover, they over-extend their credit by succumbing to subprime loans.

Many workers, upon losing their jobs, find employment with a competitor's company. They need to sell one home and buy another. In such cases banks and mortgage companies offer a self-serving service, i.e. the means to amortize the cost of buying a home. We discover however that workers today face a housing slump and (so-called) "credit crunch" - deviations from the hoped-for benevolence of Capitalism.

The anomaly is in the lender's "profit for doing good" (which in the Old Testament was zero). Today it is 85% (first year), 82% (second year), 79% (third tear), ---- and so on. This often fatal blow to a worker's dignity lies in the fact that he or she pays about $10,000 per year on a 25-year $120,000 mortgage, of which the bank receives about $8000 the first year. In the first five years homeowners "build" equity, or ownership, of their property very slowly, about 2 percent each year, while the lender collects over a third of the amount loaned. Should their new jobs also move to Mexico 3-years into their mortgage, they will not have sufficient equity to cover the down-payment for another home. They become pawns in the scam known as "teaser" loans.

This is Wall Street's big problem midway through 2007, according to Ben Bernanke, chairman of the Federal Reserve -

Credit problems rock Wall Street
By Jeannine Aversa, Associated Press writer
Published August 30, 2007 in the Goshen News

Washington - Federal Reserve Chairman Ben Bernanke is suggesting that policymakers look for ways to encourage a wider range of mortgages geared for low income and other borrowers who have been hard hit by the housing slump and credit crunch.

Bernanke, in a letter to Sen. Charles Schumer, D- N.Y., that was released Wednesday, said the Fed is keeping close tabs on financial markets and is "prepared to act as needed" to ensure that spreading credit problems that have rocked Wall Street in recent weeks don't hurt the economy. It's a message the central bank has been sending as the markets have been growing more turbulent.

Foreclosures and late payments have spiked especially for "subprime" borrowers with blemished credit histories or low incomes. Higher interest rates and weak home values have made it impossible for some to pay or to keep up with their monthly mortgage payments. Some overstreached homeowners can't afford to refinance or even sell their home.

Bernanke said the development of "a broader range of mortgage products which are appropriate for low- and moderate-income borrowers, including those seeking to refinance" might help the situation. *Such products could be designed to avoid or mitigate the risk of prepayment shock and to be more transparent with respect to their terms,* Bernanke wrote in the letter, which was dated Monday.

Mortgage foreclosures and late payments are expected to worsen in the next year and a half as low *"teaser"* rates that lured in borrowers reset to higher rates, socking homeowners. Some 2 million adjustable rate mortgages are expected to reset to higher rates this year and next. *Steep penalties for prepaying mortgages have added to some homeowners' headaches.* (Italics added.)

Bernanke said the Federal Housing Administration, a government agency that insures home loans, might be able to help.

"The Congress might wish to consider FHA reforms that allow the agency more flexibility to design new products and to collaborate with the private sector in facilitating the refinancing of creditworthy subprime borrowers facing large resets," Bernanke said.

The Bush administration is looking into ways that the FHA, part of the U.S. Department of Housing and Urban Development, may help troubled homeowners with low incomes or tarnished credit histories. >

Note especially my italics, including euphemisms, contained in this AP article (credit crunch, teaser loans, prepayment shock, homeowner's headaches and others).

An Investors Guide published October 2007 contained this interesting blurb: "Subprime loans create pain for the U.S. economy when those loans turn sour. It's like when the python swallows a pig. It takes some time for the pig to be absorbed into the python's system. Once this happens the python (i.e. economy) continues on. Unfortunately, the story does not have a happy ending for the pig."

"The pig represents companies that hold bad loans and hedge funds." Note: Treatment for indigestion is a $45 billion "Tums" from our Government.

Isn't the anomaly before God the fact that dignity for the masses is meaningless in the modern business world - and meaningless to patients in hospital beds?

The patient's bottom line is to get well at any cost ($2 trillion dollars annually for taxpayer-funded government health care for example).

The November 2007 issue of Consumer Reports contained an article titled Treatment traps to avoid that dealt with costly treatments and unnecessary medical procedures "designed to make more money for doctors, insurers and drug companies." Bone marrow transplantation, screening tests promoted nationwide to spot early heart disease, new pharmaceutical products promoted by an estimated $29 billion dollars spent each year for consumer ads, Medicaid fraud lawsuits, etc., were examples of the "I'm Number One" mindset at work within systems geared to provide expensive interventions and remedies for those conditioned to believe they need them.

The article added a second opinion, a quote from the November/ December issue of Health Affairs: "Decisions relating to payment and medical insurance coverage are driven by pressure from manufacturers, doctors and by (the real 'I'm Number One') the patient himself."

Again, the goal of altruistic Capitalism should be the Common Good; in other words, distributive justice. Capitalism should serve everyone, particularly parents and patients. Employers and government officials should do so to honor their own dignity as well as the dignity of employees and retirees, homebuyers, consumers and competitors (and the taxpayer). Government bureaucrats who manipulate great wealth, i.e. a 13.6 trillion dollar GNP for fiscal year 2007, should measure success by a moral standard - justice.

March 27, 2002

The Goshen News
Goshen, IN

Dear Editor:

We live in the Information Age. We ought to realize that information may contribute to a better understanding of reality; or, it may mislead us.

So-called "mainstream media information" fails to pass my test for trustworthiness.

Whether or not this is an accurate statement depends on the answer to only one question. Was the universe created by God? Observing harmony in nature and understanding the orderly, predictable way everything happens, those who then choose to believe all this is accidental are at best questionable sources of information.

The Sunday Goshen News reported that the "reason for increasing employment theft is a subject of debate by experts." The article was from the Associated Press. I read the article, then asked myself - was I receiving useful information or, misinformation?

The explanations for ten years of increasing work-place theft were secular explanations; "economic downturn raises tensions between employers and workers, workers feel that their employer owes them more than the pay they receive. Or, increases in work-place theft may simply indicate that employers are doing a better job of apprehending workers," and so on. The AP failed it's own test for quality journalism, i.e. both sides of every issue must be reported. The rational explanation for increasing work-place theft in a real world created by God is that Americans are becoming more sinful.

The solution for the theft problem, and the solution for behavioral problems in general, that are reported in the mainstream media is, obey God's Commandments (love one another).

Unfortunately for our children and grandchildren who will live out their lives in the Information Age, much of the information they receive about reality will not help them succeed.

Robert Jefferson

God's reward is eternal happiness. The stark contrast between monetary profit and its close tie with self-love, and heaven with its close tie to selfless love, is obvious. The contrast becomes more troublesome when one compares life-styles - consuming goods vs. consuming God (as described in His First Commandment).

It is apparent that many of our youths are lost in a tangle of opinions and choices. The over-burden of "information," particularly seductive marketing messages, hides the straight and narrow path here on earth that takes us to God's eternal Kingdom.

Proper use of freedom to bring about God's Kingdom of peace and justice everywhere on earth is evident today in religious communities, but much harder to find in the business community.

Truly, the 20th century did witness human suffering greater than any previous century, perhaps greater than the total suffering in all of human history. Simple logic will conclude that modern men and women are not in partnership with God. This raises a red flag. Stop! At least let's pause to look both ways before crossing into the third millennium AD.

We are faced with two questions. First, has benevolence from Capitalism lost its way?

Second, is it practical to return to communities modeled on a Catholic communal life of distributive justice? The answer was given by a man named Vincent McNabb: "Is anything else practicable?" (in answer to the ultimate purpose of human existence). C. S. Lewis was asked, "Can we turn back the clock?" He replied, "When the clock goes wrong, that is exactly what you do, unless you are its slave."

Our children graduate from high school and college without confidence in their ability to answer these questions.

The 10-year old girl we met in Kalamazoo (page 143) is a key to understanding the subliminal message, "I'm Number One."

Without her and a hundred million other consumers, and without a multitude of gullible investors, there would be little wealth to exchange. Capitalism would die from anemia, leaving Modern Man far worse off than if he reestablished the culture of life as it was in the thirteenth century.

> Suffering and death on a cross for the eternal benefit of mankind against short-term wealth and eternal suffering - quite a contrast.

Conclusion: Modern men and women have no defense to offer at the Last Judgment when God says, "ignorance of My Commandments is no excuse.

A separate book is needed to document the disrespect each of God's Commandments receives in the name of economic and social progress.

Substituting consumption of goods for Consumption of God is the best example - Commandment #1.

The 3rd Commandment was discarded 40-years ago when the Blue Laws were repealed, thereby opening the marketplace on the Lord's Day.

The 4th Commandment places on mankind an obligation to honor their parents by caring for them with affection and gratitude when they are unable to care for themselves. Handling the details of Free Enterprise robs many of time and opportunity to fulfill this obligation.

The 5th Commandment was repealed by the Supreme Court to accommodate man's sex drive by slaughtering the Holy Innocents he begets.

The 6th Commandment is a concession stand selling "No-Fault" divorce and adultery to 100 million Americans.

The 7th commandment is the Banking and Mortgage industry's playing field.

The 8th Commandment forbids misrepresenting the truth in one's relations with others - a playing field for those who compete for leadership and power.

The 9th and 10th Commandments cover excessive desire for (coveting) the possessions of one's neighbor (wife and goods), i.e. passion freed from sinfulness by Capitalism's gods.

"Everybody's doing it."

———————————

Customs that make it easy to be good are good customs.

CHAPTER 16

SPIRITUAL SOLIDARITY

Webster's definition of Solidarity: Unity based on community of interests, objectives, and standards.

Solidarity builds peer pressure.   Both are necessary for accomplishing the formidable and multifaceted tasks ahead; first, reordering the U.S. culture from death and despair to life and hope; second, reviving the Christian solidarity that had initially grown for 1300-years through faith in the absolute authority of the Vicar of Christ to accurately represent God on earth; and third, make peace real on earth and as permanent as sinful men and women can maintain it.

The three tasks are interconnected.   Peace is not possible unless the first and second tasks are completed successfully.

The space program was an outstanding example of political solidarity and peer pressure at work - a 10-year, highly idealistic, multifaceted goal set by President Kennedy to put a man on the moon, and return him to earth.   Kennedy united the nation by the force of his imagination (idealism) and personality.   The 1960's were witness to a nation united in President Kennedy's idea and his objective.   An Aerospace Industry sprang-up, seemingly overnight, new materials and new standards of technology were developed, an Astronaut Corps was selected and trained for one purpose; ..... You know the rest of the story.

Did faith, in other words belief and trust in an idea, and loyalty contribute to the success of the program?   You can bet on it.

Did the space program contribute to the Common Good, i.e. was it successful?   We can't know the future.   Objective reason would conclude that 50-years is too little to judge total merit and consequences from the achievement of President Kennedy's goal.

The 1940's were witness to Solidarity of a different sort.   Led by a man of the Hindu faith, Mahandas Gandhi, 300 million citizens of India stood together and won back their country from Great Britain (a Christian country).   The struggle took 20 years.   It was non-violent in principle, and prayerful. (Who will say that Jesus, Brahma and Allah are not on the same party line?) It ended without bloodshed. Sad to say man's partnership with Allah was not permanent. Muslim/Hindu Solidarity broke down in 1947 when Muslim communities made themselves into a new nation, Pakistan. Gandhi was assassinated in 1948 by a countryman.

The 1980's witnessed other instances of Solidarity. In these events Solidarity and peer pressure centered around partnership with the Catholic Church. Modern man found convincing evidence for the curative power of Solidarity in the Son of God accomplished in nations ruled by Godless men and women. People of Poland, Czechoslovakia and other communist countries united in the Body of Christ and in their own heritage. Polish citizens, flying the Solidarity banner, threw-off the Godless dictatorship of the USSR without bloodshed.

The same spiritual (prayerful) Solidarity saved the people of the Philippines from the tyranny of the Marcos regime, without bloodshed; and, solidarity through prayer, helped the people of Argentina end a war. These were examples of spiritual solidarity - citizens working nation-wide in partnership with God in mostly Catholic nations.

Objective reasoning is the modus operandi promoted in earlier chapters of this book: Common sense tells us that solidarity is necessary for achieving complex goals, whether they be idealistic in the sense that the goal seems to be virtually impossible technically, or the goal is virtually impossible because it requires collective partnership of sinful men and women with the truth of God, i.e. total agreement on social morality instituted by God and upheld by His Church.

Note that truth is a basic concern in goal achievement, because no one deliberately places his faith and trust in a liar. Solidarity based on untruths is an absurdity. The goal in the space program would not have been achieved if contractors had been generally untruthful; and, the goal of home rule in India would not have been achieved if Gandhi had not been a truthful (trustworthy) man.

The spectrum of collective achievements has two ends, absurdity at one end - man's commitment to the flesh (using St. Paul's words); and, perfection at the other - man's commitment to the spirit.

The habitual practice of Common Good hangs on whether or not each person's response to the world around him reflects God's will.

Political solidarity eventually passes out of existence in a two party democratic government when customs and the culture turn away from God. This is the lesson we have yet to learn.

Semi-Solidarity based on our Judeo-Christian heritage, with the Common Good as it's objective becomes a trumped-up solidarity with comfort as its objective. Drugs, intercourse freed from responsibility by legal abortion and confusion about right and wrong puts us on sin's slippery slope.

A question asked earlier: Does God need to tell mankind that the crowning potential good of His design came when He said, "Let there be man?"

God did not design man to be an absurdity.

Modern Man doesn't fully understand that the rest of the story takes place in hell.

Today peer pressure masquerades as "mainstream" morality fraudulently concocted by the secular media, taught in publicly funded secular schools and exemplified by Hollywood celebrities. Party-goers ask, "what went wrong?" Secularism has no answer.

Contemporary America is in deep trouble. Affluent countries around the globe are in deep trouble too, from population control, from AIDS, but also from the U.S. based religion of Marketism. The absurdity lies in the amount of damage two generations have done to the moral attitudes and cultures of Western nations and, lying about it.

Is fifty years too little time to judge the consequences of a culture based on fraudulently concocted solidarity wherein I choose to "do whatever pleases me?" And, is this kind of life absurd as the Beat Generation insists? The Answer can be found in the reality of order.

Confusion about order, i.e. multiple views of morality, is a monumental problem . One view holds with Secularism's Situation Ethics that human behavior and its consequences must be considered pragmatically. This view allows everyone, nonbeliever and believer, arbitration rights with God about this or that Commandment. The opposing view holds with Judeo-Catholic tradition - human behavior (moral or immoral), and its consequences for the Common Good, must always be ruled by the (time-tested) Ten Commandments given by God to Moses. These principles were faithfully handed down by the early Hebrews and by the will of the Holy Spirit acting through the true Church. The first is man's view of social order, leaving out Hell. The second view is social morality revealed by God deserving eternal reward.

An editorial by Donald Wildmon in the April 2001 American Family Association Journal concluded with: "Our society, and those in our Churches, would greatly benefit from a proper fear of hell. Hell is a compass point marking the Last Judgment of God - a timeless Being and an event we sorely need to acknowledge, because Divine Judgment will occur, and it matters most of all." (Reprinted with permission of the AFA Journal: Web site: www.afajournal.org.)

Justice, peace, even civility, are transient events at best if one denies the afterlife and lives as though there is no Last Judgment.

Fear of hell is our objective motive for starting a Solidarity Movement whose goal is to reorder this nation's hell-bent culture. "Thy kingdom come, Thy will be done on earth" is our subjective motive.

True moral order (reality) is God's prerogative, and free will is God's gift to mankind. It is not difficult to know true order. What is difficult is accepting that which we know in our hearts, and know from history. Choosing the one reality that dictates success, both as individuals and collectively, makes proper use of freedom of choice.

My thesis is this: Today Americans live in a reality which, like little gods, we create by virtue of freedom to control events guaranteed in the U.S. Constitution. And, history is meaningless unless it teaches two things. (1) A culture of death and despair results when men and women seek to rule over human events as though they owned God. (2) The historic Church of God is not a Church that continually protests God's will.

Supernatural Solidarity

Gothic cathedrals are an excellent example of Solidarity in God. The architecture of Cathedrals and Basilicas erected in the Middle

Ages became known as the Catholic Style. It was a universal style combining architectural innovations from many Catholic nations.

Cathedral builders copied Frankish-Norman architecture and added a pier and archivolt in the style of the Lombards. The vaulted roof and massive pillars were from Norman architecture. Builders from Charlemagne's dynasty contributed a ribbed and dome-like vault, triple apses and aisles. Pointed arches and flying buttresses were French in origin, as was stained glass - "a new art form born of faith."

The cornerstone for the Gothic crown, Notre Dame Cathedral, was laid in 1163 AD.

Note: "Hymns in stone that glorify God," describing medieval Catholic Cathedrals, is from The Age of Chivalry prepared under the guidance of Melville Grosvenor and Franc Shor, and published in 1969 by the National Geographic Society.

Solidarity in the mother of God inspired a Cathedral so wondrous that it is said to be a miraculous geometry in stone. The citizens of Chartes, a French town about 50 miles southwest of Paris, built this marvelous Cathedral in the twelfth century assisted in labor, materials and the wealth of nations throughout the Western Empire. Such was solidarity of our medieval ancestors in tribute to Mary.

Chartes Cathedral stands today, weather-worn, but exact in its geometry (including the 40-foot width of the Gothic vaults no architect thought possible). Sacredness is timeless.

The Son of Mary said: "Do this in remembrance of Me," and (long ago) the Western nations did.

The documentary DVD titled Chartes Cathedral is worth watching. It is a Janson Media production available by contacting www.janson. com.

One of the greatest gifts God bestowed on mankind is the key to unity, i.e. supernatural solidarity in the Church His Son instituted - everyone striving to use all their faculties to know God and to will nothing but what God wills. "That all may be one as you, Father, are in me ...." (Jn. 17:21).

God did not design mankind to be an absurdity is a statement worth repeating (absurd means irrational as it is used here).

The groundwork for modern absurdism - denial of absolute Truth and the (God-given) authority to proclaim it on earth, infallibly, was laid in the 16th century.

Inability of Protestant Churches to proclaim good and evil confidently and with one voice allowed absurdism to develop into Existentialism: "Without certain knowledge of what is good and what is bad, i.e. Natural Law, how can one be expected to assume responsibility for his or her acts of free will?" So said Intellectual Man, a product of the 18th century Enlightenment Movement. Intellectual Man was an atheist.

Present-day efforts to regain unity and order are hampered by conflicting historical documents describing Martin Luther's beliefs and his involvement in Church reform. Documents dealing with diabolic corruption within the Catholic Church of that time, and Luther's "95 points," tend to dismiss infallible teaching authority.

"Reformed Catholics" (in time) organized their own fallible churches in the belief that loyalty and affection was unwise for Catholic bishops and priests who were evil. Each new church denied Truth revealed in Divine (Catholic) Tradition including infallibility of the Pope and other Catholic doctrines found to be uncomfortable (contraception as an intrinsic evil is a modern example).

One item of Catholic doctrine reformed churches did not deny was that Jesus Christ, through the Incarnation, took human form to suffer and be Crucified for the sins of mankind. This, along with faith in Catholic doctrine of The Holy Trinity, Protestants accepted as Divine Truth.

Five hundred years ago an infallible pope and his seat of office (the Holy See) were indispensable for teaching the Truth about salvation. Five hundred years ago the venerated letters the twelve Apostles, St. Paul and their consecrated successors wrote to early Church members were faithfully recorded in One Bible. Today, belief in that infallible moral resource is cast aside by Protestants and too many Catholics.

Study recent history - the history of all nations during the 20th century. Then, narrow the study to the United States during the last 40-years. Look for social and political forces powerful enough to prevent Solidarity in God which is essential for world peace.

Look at Totalitarianism, easily the biggest 20th century obstacle to Solidarity for world peace. Totalitarian governments in Europe and Asia exercised brutal and oppressive power. Religion and all other aspects of daily life were strictly controlled by the state. The bitter fruits of totalitarianism are abundantly evident to modern man. Totalitarian rule, clearly contrary to the purpose for which mankind was created was advanced by Satan's will.

Optimistic humanism (liberalism), i.e. belief in the omniscience and goodness of mankind; and in the autonomy of the individual; and, pluralism, the object of which is non-judgementalism, are modern myths.

Mankind without God's graces is murderous, lustful, arrogant and greedy, as the history of every nation and every age shows.

Martin Luther said, "all are depraved."

Depravity must be met with forceful opposition, not permissiveness. History will not attest to the goodness of man until all of mankind honor God and come to realize that the wrath of God is terrible beyond imagination.

Liberalism and pluralism are fraudulently concocted tenets of the ideology of denial in that the wrath of God, the Ten Commandments, natural law and even God's existence are ignored in the public square.

Pluralism, multiculturalism and Political Correctness have evolved into rationales for non-judgmentalism. Non-judgmentalism has broadened to become radical permissiveness.

Modern pluralism nurtures disunity, not unity. Without unity there can be no support for absolute authority validated by God.

Liberation from fear of God has produced a culture of death, some call it soft-totalitarianism, in the United States and in materialistic, anti-Catholic policies of the European Union.

Twenty-first century Spiritual Solidarity for world peace must overcome hard and soft totalitarianism. Furthermore, Solidarity, as a Movement must find a way to guarantee that the fruits of modern Science and of Capitalism are never bitter, and are truly for the

Common Good of everyone everywhere on earth.

The Western world must enter the 21st century on its knees.

The collective will must be ordered to express in prayer and in heart-felt sorrow for disobeying our loving Father who is above all things; it must manifest firmness of will to resolve one's differences, first with God, then with neighbor; then, firmly resolve never to offend again; then collective penance. The grace of almighty God is at work each step of the way, as befits a loving partner.

The reason God matters most of all is because it is God who drafted the only blueprint for justice and peace in Creation - true morality fully expressed in His Ten Commandments. God's Plan is based on a relationship of mutual love.

This is the model I recommend for Spiritual Solidarity in Western nations in the twenty-first century.

CHAPTER 17

ASPERGER'S SYNDROME,

a Mild Form of Autism

The following letter to Dr. Gott was printed in his syndicated column in the Goshen News, dated June 5, 2007 -

Dear Dr. Gott:

Our 14-year-old grandson has Asperger's Syndrome. Is there a future for him? Please explain all we need to know about the syndrome. What can we do for him and where can we get help?

Dr. Gott's answer -

Dear Reader:

Asperger's Syndrome is a high functioning and relatively mild form of autism. Autism is a disorder that predominantly affects males (80 percent of all affected individuals). Of those with the Asperger's form, 90 percent are male. There is no known cause for any form of autism, but some authorities believe Asperger's has a genetic component because it appears to run in families.

Asperger's mainly affects social interaction, communication and imagination (empathy, abstract thought and flexible thinking). People with this form usually have good language skills, above average IQs, excel in visual or logical thinking, have a strong drive to identify rules and patterns in systems and analyze detail, and often specialize in skills that involve numbers, mathematics and memory. Because Asperger's is relatively mild, affected individuals are not diagnosed until after age 16 and lead relatively normal lives.

There is no blood analysis or medical test that can diagnose autism. Because people are born with it, physicians need to observe behavior from infancy.

People with autism may also have Savant Syndrome, astonishing "islands" of ability (artistic, musical, mathematical, etc.) or intelligence that is in contrast to their overall mental disability. The exact number of savants is unknown because most have profound disability (from autism, brain injury, etc.) that does not allow them to explain how and what they experience. Daniel Tammet, author of "Born on a Blue Day" (Free Press, 2007), a book about his experiences as an autistic savant) is a notable example of an individual with Asperger's. He is proof that there is hope for a relatively normal life despite his autism. He is also a blessing to doctors studying Savant Syndrome because he is not profoundly disabled, as are most savants.

Your grandson will most likely lead a relatively normal life despite his Asperger's. He should be under the care of a neurologist and/ or psychiatrist. Your love and support are necessary. >

I wrote a letter to Dr. Gott voicing mild disapproval of his assumption that their 14 year-old grandson should be under the care of a psychiatrist or neurologist -

June 7, 2007

Dr. Peter Gott
c/o United Media
200 Madison Avenue
New York, NY
Ref: Your June 5th Column titled, *Asperger's Syndrome a Mild Form of Autism*

Dear Dr, Gott:

Five years ago our 13-year-old grandson was placed in the care of a psychiatrist, after a number of reprimands by his school Principal. The diagnoses was neurological disorder he called Asperger's Syndrome. The psychiatrist gave us Hans Asperger's report on this form of mental disability and said our grandson lacked social awareness and the skills needed to connect with the world around him.

I was seventy four years old when I read the report, that being the first knowledge I had of Asperger's work. My "strong drive to identify patterns" found that much in the pattern of adjectives in the report fit me.

I lack what the report called "social awareness." As a student my social interaction skills were minimal. I recall the names of only three high school classmates that I found likeable. Three names I remember from college, and from graduate school, no one that I remember. Participation in alumni gatherings was never in my range of interests. Did I lack empathy? Yes and no. Did I lack social awareness? Yes and no. Looking back, particularly with this new insight, I believe what Hans Asperger called "mental disability" turned out (for me) to be what I call a "saving influence." Innate ability to analyze detail helped me see, for example, that connecting with the world around me depended on whether or not I applied God's rule - the Golden Rule. I discovered on my own that the pattern of behavior that best suits my drive for control and is most logical is: "Do unto others as I would have them do unto me."

Desire for control is my negative side. I have a strong drive to control all that is within my ability to control and to know where to draw the line.

I felt obliged to give my employer my best efforts in return for the wage I received. I felt inclined to cooperate with fellow-workers and assist those who asked. Looking back I see professionalism and a devious, shallow compassion for those around me.

I am a loner without a sense of loneliness. Yet, I was open to love. I love my wife and my children and I was genial with others.

My ability to think logically required (in fact demanded) objectivity. The pattern of controlling others must include the mental ability to control oneself. I discovered that objectivity is the vanguard for order, not disorder. Self control goes a long way, not only in regard to acceptance, but it hid my so-called "mental disability" (even from me).

I found that society has a overly optimistic view of IQ. IQ is not measured by the knowledge one possesses. IQ is measured by the language skill to communicate to others my small part of the vast knowledge God has revealed to mankind.

The gifts I received, perhaps to offset my autism, have not brought disorder to my life. (In The Sound of Music the Mother Abbess said to Maria: "When God closes a door somewhere He opens a window.")

No psychiatrist could have convinced me of the importance of people around me. I learned through on-the-job-training assisted by the language skills of Ursuline sisters, Xavierian brothers and Jesuit professors. >

Asperger's Syndrome truly blends contrasting ways of living one's life. In fascination I now wonder, why did God block my desire for social interaction but not for love of family.

Did I choose logical thinking to be my modus operandi, or did God make it so? Is it logic that locates high in a tree the window God opened for viewing my surroundings?

Eighty years of semi-detachment from society allows me to fit pieces together in that puzzle of life mentioned earlier.

I start with the piece I call the keystone - God. This is the logical place to start, because it is the place where everything starts.

Nonbelievers who lose the keystone must worry because deep in their subconscious they know that solving the puzzle of life is meaningless without God. They become angry when told the truth about their hopeless worldview.

Hans Asperger identified a pattern of behavior of patients who are deficient in or lack "social awareness." He noted that they scored high when tested for their ability to explain complex problems in simple terms, and for logical thinking.

I choose the following article to emphasize anger in those secularists who are atheists, and to show the irrationality in both their worldview and the worldview of the AP Wire Service -

Angry atheist books sell, revealing new intensity to public
angst over faith
AP Wire Service article written by Rachel Zoll
Printed in the Goshen News on May 25, 2007

The time for polite debate is over. Militant atheist writers are making an all-out assault on religious faith and reaching the top of the best seller list, a sign of widespread resentment over the influence of religion in the world among nonbelievers,

Christopher Hitchens' book, God Is Not Great: How Religion Poisons Everything, has sold briskly ever since it was published last month, and his debates with clergy are drawing crowds at every stop.

Sam Harris was a little-known graduate student until he wrote the phenomenally successful The End of Faith and its follow-up, Letter to a Christian Nation. Richard Dawkins' The God Delusion and Daniel Dennett's Breaking the Spell: Religion as a natural Phenomenon struck similar themes - and sold.

"There is something like a change in the Zeitgeist," Hitchens said, noting that sales of his latest book far outnumber those of his earlier work that had challenged faith. "There are a lot of people, in this country in particular, who are fed up with endless lectures by bogus clerics and endless bullying."

Richard Mouw, president of Fuller Theological Seminary, a prominent evangelical school in Pasadena, Calif., said the books' success reflect a new vehemence in the atheist critique.

"I don't believe in conspiracy theories," Mouw said, "but it's almost like they all had a meeting and said, 'Let's counterattack.'"

The war metaphor is apt. The writers see themselves in a battle for reason in a world crippled by superstition. In their view, Muslim extremists, Jewish settlers and Christian right activists are from the same mold, using fairy tales posing as divine scripture to justify their lust for power. Bad behavior in the name of religion is behind some of the most dangerous global conflicts and terrorist attacks in the U.S., London and Madrid, the atheists say.

As Hitchens puts it, "Religion kills." (My claim is: Man-made morality Hitchens worships causes more suffering than any religion.)

The Rev. Douglas Wilson, senior fellow in theology at New Saint Andrews College, a Christian school in Moscow, Idaho, sees the books as a sign of secular panic. Nonbelievers are finally realizing that, contrary to what they were taught in college, faith is not dead, he says.

Signs of believers' political and cultural might abound.

Religious challenges to teaching evolution are still having an impact, 80 years after the infamous Scopes "Monkey" trial. The dramatic growth of home-schooling and private Christian schools is raising questions about the future of public education.

Religious leaders have succeeded in putting some limits on stem-cell research.

And the recent U.S. Supreme Court decision upholding a national ban on the procedure critics call "partial-birth abortion" - the first federal curbs on an abortion procedure in a generation - came after decades of religious lobbying for conservative justices.

"It sort of dawned on the secular establishment that they might lose here," said Wilson, who is debating Hitchens on christianitytoday. com and has written the book Letter from a Christian Citizen in response to Harris. "All of this is happening precisely because there's a significant force that they have to deal with" (my comment, first they have to deal with their conscience).

Indeed, believers far outnumber nonbelievers in America. In an 2005 AP-Ipsos poll on religion, only 2 percent of U.S. respondents said they did not believe in God. Other surveys concluded that 14 percent of Americans consider themselves secular, a term that can include believers who say they have no religion.

Some say liberal outrage over the policies of President Bush is partly fueling sales, even though Hitchens famously supported the invasion of Iraq.

To those Americans, the nation's born-again president is the No. 1 representative of the religious right activists who helped put him in office. Bush's critics see his Christian faith behind some of his worst decisions and his stubborn defense of the war in Iraq. >

The war metaphor is "apt" in another way. At the battle for Bastogne in 1944 the Germans had surrounded the town defended by the 101st Airborne division. General Anthony McAuliff, the American Commander, received an ultimatum from the German Commander: "Surrender or face destruction." McAuliff answered: "Nuts."

My answer to battling atheists who demand that I surrender my religious faith is "Nuts," - the edible kind. Who but an all-loving God attends to our trivial pleasures.

If this all-out assault by atheists truly is a battle for reason, I demand their surrender before my God who lavishes such love for mankind manifest in infinite ways marvelous to behold - peanuts, almonds, butternuts, cashews, English walnuts, black walnuts, chestnuts, hazelnuts, hickory nuts, pecans, pistachio and macadamia nuts, etc., each having a distinct taste. To make our enjoyment real, God provides each mouth with receptors able to distinguish one variety from another.

I responded to the "Angry atheist" article with the following letter to the editor of the Goshen News -

Dear Editor:

After reading the article Angry atheists books sell, revealing new intensity to public angst over faith, I had to confirm the meaning of angst. It fits, except for that word "public," meaning shared by all of the people.

The same article reports results of a 2005 AP-Ipsos poll wherein "2 percent of U.S. respondents said they did not believe in God;" and, "other surveys concluded that 14 percent consider themselves secular."

Ten percent of this nation's adult population is approximately 30 million people. That number is more than enough to make atheist authors very rich.

Conclusion: Authors of atheist books are "singing to the choir."

Atheist writers see themselves in a battle for reason in a world crippled by superstition. Do I need to look up the meaning of reason too? If reason is defined as proper use of the mind, (logical thinking) atheist writers need to examine a seed from an orange.

The mind easily grasps the truth that orange trees grow from orange seeds. One tree produces hundreds of oranges in season and repeats this feat season after season. Botanists know enough about orange seeds to cultivate hybrid varieties of orange trees that produce seedless oranges. Botanists also know that the intelligence to invent the first orange seed far surpasses human intelligence.

If, as atheists say, seeds came about accidentally, they should check out the meaning of accident. >

Analyze, analyze, analyze - everything, especially puzzles, must be analyzed. Would knowing what I now know about myself change my beliefs? Truth cannot change and is never unreasonable.

Would I change my view of what the future holds for my children and grandchildren? No. Would I reevaluate my view of atheists and other pompous people who imperil that future by greatly offending God? (Changing my heartfelt disgust of their lies to heartfelt concern for their salvation would help me avoid their fate.)

Would I change what I have written? No. I believe twenty-first century battles are about salvation. Salvation is all about faith in action. Question your faith in God and you will discover reason at work.

I believe the modern Western world is itself crippled, not by religion, but by the opposite of religion - a pompous sense of self-importance.

The atheistic and secular culture of death became a force to be confronted in the 1960's and 1970's. It represents a total reversal of the traditional worldview of life's meaning given in historical accounts of Western civilization from the first century AD to the thirteenth century. And, a reversal of universal belief in a Supreme Being (or Beings) that is as old as history.

I believe and fear that under God's Plan one's emphasis on self-importance must end in hell. Christopher Hitchens was correct in seeing something like a change in the Zeitgeist. The movement toward intellectual, moral and cultural failure is gaining strength at this junction/juncture in time. Dignity, honesty, duty to serve God and neighbor - common good, really are being sacrificed to the gods of pleasure, as they were before the call of Abraham and the founding of Judaism.

Hitchens and his cadre of fellow-travelers in the liberal media, in the Judicial and Legislative branches of government, in Public Education and in an amoral marketplace have made political correctness (broadmindedness) a bogus criterion for determining the model for morality - man or God. Civilizations have risen and fallen on these determinations.

If, as many Christian scholars believe, Satan chose the twentieth century to do his greatest harm; then, the doors Satan closed are those leading us to God. The windows Satan opened are those leading us to Hell.

Without unity in one body, Christians today (a vast majority) can only endure the ridiculous lies about bad being good and good being bad.

My manner must appear condescending throughout these chapters. It is the arrogance of Asperger's Syndrome. However, the mirror looks past me as well as at me. My window, though not itself real, truly is a mind's logical thinking about God's reality - the only reality that has a credible beginning and a wonderful end.

I see in the mirror both sides of Man - Whole Man and Modern Man, standing before God at the last Judgment. The image is clear enough to recognize an aura of humility surrounding Whole Man; and, an aura of arrogance surrounding Modern Man.

CHAPTER 18

UNITY IN ONE BODY

At this singular juncture in time mankind must choose either to continue driving wildly toward paganism, as we have done for the past forty years, or turn toward God with firm resolve to pray that He grant us pardon for the contemptible sins (abortion, sodomy, adultery, hate and the rest) for which we are accountable. And pray that He will give us His grace to come together as of old.

St. Paul brought Gentiles and Jews together in One Body. But, first he himself was converted. Unity will not be accomplished without conversion.

In One Body, we can conquer modern barbarians as One Catholic Body and Catholic teaching conquered barbarians a thousand years ago. Modern barbarians are no different than barbarians of old. All possess God's gift of common sense.

Truth never changes. The quote (Chap. 3) from King Edwin of Northumbria is true today as it was true in the seventh century: "This new teaching reveals more certain knowledge than from our pagan gods of what went before this life and what follows."

Truth is - Man was created to worship God, not self.

The claim made in the Introduction is: The reality of One God is made a myth today so that we can have ethics as our plaything.

Stanley Marrow writes in Paul, His Letters and His Theology: "Few are those who rightly appreciate, not the struggle itself, but the resolve to undertake it. Fewer still are they who can comprehend what is involved in such reversal. .... Whatever happened to Paul on the road to Damascus altered his life radically, reversed the scale of his values, and made his vision of all things (his Zeitgeist) utterly new." (See page 105 for the book's publisher.)

Paul's sinful human nature was not altered. Marrow points to the Letter to the Romans, where St. Paul says (in 7:21-23): "So I find it to be a law that when I want to do right, evil lies close at hand. For I delight in the law of God, in my inmost self, but I see in my members another law at war with the law of my mind and making me captive to the law of sin which dwells in my members" (7:21-23).

Sin is a constant. Fortunately, God's gifts of His grace and His mercy are also constants.

My closing observation: Common sights as one travels across America are a church on a hill, churches on busy streets, churches in vacated stores, churches alongside Court Houses, churches taller than commercial buildings; churches outnumbering beauty shops and barber shops combined. Each of these, Churches, Synagogues, and Mosques, hold their own definition of the One God who spoke to Abraham.

America truly is a nation under God. But, is it a Male or Female God? Is it a nation that proclaims Absolute Truth with a capital T, or is it Modern Man's truth with a small case t? Are we One Body strong enough to maintain a just society?

Our children want to know.

FINALE

The analogy of a fallen bridge is used here as a means to better understand the prediction of C. S. Lewis I discovered in a book titled C. S. Lewis for the Third Millennium written by Peter Kreeft (published in 1994 by Ignatius Press, San Francisco, CA).

In a manner of speaking Western Man has come to a juncture in time or, if you will, a crucial predicament on our path to the future. There is no going back. Modern Man must choose the path that takes him and her to heaven; or, the path that takes them and their children to hell will be theirs by default.

The influence of secularism on the Western world has produced, in only forty years, a culture that treats morality as a private matter. One of many consequences is that God's Truth about morality has been pushed out of the public square.

History teaches that man is moral choice, and cultures that remove or minimize God in order to have morality as its plaything are cultures of death that soon turn to paganism.

As ironworks corrode due to chemical reaction, and bridges fall, so goodness in mankind corrodes due to reaction with atheism's ideology of denial, and mankind falls.

Proof that our children will witness the failure of the Western world and the United States is shown through objective reasoning promoted in earlier chapters. Proof that unity (Solidarity) in the Body of Christ prevents failure comes from unbiased historians.

Unity in the Body of Christ is a five hundred year-old work in progress known as the Ecumenical Movement. The problem is that Christianity honors the Edict of Milan's granting everyone freedom to follow their own religious convictions. The key to achieving sacred unity collectively is persuasion not coercion.

Ecumenism is the best way to unite the many branches of Christianity; but time is short. Reason is a quicker way if the Holy Spirit provides guidance. Start with what is self-evident: The existence of almighty God who does not speak different truths to different people. Reflect upon God's words to Moses in Deuteronomy 18:18-19, then vote as your conscience directs.

In the preceding chapters I say "Go to Hell" (but not in those words) to those responsible for the corrosion of goodness and the disruption of sacred unity that existed in (C. S. Lewis called it) the century of excellence. My intention is honorable and judicious. It is honorable to warn sinners that dying while separated from God will invite the wrath of God. It is judicious to heed the warning God gave to Ezekiel (3:18-19) -

> "If I say to the wicked man, you shall surely die; and you do not warn him or speak out to dissuade him from his wicked conduct so that he may live; that wicked man shall die for his sin, but I will hold you responsible for his death. If, on the other hand, you have warned the wicked man, yet he has not turned away from his evil nor from his wicked conduct, then he shall die for his sin, but you shall save your life."

God then said-

> "If a virtuous man turns away from virtue and does wrong when I place a stumbling block before him, he shall die. He shall die for his sin, and the virtuous deeds shall not be remembered; but I will hold you responsible for his death if you did not warn him. When, on the other hand, you have warned a virtuous man not to sin, and he has in fact not sinned, he shall surely live because of the warning, and you shall save your own life." (3:20-21)

Index for Subheadings and Titles

292

LaVergne, TN USA
11 September 2009
157517LV00002B/30/P